PARALEGAL LITIGATION AND PRACTICE LIBRARY FROM WILEY LAW PUBLICATIONS

BANKRUPTCY LAW AND PROCEDURE: A GUIDE FOR PARALEGALS (THIRD EDITION)
Steven N. Berger, J. Daria Westland, and Thomas J. Salerno

CONSTRUCTION LITIGATION FOR PARALEGALS: CLAIMS PREPARATION AND MANAGEMENT
Dianne D. Zalewski and Cheryl D. Evans

DEPOSITION MANUAL FOR PARALEGALS (SECOND EDITION)
Christine Bergren Greene

ESTATE PLANNING AND ADMINISTRATION FOR PARALEGALS
Charles P. Nemeth

EVIDENCE HANDBOOK FOR PARALEGALS
Charles P. Nemeth

LITIGATION GUIDE FOR PARALEGALS: RESEARCH AND DRAFTING
Cynthia Montiero Osborne

LITIGATION ORGANIZATION AND MANAGEMENT FOR PARALEGALS
Lynn M. Randall

LITIGATION PARALEGAL (SECOND EDITION)
Phillip J. Signey

PARALEGAL BOOK OF LETTERS
Wiley Law Publications Editorial Staff

PARALEGAL CAREER GUIDE
Chere B. Estrin

PARALEGAL DISCOVERY: ORGANIZATION AND MANAGEMENT
Joyce Samson and Dianne Zalewski

PARALEGAL DISCOVERY: PROCEDURES AND FORMS
Pat Medina

PARALEGAL DRAFTING GUIDE
Dorien S. McClellan

PARALEGAL LITIGATION: FORMS AND PROCEDURE
Marcy Davis Fawcett

PARALEGAL LITIGATION: FORMS AND PROCEDURE (DISK EDITION)
Marcy Davis Fawcett

PARALEGAL MANAGEMENT HANDBOOK
Maureen Brophy and Patsy Pressley

PARALEGAL MEDICAL RECORDS REVIEW
Kristyn Appleby and Joanne Tarver

Paralegal Trial Handbook
Beverly Hutson

Personal Injury Paralegal
Burgess Eldrige

Personal Injury Paralegal: Procedures and Forms
Joyce Walden

Personal Injury Paralegal: Procedures and Forms (disk edition)
Joyce Walden

Real Estate Foreclosure: Paralegal Practice and Procedure
Charles P. Nemeth and Grayson P. Van Horn

ESTRIN SERIES

Computerized Litigation Support
Despina C. Kartson and Norman F. Strizek

How to Survive in a Law Firm: Client Relations
Dana Graves, Jill Levin and Nancy Pulsifer

Medical Malpractice Guide for Paralegals
Stephanie A. Danelson

The Paralegal's Role at Trial
Kerri W. Feeney

Smart Litigating with Computers
Patricia S. Eyres

PARALEGAL BOOK OF LETTERS

SUBSCRIPTION NOTICE

This Wiley product is updated on a periodic basis with supplements to reflect important changes in the subject matter. If you purchased this product directly from John Wiley & Sons, Inc., we have already recorded your subscription for this update service.

If, however, you purchased this product from a bookstore and wish to receive (1) the current update at no additional charge, and (2) future updates and revised or related volumes billed separately with a 30-day examination review, please send your name, company name (if applicable), address, and the title of the product to:

Supplement Department
John Wiley & Sons, Inc.
One Wiley Drive
Somerset, NJ 08875
1-800-225-5945

For customers outside the United States, please contact the Wiley office nearest you:

Professional and Reference Division
John Wiley & Sons Canada, Ltd.
22 Worcester Road
Rexdale, ONT M9W 1L1
CANADA
(416) 236-3580
Phone: 1-800-263-1590
Fax: 1-800-675-6599

John Wiley & Sons, Ltd.
Baffins Lane
Chichester
West Sussex, PO19 1UD
UNITED KINGDOM
Phone: (44) (243) 779777

Jacaranda Wiley Ltd.
PRT Division
P.O. Box 174
North Ryde, NSW 2113
AUSTRALIA
PHONE: (02) 805-1100
Fax: (02) 805-1597

John Wiley & Sons (SEA) Pte. Ltd.
37 Jalan Pemimpin
Block B # 05-04
Union Industrial Building
SINGAPORE 2057
Phone: (65) 258-1157

PARALEGAL BOOK OF LETTERS

WILEY LAW PUBLICATIONS
EDITORIAL STAFF

Editors
Colorado Springs, Colorado

Wiley Law Publications
JOHN WILEY & SONS, INC.
New York • Chichester • Brisbane • Toronto • Singapore

This text is printed on acid-free paper.

Library of Congress Cataloging-in-Publication Data

ISBN 0-471-04145-9

Printed in the United States of America

10 9 8 7 6 5 4 3 2

PREFACE

The *Paralegal Book of Letters* is a self-help guide to composing those pieces of correspondence that are vital and necessary in supporting client matters no matter how complex. It is designed to ease the frustration of tending to one of the administrative functions of a case, namely, relaying information to any party related to the matter at hand. This information can be time-consuming in preparation, but is overwhelmingly important to the management and conduct of a case. Such seemingly unimportant correspondence such as cover or transmittal letters can become crucial in eliminating culpability and liability. Correspondence is also the recorded history of the case which one can refer to for clarification of facts or events. Because correspondence can be so critical in a case, Wiley Law Publications has assembled many of the letters available from its extensive paralegal reference library into one easy-to-use guide.

The book is designed to contain only letters with no explanatory text. It is assumed that the reader's compositional and cognitive skills are of the highest quality. The book is further designed to take a case from start to finish. From initial client contact through disposition of the matter, the letters contained herein will greatly aid in communicating information, requests, or actions to be taken in a case with the clear precision necessary to effective representation.

As to the contents of the book, **Chapters 1** and **2** deal with the preliminary matters such as interviewing the client, notification of representation, obtaining medical records, and contacting witnesses. **Chapter 3** concerns initiating the case and has examples of transmittal letters to accompany the necessary pleadings. Many times after pleadings are filed, it is deemed to be in the best interest of the client to settle the matter. **Chapter 4**, therefore, provides a broad range of correspondence with regard to stipulation and settlement issues. If it is determined that a trial will be necessary, **Chapters 5** through **9** deal with all of the discovery devices available to litigants. Discovery is where the case is won or lost, and proper recording of requests for production or documents produced or required is crucial. Once discovery is accomplished, the matter can proceed to trial. Keeping the client and all other parties notified of specific dates at this juncture is of prime importance. **Chapter 10** deals with various situations which may arise during trial and after judgment. **Chapter 11** concerns the small details left after the trial is over. Generally, these letters refer to execution of the judgment and receipt or payment of funds awarded or statutorily required.

Chapter 12 breaks from the litigation-related letters to provide assistance with managing the law office itself. Many paralegals who have achieved management level responsibilities will find these extremely helpful in dealing with staffing the office and handling personnel matters. These matters in particular can be vexing when one is involved in complex litigation or the daily routine of the office. The examples in **Chapter 12** will, hopefully, ease the stress of having to change gears in the middle of an assignment.

It is hoped that the benefits derived from this book will be many. The book has been designed to include letters that are directed primarily toward very specific situations as well as some standard ones. Litigation is rarely cut and dried and neither, for that matter, is law firm life in general. This book, therefore, has avoided the pedagogical approach to letter writing and instead concentrates on as many diverse situations as can be imagined when one deals with the law. When time is of the essence, the examples need to be at your immediate disposal. If it is found that this book eases the burden of case management, and relieves some of the accompanying stress, then it has fulfilled its mission.

Colorado Springs, Colorado
February 1994

MICHAEL VETRANO
Editor
Wiley Law Publications

ACKNOWLEDGMENTS

The editor would like to acknowledge the work and dedication of the editorial staff at Wiley Law Publications who assisted in the assembly and production of this valuable project, and in particular, the talents of Cheri Paulson and Karen Kressin, without whom this book would not have been possible.

SUMMARY CONTENTS

DETAILED CONTENTS

CHAPTER 1

CLIENT INTERVIEW AND INITIAL MATTERS

LETTER 1-1
LETTER CONFIRMING FIRST APPOINTMENT

[Date]

[Name]
[Address]

Dear [Name]:

Thank you for contacting our office. We have scheduled an appointment for you with [Name] who is one of our associates specializing in wrongful termination.

Please bring the following documents with you to your interview:

1. All correspondence and memos from any of the proposed defendants.

2. Any photos, reports, personnel file, office manual, etc.

3. Any supporting documentation for damages (medical bills, invoices, leases, contracts, payroll stubs, etc.).

Enclosed with this letter is our standard New Client Questionnaire. Please take some time before the interview to complete this form and bring it with you. Your appointment is set for [date] at [time] at the offices of [Law firm name] [Address].

If you are unable to keep this appointment, please call me at [Phone number] and I will reschedule your appointment.

We are looking forward to meeting you and hope that we can be of service to you.

Sincerely,

____

[Name]
Legal Assistant

LETTER 1-2
LETTER DECLINING REPRESENTATION 1

[Date]

[Name]
[Address]

Dear [Name]:

This will confirm the conversation that we had during your initial interview on [Date]. As I indicated at that time, I have determined that it is not economically feasible for our firm to investigate or pursue an action on your behalf. I have, therefore, not opened up a file for such a claim. This is not to say that you do not have a case, but rather that our firm would not be interested in handling such an action.

This is to further advise you that the statute of limitations for your cause of action will expire on or about [Statute of limitations date]. I would, therefore, suggest that you seek the advice of another attorney immediately.

I am sorry that we could not be of service to you.

[Attorney]

LETTER 1-3
LETTER DECLINING REPRESENTATION 2

[Date]

[Name]
[Address]

CERTIFIED MAIL: RETURN RECEIPT REQUESTED

Dear [Name]:

Thank you for your visit to our office concerning your possible medical malpractice claim against [Name]. As was explained to you at the interview, our firm has elected not to take your case, as your particular type of lawsuit falls outside our principal area of practice.

If, however, you are still interested in pursing this matter, please be advised that you only have until [Statute of limitations date] within which to file a complaint under the [State] statute of limitations. You may wish to get in touch with [Attorney name], a partner with the firm of [Law firm name], who is an expert litigator specializing in your type of problem.

We wish you the best of luck in pursuing your claim to its conclusion. If we can be of assistance to you in the future, please do not hesitate to contact us again.

Sincerely,

____
[Attorney]

LETTER 1-4
LETTER DECLINING REPRESENTATION 3

[Date] Certified Mail: Return Receipt Requested

[Name]
[Address]

Re: Potential Medical Malpractice Suit

Dear [Name],

As you are aware, you have consulted with this office concerning a potential medical malpractice lawsuit arising out of an incident which occurred on or about [Date]. Through various consultations, we have concluded that it would not be advisable for this firm to become involved in this lawsuit. We appreciate very much your consideration of our firm but we regret to inform you that <u>we cannot represent you in this matter</u>.

Please understand that by our declination of representation, we mean to imply no judgment concerning the merits or demerits of your case. We make absolutely no statement, either implied or expressed, about your chances of success in any lawsuit you may deem to file over the unfortunate events you recounted to this office. All we mean to do by this letter is to express our gratitude in thinking of us and advise you that the facts of your case do not justify any further action by this office in representing you in this potential lawsuit.

Accordingly, we felt it best to advise you immediately that <u>we will not be handling your case</u>. We would not want you to sit idly by under the assumption that this firm might be conducting this matter on your behalf, allowing the statute of limitations to expire. If you desire to pursue this matter any further, you should annotate other lawyers of your contact immediately. You should be advised that there is a statute of limitations with respect to any lawsuit filed by you, based upon the date of your surgery, [Date]. The statute of limitations in your case will expire on [Statute of limitations date].

After the statute of limitations expires in your case, you will no longer be able to pursue your lawsuit. Therefore, should you desire to proceed any further with this case, you should do so allowing your new attorney ample time to file a lawsuit prior to that date, should he feel that one is justified.

Thank you once again for your consideration and accept our sincere apologies and regrets that we cannot be of more service to you.

Very truly yours,

____

[Attorney]

LETTER 1-5
LETTER DECLINING REPRESENTATION 4

[Date] Certified Mail: Return Receipt Requested

[Name]
[Address]

Re: Potential Medical Malpractice Suit

Dear [Name]:

As you are aware, you have consulted with this office concerning a potential personal injury lawsuit arising out of an incident which occurred on or about [Date]. Through various consultations, we have concluded that it would not be advisable for this firm to become involved in this lawsuit. We appreciate very much your consideration of our firm but we regret to inform you that <u>we cannot represent you in this matter</u>.

Please understand that by our declination of representation, we mean to imply no judgment concerning the merits or demerits of your case. We make absolutely no statement, either implied or expressed, about your chances of success in any lawsuit you may deem to file over the unfortunate events you recounted to this office. All we mean to do by this letter is to express our gratitude in thinking of us and advise you that the facts of your case do not justify any further action by this office in representing you in this potential lawsuit.

Accordingly, we felt it best to advise you immediately that <u>we will not be handling your case</u>. We would not want you to sit idly by under the assumption that this firm might be conducting this matter on your behalf, allowing the statute of limitations to expire.

As you are aware, because of the impending expiration of the statute of limitations, this office on [Date of complaint] filed a complaint in pro per, making you your own attorney of record in this matter. We suggest that if you desire to pursue this matter any further, you contact another lawyer of your own choosing immediately. Please be advised that there are various deadlines that are associated with the filing of a lawsuit. The following is a summary of these deadlines:

Original Complaint filed	[Date]
Last day to file the original summons with the court	[Date]
Last day to serve all defendants with a copy of the summons and complaint	[Date]
Last day to bring your case to trial	[Date]

Based upon these imminent deadlines, should you decide to further pursue this case, you should do so with much haste and in such a fashion that your new attorney will be allowed ample time to prepare your case and adhere to the above-referenced deadlines.

Thank you once again for your consideration and accept our sincere apologies and regrets that we cannot be of more service to you.

Very truly yours

____

[Attorney]

LETTER 1-6
LETTER DECLINING REPRESENTATION IN CASE AGAINST THE VETERANS ADMINISTRATION

[Date]

CERTIFIED MAIL
RETURN RECEIPT REQUESTED

PERSONAL AND CONFIDENTIAL

[Name]
[Address]

RE: [Name]
[Reference number]

Dear [Name]:

As you know, this office filed a claim on your behalf against the Veteran's Administration Hospitals in [Place] and [Place] on [Date of claim]. Thereafter you provided us with medical records which we have reviewed along with your narrative letter enclosing further documentation.

To date, this office has received the enclosed letter from [Name], Veteran's Administration District Counsel. After reviewing this matter, we have decided that we are unable to represent you in a medical malpractice action against the United States of America and the Veteran's Administration. As you know, a claim must be filed within two years of the date of accrual of injury. The government then has six months to deny your claim or the claim will be automatically denied by operation of law U.S.C. §2675(a). If your claim is not formally denied by letter, but rather is deemed denied by operation of law, the date of that denial will be [Date], six months from the date of filing of your claim on [Date of claim]. You must then file your lawsuit by [Date], one year after that denial. If you do not file within one year after the date of denial or the deemed denial date, your claim will be forever barred by the statute of limitations.

I strongly urge you to seek other counsel regarding this matter. I would be happy to discuss it further with you or your new counsel. With this letter, I am enclosing all materials you have provided to this office, and all correspondence we have received relating to this claim including copies of our certified letters to the Veteran's Administration presenting your claim, along with copies of certified mail return receipts indicating receipt of the claim.

Thank you for contacting our office. I am sorry we could not be of further assistance and hope that this matter is resolved satisfactorily for you.

Very truly yours,

____

[Attorney]

LETTER 1-7
LETTER DECLINING REPRESENTATION WITH A GOVERNMENTAL NOTICE PROVISION

[Date]

[Name]
[Address]

Dear [Name]:

Thank you for contacting my office with respect to your potential claims arising out of surgery which you had at [Name of public hospital] on [Date]. From the information provided to my office, I do not feel you have a case which I would recommend you pursue. However, opinions of attorneys may differ and if you do wish to pursue this matter from a medical malpractice perspective, you should contact another attorney immediately.

Because the [Name of public hospital] is a governmental entity, in order to bring a suit against them you must file a notice of your claim within 180 days after the date of discovery of the injury, regardless of whether you knew all of the elements of your claim or whether you had a cause of action for such injury. The notice must contain your name and address; the name and address of an attorney, if you have one; a concise statement of the basis of your claim, including dates, times, place, and circumstances of the act, omission, or events complained of; the name and address of any public employee involved, if known; a statement of the nature and extent of the injury claimed to have been suffered; and a statement of the amount of the monetary damages being requested. You must then serve the notice by personal service or by registered mail with the Attorney General and a member of the Board of Regents and the administrator of the Hospital.

In addition to the governmental notice provision, there is a statute of limitations, or a time period beyond which you may not file a case in court against a physician, health institution, or health care providers. In [State] that statute of limitations is two years from the date both the injury and its cause are known or should have been known in the exercise of reasonable diligence. Thus, in your case, your statute of limitations would be two years from that date on which you received the care that you believe to be a problem. Therefore, your statute of limitations would run on [Date statute of limitations runs]. [From the limited information provided to my office, I am unable to determine the precise date the statute of limitations would expire.]

If you have any questions regarding the notice provision to the state or your statute of limitations, please feel free to call.

Once again, thank you for contacting this office.

____
[Attorney]

LETTER 1-8
CLIENT CONFIRMATION LETTER

[Date]

[Name]
[Address]

Re: Accident Date: [Date]

Dear [Name]:

Pursuant to your visit to our office on [Date], this letter will serve to confirm your representation by this firm for any and all claims arising from your accident of [Accident date], occurring at the intersection of New York and Florida Avenues, N.W., in Washington, D.C., when your vehicle was struck by the automobile operated by Ms. Jane Smith of Washington, D.C. As I advised you in my office, do not discuss your accident with anyone. If you are contacted by telephone, in writing, or in person concerning this accident, show them this letter and your signed contract, and ask them to contact this office immediately.

Additionally, I would like to reiterate the main points of our discussion:

1. Your next appointment with Dr. [Name] is [Date], at [Time]. Each time you see the doctor, please call or stop by my office and speak to my paralegal, [Name], who took your statement earlier today, concerning your prognosis.

2. Once you return to work, please let us know, so that we may write to your employer for loss of wages information.

3. You should arrange to obtain estimates of damage to your vehicle as soon as possible. Insurance companies prefer a minimum of two (2) estimates from local garages, and one (1) from the local dealer. Once you have these estimates, please come by or call our office so that we can make arrangements to have your vehicle repaired.

If you have any questions, please do not hesitate to contact me.

Sincerely,

____

[Attorney]

LETTER 1-9
ACKNOWLEDGMENT LETTER TO CLIENT/DEFENDANT

[Date]

[Defendant's Name]
[Defendant's Address]

Re: [Name of Case]

Dear [Defendant's Name]:

This law firm has been retained by your insurance carrier, [Name of insurance company] to represent you relative to the above referenced matter. During the course of this litigation we will need to consult with you, and naturally desire your full cooperation, in the defense of this legal action in accordance with the provisions of your insurance contract.

It is essential that we know of your current address and telephone number at all times. Should you move, even temporarily, please advise us as we may need your assistance and cooperation in answering some legal inquiry.

Since this lawsuit concerns our mutual interests, please do not discuss this matter or give any written or oral statements to anyone other than a properly identified representative of this office or [Name of insurance company]. If you have any questions, please do not hesitate to call us.

In order that we may properly and effectively defend this lawsuit in your behalf, it is imperative that we be furnished copies of all correspondence and other documents you may have accumulated in connection with this incident. Please forward the requested documentation to me as soon as possible. I would appreciate it if you would address this question at your earliest possible convenience.

Respectfully yours,

____

[Attorney]

LETTER 1-10
LETTER TO NEW CLIENT AFTER CASE HAS BEEN ACCEPTED

[Name]
[Address]

Dear [Name]:

It was a pleasure meeting with you on [Date], and we are pleased to be given the opportunity to represent you in this action.

As we discussed in our meeting, my legal assistant, [name], will be contacting you periodically so that we can be updated on your medical care and treatment. It is important that you keep copies of all medical bills which are mailed to you as well as any correspondence you may receive from the defendant or his insurance company.

We have written a letter of representation to [Insurance company] the defendant's insurer, a copy of which is enclosed for your records. You will note that we have requested all communications regarding this incident be directed to us rather than to you. It is important that you do not discuss your case with anyone outside of your immediate friends and family, treating physicians, and, of course, this office. It might be helpful for you to keep a journal in which you could jot down the dates of all doctor's appointments and your recollection of medical advice given at each appointment. You might also wish to include in the journal any pains, aches, or other symptoms which you are feeling at the moment. This is a useful way of charting your recovery, which we hope will be prompt.

We will advise you as soon as we have been contacted by an [Insurance company] representative. It is our intention to gather your medical records and bills, wage loss verification, and other items of special damage to present to the adjustor in the form of a settlement package within the next 60 to 90 days. We are hopeful that upon receipt of this settlement package, the insurance adjustor will enter into meaningful negotiations with our office. Should we fail to achieve a satisfactory settlement offer from the insurance company, we will, of course, proceed to file an action on your behalf. We have one year from the date of your accident to do so, and we will keep you advised as that time approaches.

If you have any questions at all, please do not hesitate to contact my legal assistant, [Name] or myself. We look forward to working with you in this action. Best wishes for a prompt and complete recovery.

Sincerely,

____

[Attorney]

LETTER 1-11
REPRESENTATION LETTER TO CLIENT

[Date]

[Name]
[Address]

Dear [Name]:

Thank you for the opportunity to represent you in your personal injury claim as a result of the accident/incident of [date].

Our office will initially investigate your case and in some cases we will hire a special investigator to interview you and obtain statements from any witnesses who may exist. The investigation will be conducted also to obtain photographs and to assemble all the information that is available as to how the accident/incident occurred and who is responsible. Photos of the accident scene and your injuries before the cuts and bruises have had a chance to disappear and heal will probably also be taken.

As the investigation is being conducted, our office will prepare a letter to each of your physicians and request medical records. We may also wish to contact the physician to personally interview him prior to requesting a written report.

Your insurance company or, if you do not have any insurance, the defendant's insurance company, will wish to have a list of out-of-pocket expenses from you with copies of supporting documentation. These are called special damages, which include doctor bills, hospital bills, medical bills, any loss of earnings or income which occurred as a result of the accident, and any property damage. For items of property damage, if you have repair estimates and photographs of your automobile, please provide those to us as well.

You should not discuss the details of your accident or your injuries with people who are not entitled to that information. Any inquiries from the persons responsible for your injuries or their representatives, including their insurance company, should be referred to our office. If an insurance company representative comes to you or contacts you, you are to inform him that you are represented by our law firm and refer him to us for any information he seeks. DO NOT MAKE STATEMENTS TO HIM. If you have already made statements to any insurance company representative, or anyone else, notify us immediately of these statements and we shall obtain a copy of them.

<u>Information regarding your medical treatment.</u>

You are entitled to the best medical care available to cure or to minimize the permanent effects of your injury. It is essential that you obtain copies of bills and receipts for all expenditures made by you. The financial loss suffered by you is sometimes less important than the effects of the injury. We need your assistance to keep us informed of the effects of the accident on your life and in furnishing information as to where we can get credible and admissible testimony to prove the effects of your injuries on your life. One of the jobs of the legal assistant handling your case is to accumulate all these medical records and expenses. It is essential that you communicate with her during the course of your medical treatment with any questions you may have regarding your treatment.

You should continue to go to a doctor as long as your injuries continue to bother you. You should cooperate with your doctor in every way and should relate to him truthfully and fully all symptoms you have that were a result of this accident. You should answer all questions that he asks you. Medical treatment often takes time to produce results. You cannot expect a doctor to give effective testimony about your condition at the time of trial if several months have elapsed since he last examined you. Also, insurance companies will often treat this failure to obtain medical treatment as evidence that there was no injury or that you are exaggerating. Naturally we do not want you to fake or exaggerate anything, but as long as there is something legitimately wrong with you, in order to help the doctors make their diagnosis and avoid a distortion of your medical picture by the insurance company, you should continue to obtain the medical care you need.

If you have had prior injuries, particularly to the same area of the body, you must let us know. This information often appears in medical records and it is not in your best interest to attempt to hide that fact. As long as we are made aware of any prior or subsequent injuries, we can deal with that fact.

One of the most significant factors affecting the value of your lawsuit is whether or not we can establish by doctor testimony that you have suffered a permanent injury because of the accident. Doctors know from experience that the full extent of a person's injuries is not known for several months after the accident. It is important for you to advise us of your medical progress, including when your doctor refers you for physical therapy or to another doctor in a different specialty. We will then be able to get complete copies of all your records, which is of utmost importance in documenting your case.

Do not talk about your case or your lawyers when you see your doctor. You do not want to give the impression that you care more about collecting money than you do about getting well.

The value of your case.

Some insurance companies, in cases in which the liability or fault is clear, relate the value of the case to the special damages. It is often unrealistic to evaluate your case on such factors because the major factors, including your physical pain and suffering and the loss of your capacity to lead a normal life, may have a greater impact on the value of your case.

After we have assembled all the information, we will make the best estimate of the least jury verdict we could obtain, the highest jury verdict we could obtain, and the probable jury verdict. These figures are based on our experience as well as research that we have regarding jury verdicts for similar cases in our area.

In those cases where there is some question as to whether we can win, we think it is necessary to discount the probable jury verdict by the percentage of our chances of winning. For example, if we estimate in a hypothetical case that we could obtain a jury verdict in the amount of $10,000 but that we have only a 50–50 chance of winning, we believe that for settlement purposes the value of the case is approximately $5,000.

Automobile accident cases. [Omit when not applicable]

There are special factors that influence the value of your case. These factors also affect whether or not we will be able to file a lawsuit on your behalf.

Many legislatures have greatly limited the rights of people to recover for injuries sustained in automobile accidents. In states where no-fault laws are applicable, the theory of no-fault is that it will permit limited recovery for some of your medical bills and some of your lost wages from your own insurance company even if you caused the automobile accident. However, the rights of injured people who are not at fault are sometimes also limited: they may be able to sue the people who have injured them only if they have permanent injuries or meet other threshold requirements. For example, in some jurisdictions you must have incurred $2,500 in medical bills, a permanent disfigurement, or a permanent injury.

There are situations when the driver of the other vehicle had no automobile insurance or had automobile insurance in the least amount that can be carried by law. It is therefore necessary for us to know whether you have a policy of automobile liability insurance and whether you have purchased uninsured motorist coverage on that policy. In most states an injured person is permitted to make a claim for his pain and suffering under his own insurance policy if he has uninsured motorist coverage. Sometimes this coverage may be the only source of recovery for you or your family for the negligence of another driver.

Filing the lawsuit.

In some jurisdictions you are permitted to file a lawsuit only if you have met the threshold requirements, and within two years from the date of the accident. This time period is provided for by law and once that time period has elapsed you are forever barred from pursuing your claim. We usually will not initiate a lawsuit until the permanency of your injuries becomes known or until this time period is about to run, whichever comes first. If a lawsuit is filed, you are the plaintiff. A complaint filed on your behalf states the reasons why we believe you have a cause of action against the defendant and sets forth the claims we are making. The defendant has 20 days after he has been served with the papers of the lawsuit to respond or answer that claim. Often the defendant will claim that you contributed to your own injuries.

Many clients want to know how much we are going to sue for. In order not to be prevented from recovering a larger amount than what is possible, we try not to request a specific amount. We are therefore able to recover an amount proportionate to the nature and extent of your injuries.

During the course of the lawsuit, we will take testimony from all witnesses and doctors who may be involved in the case.

The attorney for the defendant will send written questions, known as interrogatories, which must be answered under oath in writing. The attorney for the defendant will also take your deposition. A deposition is oral questions given to you under oath in an informal setting. Your attorney will be present with you during this time and he will adequately prepare you prior to your deposition.

This phase of the lawsuit is called discovery and its purpose is to attempt to narrow the issues for trial.

There are certain items of damages that you are entitled to recover in most lawsuits. These include:

1. past pain and suffering,

2. future pain and suffering,

3. loss of income,

4. future loss of income and loss of earning capacity,

5. out-of-pocket expenses, such as doctor bills or other medical bills and property damage for which you have not been reimbursed, and

6. loss of consortium on behalf of the noninjured spouse.

Loss of consortium is the loss of services of an injured spouse in all ways that the spouse renders service to his or her mate, including housekeeping, lawn mowing, maintenance, cooking, companionship, and sexual relations.

We will not settle your claim without your permission and we are bound to advise you of any offers of settlement that are made to us on your behalf.

The following is a list of important things that you can do to help us in our representation. This list is designed to help you furnish us with information that is of great importance in preparing your case for both trial and settlement purposes. You should keep us informed of any changes that may occur. Items of information we need from you are as follows:

1. A diary of your activities, with emphasis on restriction of the activities caused by your injuries, specific pains and the frequency of them, the frequency of medications taken, and the kind of medication. This diary may be useful to refresh your memory as to occurrences that might be forgotten. This should be kept personal and may be as simple as jotting remarks on a calendar when appropriate.

2. Keep any physical objects such as shoes or clothing that you had on at the time of the accident. We may need to use them as evidence at trial.

3. Provide our cffice with itemized receipts of (a) hospital bills, (b) doctor bills, (c) ambulance bills, (d) nursing bills, (e) drug bills, and (f) all other expenses you incurred as a result of the accident, including (i) travel to and from the doctor's office and any time you have missed from work as a result of these office appointments, and (ii) additional help around the home or business that you have required (including babysitters or domestic or yard help).

4. The names of neighbors, friends, employees, or relatives who knew of your activities both before and after the accident.

As you think of any other information that you think should be added to this list, please let us know. The more information we have, the better job we can do for you. Please do not hesitate to call the legal assistant or myself with any questions you might have. We will do our best to represent you fairly and aggressively and will keep you informed of the progress of your case.

____

[Attorney]

LETTER 1-12
RETENTION LETTER AGREEMENT—BANKRUPTCY

[Date]

[Name]
[Company]
[Address]

Dear [Name]:

When you return a signed copy of this letter to me, you will have agreed as follows:

1. [Law firm] will represent [Company] in [Company's] Chapter 11 bankruptcy.
2. [Law firm] will charge [Company] at its standard hourly rates for this representation.
3. [Law firm] will require a retainer of $50,000 to be paid before it will represent [Company]. The retainer will be held in our trust account pending authorization of the bankruptcy court to apply funds from the retainer to our outstanding bills.
4. [Name] and [Name] agree to guarantee the payment of any fees charged but not covered by the retainer or funds from [Company].

We look forward to working with you.

Sincerely,

[Attorney]

WE AGREE TO THE ABOVE TERMS

[Company]

By ________________________
Its President

____
[Name], personally

LETTER 1-13
REPORT TO CLIENT REGARDING REPRESENTATION

[Date]

[Name]
[Company]
[Address]

Re: [Case name]
Your Claim No. : [Number]
Insured : [Name]
Date of Loss : [Date]
Our File No. : [File number]

Dear [Name]:

I have been assigned to handle this file. Please address all further communications to my attention. Plaintiff has propounded a request for production of documents which I enclosed for your review, together with a copy of our proposed response. Please execute the enclosed verification and return it to me at your earliest convenience, together with a copy of your workers' compensation file. I will go through the files and remove all privileged documentation prior to production.

Should you have any questions, please do not hesitate to contact me. I look forward to working with you on this file.

Very truly yours,

[Attorney]

Enclosures: Request for Production
Proposed Responses
Verification

LETTER 1-14
LETTER INTRODUCING
INSURANCE CARRIER'S ATTORNEY TO INSURED

[Date]

[Company]
[Address]

Re: [Case name]
Our File No. : [Number]
WCAB Case No. : Unassigned
Claim No. : [Number]
DOI : [Date]

Gentlemen:

We are attorneys employed in the Field Litigation Division of the Law Department of [Insurance company]. Our firm has been designated to represent and defend your interests in the above-captioned litigation.

It may be necessary for us to contact you from time to time in regard to our handling of this case. Please insure that you keep us advised of any changes in your telephone number or address so we will be able to contact you. In addition, please let us know the name and title of the person to whom you would like us to report.

Should anyone approach you seeking information regarding this case, other than our office, your insurance company, or their authorized representative, please refrain from providing any information and direct that individual to contact our offices.

If you have any questions regarding the status of the above referenced workers' compensation case, please feel free to contact us at any time.

Very truly yours,

[Attorney]

LETTER 1-15
DUAL REPRESENTATION LETTER

[Date]

[Name
[Address]

RE: Mr. & Mrs. [Name]—Estate Planning
Our File No. [Number]

Dear [Name] and [Name]:

When you both were in my office for our initial meeting on [Date], I explained to you four alternatives for representation in your estate planning: that one of you could use me and the other could use an attorney from another firm; that each of you go to a different other attorney from a different other firm; that I could counsel you both together as joint clients; that I could counsel you separately as separate clients if either of you so chose. You both opted to have me represent the two of you jointly, rather than separately, and rather then either or both of you going to another attorney or other attorneys. However, I write this letter in order to repeat, and also supplement, what I told you both at that meeting, so that each of you can review and further consider your initial decision. Of course each of you is free to consult or switch to a lawyer from one or more other law firms at any time, despite your signing and returning this letter to me.

In negotiating any contract between two parties each of the parties should, except in the most extraordinary of circumstances, be represented by an attorney from a different firm. This is because a contract, once entered into, binds both parties and therefore cannot be changed unilaterally by either. In the estate planning field, marriage or pre-marriage contract (or a contract to make a will in those jurisdictions, other than Louisiana, that permit this) is an example of such a contract requiring separate-firm representation.

By contract the establishment of gifts (outright or in trust) and the preparation of wills are examples of noncontractual, individual actions that leave each person free to make unilateral changes in his or her future plans without knowledge or acquiescence of any other person. Since your estate planning does not involve any planned marriage contract, each of you is free to make any desired changes in your plan unilaterally, regardless of what lawyer each of you uses. Therefore, the choice of having me represent both of you jointly (on the one hand) or separately (on the other hand) is available to each of you, and I therefore am detailing the differences.

On the one hand, if I were to represent both of you jointly, I would have to immediately tell the other anything which one of you later told me in confidence that related to his/her estate planning, since not to reveal such information to the other would be a violation of the attorney-client joint relationship. This might inhibit each of you from telling me something in confidence that you thought I needed to know, because you would realize that I would be forced to disclose it to the other.

On the other hand, if I were to represent each of your separately, I would have to keep in confidence, and conceal from the other, anything later told me in confidence by one of you even though it prejudiced what the other relied upon in making his or her own estate plan, including such difference as how each of you would like to transfer your property or your interest in community property by gift or at death, as how each of you would like to have your income, gift and estate taxes allocated and paid, and as how each of you would like your interest in community property to be managed and controlled.

However, there might be or might arise disputes between you as to which assets are separate and which are community, or whether (or how much of) any reimbursement should be made from the community to the separate estate of either of you (or vice versa), and I would not in any event be able to represent either of you in resolving any such dispute; if such a dispute were to arise I would tell each of you to go a different law firm.

This written explanation is designed to make it certain that each of you fully understands the consequences of the joint representation you previously opted for. In order that the file can reflect this, and assuming that neither of you wishes to change your mind, each of you should sign the enclosed copy of this letter and return it to me for the file.

With kindest regards to each of you.

Sincerely,

____

[Attorney]

LETTER 1-16
CONFIRMATION FROM CLIENTS OF DUAL REPRESENTATION

[Date]

[Name]
[Address]

Dear [Attorney]:

I hereby agreed to, and reconfirm my previous decision, to have you represent me and [Name] jointly. While as to others you are to keep in strict confidence everything that either one of us reveals to you, I hereby authorize and direct you to tell [Name] anything which I reveal to you about my estate plan while we are married, even information which I reveal to you outside of [Name]'s presence. I understand that [Name] will be giving you the same authorization and direction.

[Signature]
[Date]

Dear [Attorney]:

I hereby agreed to, and reconfirm my previous decision, to have you represent me and [Name] jointly. While as to others you are to keep in strict confidence everything that either one of us reveals to you, I hereby authorize and direct you to tell [Name] anything which I reveal to you about my estate plan while we are married, even information which I reveal to you outside of [Name]'s presence. I understand that [Name] will be giving you the same authorization and direction.

[Signature]
[Date]

LETTER 1-17
LETTERS OF CONSERVATORSHIP

DISTRICT COURT, COUNTY OF [ ], STATE OF [ ]

Case No. [ ], Division [ ]

LETTERS OF CONSERVATORSHIP

IN THE MATTER OF THE ESTATE OF
[minor],
A Protected Person.

WHEREAS, on this [ ] day [month, year] [conservator] was appointed or qualified as Conservator of the Estate of [minor], a protected person, by this Court or its Registrar, with all authority pertaining thereto;

NOW THEREFORE, these Letters of Conservatorship are issued as evidence of such appointment or qualification and authority.

WITNESS my signature and the Seal of this Court on this [ ] day of [month, year].

(Seal of Court)

(Deputy) Clerk or Registrar of Court

CERTIFICATION

Certified to be a full, true and correct copy of the original in my custody and control and to be in full force and effect as of [date].

(Deputy) Clerk of the Court

LETTER 1-18
PRELIMINARY CASE EVALUATION LETTER TO CLIENT 1

[Date]

[Name]
[Company]
[Address]

Re: [Case name]
Our File No. : [Number]
WCAB No. : Unassigned
Claim No. : [Number]
D.O.I. : [Date]

Dear [Name]:

INITIAL EVALUATION

I have now had an opportunity to review in detail all of the materials which were sent along with this file for defense of the workers' compensation case. The following will provide you with my initial evaluation and suggestions for further handling.

FACTS

The applicant, then a 34 year old roofer employed by [Company] was driving northbound on the 55 freeway in Orange County on his way to a job site when he was rear ended in stop and go traffic. This specific injury occurred on [Date]. The applicant apparently worked that day, but has not returned to work since. After waiting a few days, he sought medical treatment through his employer, who referred him (at Travelers' suggestion) to the [medical center] for treatment. He later began treating with neurosurgeon [Doctor's name], M.D., who had treated the applicant previously for a 1987 workers' compensation injury.

Dr. [Name] found problems in both the applicant's cervical and lumbar spine. On [Date], the applicant underwent surgery at L4-5 (the site of a previous September 1987 laminectomy). On [Date], he underwent surgery at C5-6. On [Date], Dr. [Name] found the applicant to be permanent and stationary and ready to participate in vocational rehabilitation.

ISSUES

AOE/COE is not an issue in this case, inasmuch as the injury was accepted as industrial. It appears that the applicant was paid temporary total disability benefits from [Date] through [Date], when he began receiving vocational rehabilitation maintenance allowance. He is a maximum wage earner for purposes of calculating his TD, VRMA, and PD rates.

Because of the applicant's prior workers' compensation injury, apportionment will be the central issue in this case. Dr. [Name] has found that there is no apportionment with respect to the cervical spine, but that 50% of the applicant's permanent disability is apportionable to this accident. However, the work restriction imposed by Dr. [Name] (no heavy work; equivalent to a 30% standard rating) does not specify whether it is related to the cervical or lumbar spine (or both).

We will need to review both Dr. [Name]'s reports concerning the applicant's previous injury as well as his prior workers' compensation case. These have been requested.

STATUS OF MEDICALS

The applicant is now post-two surgeries and permanent and stationary according to his treating physician, Dr. [Name]. Dr. [Name] does find that the applicant will need future medical care during his lifetime, but the nature of this care is not specified.

VOCATIONAL REHABILITATION

VRMA payments have begun, and the applicant should be immediately enrolled in a vocational rehabilitation program, if this has not already been done. Since I do not have any information concerning his educational or employment background, I cannot comment as to the likelihood of his success in vocational rehabilitation. The fact that he took on a physically strenuous job after a prior laminectomy leads me to believe that, despite all efforts to retrain him to something more sedentary, he will probably take on a strenuous type of job after completing his program.

SUGGESTIONS FOR FURTHER HANDLING

We have requested the complete records of Dr. [Name] as well as the applicant's prior WCAB case. (Incidentally, if you have the WCAB case number, it would be very helpful in locating that file.) Once we have received that information, we will be in a position to render an opinion concerning settlement of the permanent disability. However, assuming that the work restriction applies to the lumbar spine, I would expect that the case would be settled for approximately half of the 38% adjusted PD rating of Dr. [Name]'s report, plus a substantial premium for a C&R if surgery is, in fact, a future possibility. Dr. [Name]'s P&S report is not very thorough with respect to whether the applicant may have lost motion in his neck, but we would, certainly, argue that any loss of motion in the neck should be subsumed under the heavy work restriction.

I will let you know as soon as we have received the requested records. In the meantime, please keep me informed as to the applicant's status in vocational rehabilitation, having the vendor copy me on all of the status reports. Should there be any difficulties in the rehabilitation process, we will, of course, be happy to assist you in handling them.

Very truly yours,

[law firm]

By

[attorney]

LETTER 1-19
PRELIMINARY CASE EVALUATION LETTER TO CLIENT 2

[Date]

[Name]
[Address]

Dear [Name]:

We are in receipt of the [Case name] file which you forwarded to us on [Date]. We would like to thank you for referring this file to us.

(Because of the improper service of this complaint on [Date], our first action will be to file a motion to quash service.) All (other) components of the complaint seem to be in order, and (as soon as proper service is effected,) we will proceed immediately with an answer. As usual, we will forward our standard predeposition interrogatories to the plaintiff when we file our answer.

Our investigation will begin by obtaining a copy of the accident report and a visual inspection of the scene. We also plan to order a history of accidents at that intersection from the Highway Department.

As soon as we have received the plaintiff's answers to interrogatories and have evaluated the above information, we will forward to you our initial suit evaluation.

Thank you again for the referral. We appreciate your continued confidence.

Respectfully yours,

____
[Attorney]

LETTER 1-20
LETTER REQUESTING MISSING PLEADINGS

[Date]

[Name]
[Address]

Regarding: [Case Name]
[Case Number]

Dear [Name]:

Thank you for responding to the request for copies for pleadings that were [served/mailed] on behalf of our client, [Client's name], on [Date]. However, certain documents appear to be missing. We would appreciate receiving the following documents, which appear to have originated in your office:

1. Your answer to plaintiff's complaint;
2. Your responses to plaintiff's 2d set of interrogatories;
3. Your admissions to deft. [Name]'s RFA;
4. Your motion to compel, for which we have only a notice.

Thank you for your assistance. If you have any questions, please do not hesitate to call.

Very truly yours,

[Legal Assistant]
Legal Assistant to
[Attorney]

LETTER 1-21
SUMMARY-OF-PLEADINGS LETTER FROM ATTORNEY RECENTLY ENTERING CASE

[Date]

[Name]
[Address]

Dear [Name]:

The following is a summary of pleadings in this case before we entered it.

Complaint: Plaintiff filed a complaint for personal injuries on [Date]. As you know, you were not served until [Date of service], almost one-and-a-half years later. Plaintiff's complaint did not name [corporation], but their answer below indicates that they were served as Doe 2.

Cross-complaint: [Corporation]'s attorney signed a cross-complaint for indemnity, apportionment of fault and declaratory relief on [Date] but, again, you were not served until [Date of service].

Demand for Jury: [Corporation] served this pleading on plaintiff on [Date of service].

Answer to Complaint: [Corporation] served as Doe 2, served its answer to plaintiff's complaint on [Date of service].

Request for Statement of Damages and Response: After [Corporation] served a request on [Date of service] plaintiff served her response on [Date of service]. Plaintiff's responses listed [Amount] for health care providers and [Amount] for estimated general damages. Plaintiff stated "unknown" in response to future medical, loss of earnings and other special damages.

At-issue memorandum: Plaintiff did not request a jury trial, which she estimated at [Number] days.

Status Conference Evaluation Questionnaire: On [Date] plaintiff listed total medical expenses to date of [Amount] loss of earning to date of [Amount] and [Amount] in general damages.

COMMENTS: Depending on the trial date, I may obtain the records of plaintiff from medical physicians and facilities whose records we have not yet received but who were mentioned in various pleadings. If you have any recommendations or questions, please do not hesitate to contact me.

Very truly yours,

____

[ATTORNEY]

LETTER 1-22
LETTER TO PREVIOUS ATTORNEY REQUESTING CLIENT FILE

[Date]

[Name]
[Address]

Dear [Former Attorney]:

[Name], your previous client, has consulted our law firm regarding representation for injuries she received in an accident which occurred on [Date]. We understand that you were the attorney of record for [Name] and that your firm handled her case from approximately [date on client's copy of prior retainer agreement] until approximately [Date], at which time [Name] sent the enclosed letter to you (or caused and expressed clear intent to dismiss attorney), indicating her intention to seek new counsel and requesting the return of her original documents and client file.

We would like to arrange a specific date and time for [Name] to come to your office and pick up her documents. Please contact our office within the next ten (10) days to set a time.

[Name] has retained our law firm to represent her and we have prepared a standard Substitution of Attorney form for your signature. Please execute this form and return it to us. We will be happy to send you a file-endorsed copy of the substitution for your records.

Your cooperation will be appreciated in expediting the transfer of [Name]'s file so that we may file an appearance on her behalf and protect her interests in this lawsuit.

Thank you for your anticipated professional courtesy.

Sincerely,

____

[Name of Attorney named on
Substitution of Attorney who
will become attorney of record]

LETTER 1-23
LETTER REGARDING MISSING ITEMS

[Date]

[Name]
[Address]

Re: [Case name]
DOI: [Incident date]
Case No.: [Court case number]
File No.: [Your firm's case file number]

Dear [Attorney]:

Thank you for responding to the request for copies of pleadings served by our client, [Name of client], on [Date].

However, certain documents appear to be missing. We would appreciate receiving copies of the following documents, which appear to have originated in your office:

1. ____
2. ____
3. ____

Thank you in advance for your assistance. If you have any questions, please do not hesitate to call.

Sincerely,

[Name]
Legal Assistant to
[Attorney's name]

LETTER 1-24
LETTER REGARDING MISSING ITEMS (ALTERNATE)

[Date]

[Name]
[Address]

Re: [Case name]
DOI: [Incident date]
Case No.: [Court case number]
File No.: [Your firm's case file number]

Dear [Attorney]:

This office has substituted in as attorney for [Client]. Upon review of the files received from [Prior attorney], it appears that certain documents are missing.

We would appreciate receiving copies of the following documents, which appear to have originated in your office:

1. ______________________________
2. ______________________________
3. ______________________________

Thank you in advance for your assistance. If you have any questions, please do not hesitate to call.

Sincerely,

[Name]
Legal Assistant to
[Attorney's name]

LETTER 1-25
LETTER TO MEDICAL PROVIDER RE: DEFERRED PAYMENTS

[Date]

[Medical Provider]
[Address]

Re: [Name of Client]
[Date of Accident]

Gentlemen:

Our office has been retained by [name of client] to represent him in his claim for injuries and damages arising from an automobile collision on [date of accident].

Enclosed is an authorization signed by [name of client] which promises to pay medical charges and services billed to him upon settlement or verdict against the party responsible for the collision.

We anticipate that it will be six months to one year before the full extent of [name of client]'s damages are known and we will then be in a position to discuss settlement. Although [name of client] has a meritorious claim, he has no medical insurance to meet his ongoing expenses. If you can cooperate with him in this matter by agreeing to defer receipt of payment until we receive funds through the civil suit, he should be able to pay your account in full.

Thank you for your patience and cooperation.

[Signature]

LETTER 1-26
LETTER TO CREDITORS TO PREVENT HARASSMENT

[Date]

[Creditor's Name]
[Address]

Re: [Name of Client]
Date of Accident: [Date]

Gentlemen:

This office represents [name of client] as a result of damages and injuries received in a collision which is referenced above. [Name of client] did not have insurance coverage available at the time of this incident. When and if recovery is made on behalf of [name of client], the amount of your bill will be protected.

Thank you for your patience and cooperation in this matter.

[Signature]

LETTER 1-27
LETTER OF CLIENT'S AGREEMENT TO PAY

[Date]
[Creditor]
[Address]
[City, State, Zip]

Re: Patient/Client's Name: [Name]
Treatment date or Patient #: [Date]

Dear [Creditor]:

Enclosed please find an agreement signed by [client's name] which states that payment will be made for medical services provided by you from any monies received from either trial or settlement of a legal claim for damages which [client's name] has as the result of an automobile collision on [date of accident]. Payment to you will be made in the same proportion for which damages for these medical expenses are recovered.

Although [client's name] has no applicable insurance [him/her]self, the party who we believe is responsible for these charges being incurred is insured and [client's name] legal position is favorable.

This agreement to pay is made in consideration of an understanding that you will agree to await the completion of our legal representation before you decide whether you shall avail yourself of any collection procedures. Please understand that our ability to conclude this case will largely be dependent upon the rate of [client's name] medical progress over which, of course, we have no control. However, we agree to keep you informed of such progress as you may make inquiry.

If you agree to this proposal, then we shall, furthermore, agree to presume that your charges are both "reasonable" and "necessary." However, in the event you choose to disregard this offer and commence collection related activities against [client's name], then we reserve the right to disregard this presumption and to fully contest such matters.

We shall assume that you are in agreement with this arrangement until such time as we receive notice that [client's name] has become the subject of collection activities.

Thank you for your cooperation and please do not hesitate to contact me if at any time you have questions concerning our progress towards settlement. Until then, please forward copies of all charges directly to my office to the attention of my secretary, [secretary's name].

Very truly yours,

[Signature]

LETTER 1-28
LETTER OF REPRESENTATION TO CLIENT'S INSURANCE CARRIER

[Date]

[Insurance Company]
[Address]

Re: Your Insured: [Name]
Claim Number: [Name]
Date of Loss: [Name]
Claimant: [if insured is other than person making the claim]

Dear [Insurance Adjustor]:

Our office has been retained to represent [client] in his claim for injuries and damages as a result of the accident of [date].

Please provide our office with a complete copy of your PIP file and ledger sheet regarding payments made on [client]'s behalf. If there are bills that have been submitted and not paid, please provide copies of those bills and a brief explanation for the nonpayment. I have enclosed a release so that you may comply with this request.

I would appreciate receiving this information within the next two weeks. If this is not possible, please let us know. We will be happy to reimburse for any costs of copying. Thank you for your courtesy and cooperation.

[Signature]

LETTER 1-29
LETTER TO CLIENT'S CARRIER REQUESTING PIP INFORMATION

Re: Uninsured/Underinsured Motorist Claim

[Date]

[Carrier Name]
[Address]

Re: Your Insured: [Name]
Claim Number: [Number]
Date of Loss: [Name]
Claimant: (if insured is other than person making the claim)

Dear [Adjustor]:

Our office has been retained to represent [client] in his claim for injuries and damages as a result of the accident of [date].

Please provide our office with a complete copy of your PIP file and ledger sheet regarding payments made on [clients] behalf. If there are bills that have been submitted and not paid, please provide copies of those bills and a brief explanation for nonpayment.

Our preliminary investigation reveals that the party at fault did not have insurance [or had only minimal limits of coverage] at the time of this accident. Please be advised that we intend to pursue a claim against our client's uninsured motorist coverage [or underinsured motorist coverage]. I have enclosed an affidavit from the defendant driver indicating that he did not have any automobile insurance coverage on the date of the accident.

In order to avoid a conflict of interest, we would appreciate it if you would assign a separate adjustor to handle the uninsured/underinsured motorist portion of this claim.

We will be happy to reimburse you for any costs of copying the PIP file. I would appreciate receiving this information within the next two weeks. If this is not possible, please let me know. Thank you for your courtesy and cooperation.

[Signature]

LETTER 1-30
NOTIFICATION OF REPRESENTATION OF INJURED WORKER

[Date]

[Insurance company]
[Address]

RE: Applicant: [Name]
Employer: [Employee name]
Date of Loss: [Date]

Dear Sir/Madam:

This office represents the above referenced applicant in his/her workers' compensation case against the above referenced employer. Enclosed herein please find the Disclosure Statement noticing this representation.

It is our understanding that a claim has previously been submitted on this matter. However, if a claim has not previously been submitted, enclosed is a claim form completed and signed by our client, serving as your notice of claim. Also enclosed please find an Information Request form for your response.

Demand is hereby made for service of all medical reports and records concerning the applicant. Further, demand is hereby made upon defendants, and each of them, for a copy of any statements taken of the applicant.

If ninety days has lapsed since the written claim, please inform us if the claim has been rejected.

Very truly yours,

[Law firm]

[Attorney]

DISCLOSURE STATEMENT

You are not required to be represented by an attorney in the handling of your workers' compensation case.

If you choose to be represented by an attorney, your attorney's fees will be deducted from your benefits. Attorney's fees normally range from 9% to 12% of the benefits awarded. The actual amount of your attorney's fee will depend on the complexity of your case. The fee has to be approved by the Workers' Compensation Appeals Board. If your attorney has also represented you before the Rehabilitation Unit, there may also be a fee in conjunction with this representation.

There are certain circumstances where your employer or his/her insurance carrier may be liable for the attorney's fees. (Statutory section).

However, at no charge you may contact the Office of Benefit Assistance and Enforcement and talk to an Information and Assistance Officer regarding questions concerning your workers' compensation benefits. He/She may be able to resolve your problems without the need for litigation. **Call this toll-free number:** [Telephone number]

If you choose to be represented by an attorney, you and your attorney must sign this form. A copy of this form must be sent to your employer. (Labor Code Section 4906). If at any time you no longer wish to be represented by the attorney, you may withdraw from representation by notifying the attorney. If you withdraw from representation, you will still be responsible for the fee amount found by a workers' compensation judge to be the fair value of any work the attorney did in your case.

Employee's Signature [Employee] Date [Date]

Attorney's Signature [Attorney] Date [Date]

Attorney: ***Give a copy to the employee***

LETTER 1-31
LETTER INTRODUCING ATTORNEY OF RECORD

[Date]

[Name]
[Company]
[Address]

Re: [Case name]

Our File No.	:	[Number]
WCAB No.	:	Unassigned
Claim No	:	[Number]
D.O.I.	:	[Date]

Dear [Name]:

Thank you for the recent forwarding of the above-captioned workers' compensation file. I will be the attorney of record handling this matter and will be forwarding an Initial Evaluation Report detailing this claim with my recommendations within 30 days of receipt of this file.

Kindly send all correspondence regarding this case to my attention, together with any specific instructions or employer information.

Thank you for your courtesy and cooperation regarding this matter.

Very truly yours,

[Attorney]

LETTER 1-32
REQUEST OF WORKERS' COMPENSATION CARRIER FOR COPY OF COMPLAINT FROM INJURED WORKER'S ATTORNEY

[Date]

[Attorney name]
[Address]

Re: [Case name]
Our Client: [Name]
Our File No.: [Number]
Date/Injury: [Date]

Dear [Name]:

Please be advised this office represents [Name] in its efforts to be reimbursed for workers' compensation benefits paid to or on behalf of [Name] subsequent to a [Date] automobile accident. If your office filed a complaint on behalf of [Name] for damages and injuries sustained in the [Date] automobile accident, please serve such complaint on this office as required by Labor Code §3853. In the event no complaint has been filed, and any settlement negotiations unproductive, I suggest respective offices concurrently file complaints and stipulate to consolidation of the complaints. As a practical matter, if the initiation of lawsuits is performed simultaneously, discovery can be coordinated, and costs and tasks shared between counsel.

Subsequent to your review of this letter, please call me and provide me with an oral report on the filing status of a complaint and/or any settlement negotiations.

If you have any questions regarding this matter, or requests of this office, please do not hesitate to contact me. I look forward to hearing from you in the near future regarding the filing status of the complaint.

Very truly yours,

[Attorney]

LETTER 1-33
TRANSMITTAL TO DEFENDANT'S INSURANCE COMPANY OF COPY OF COMPLAINT IN SUBROGATION

[Date]

[Name]
[Insurance Company]
[Address]

Re: [Case name]
Your Insured : [Name]
Your Claim No. : [Number]
Date of Loss : [Date]
Our File No. : [Number]

Dear [Name]:

This law firm has been retained by [Insurance company] to represent its interests in the above-reference case. [Insurance company] is the workers' compensation carrier for [Name]. [Name] was in the course and scope of his employment with [Name] at the time he was injured in an automobile accident on [Date].

Our research indicates that the accident was entirely the fault of your insured driver, [Name]. [Insurance company] has been required to pay for medical expenses and/or compensation due to injuries suffered by [Name]. [Insurance company] will be looking to [Name] and [Name] Insurance for reimbursement for all money paid to or behalf of [Name].

I enclose with this letter for your convenience a courtesy copy of the Complaint in Subrogation which I have prepared for filing in the [Location] Court. This will be a fast track case and I will be required to serve [Name] with the Summons and Complaint within 60 days of filing. I therefore request you call me as soon as possible to discuss possible negotiated settlement of the claim. With your cooperation and that of [Name], we may be able to avoid protracted litigation.

Very Truly Yours,

[Attorney]

LETTER 1-34
LETTER FROM WORKERS' COMPENSATION CARRIER TO DEFENDANT REGARDING INTENT TO SEEK REIMBURSEMENT

[Date]

[Name]
[Address]

Re: [Case name]
Our Insured : [Name]
Date of Loss : [Date]
Our File No. : [Number]

Dear [Name]:

This law firm has been retained by [Insurance company] to represent its interests in the above-referenced case. [Insurance company] is the workers' compensation carrier for [Name]. [Name] was in the course and scope of his employment for [Name] at the time he was injured in an automobile accident on [Date].

Our records and research indicate that you were driving the other motor vehicle in the subject accident. Our records also indicate that you were responsible for the accident. [Insurance company] has paid money to or on behalf of [Name] for medical expenses and compensation as a result of the injuries he sustained in the accident. Because we believe you to be liable, we will be looking to you and your liability insurance carrier for reimbursement of the money paid to or on behalf of [Name].

I understand that you are insured by [Name] Insurance Companies for the loss involved in this lawsuit. I suggest you contact [Insurance company] immediately about this claim. I have also written [Insurance company] and requested they contact me.

I would prefer to resolve this matter without litigation. However, if no settlement can be negotiated I will be required to file a Complaint in the immediate future. In that case, you will be made a defendant and served with the Summons and Complaint.

Should you have any questions or comments, please call our office.

Very Truly Yours,

[Attorney]

LETTER 1-35
LETTER FROM WORKERS' COMPENSATION CARRIER'S ATTORNEY REQUESTING CERTAIN INFORMATION

[Date]

[Attorney name]
[Address]

Re: [Case name]
Our Insured : [Name]
Date of Loss : [Date]
Our File No. : [Number]

Dear [Name]:

Please be advised I am the attorney handling [Insurance company]'s Complaint-in-Intervention in the above referenced case. Responding to your recent correspondence to [Name] at [Insurance company], I enclose copies of the latest payment summary and detail showing payments made to or on behalf of [Name] by [Insurance company].

I trust that you will by now have received our Complaint-in-Intervention. Please advise me of any calendar dates, such as Status Evaluation Conferences or depositions. Should you have any questions or comments concerning the workers' compensation claim, or any other aspect of the action, please do not hesitate to call. I sincerely appreciate your professional courtesy and cooperation.

Very truly yours,

[Attorney]

LETTER 1-36
NOTIFICATION TO OPPOSING COUNSEL OF REPRESENTATION OF INSURANCE CARRIER AND DEFENDANT

[Date]

[Name]
[Address]

Re: [Case name]
Our File No. : [Name]
WCAB No. : Unassigned
Claim No. : [Number]
D.O.I. : [Date]

Dear Mr. Hite:

This office has been retained to represent the interest of [Insurance Company] and [Name] in the above-referenced case. Please direct all future correspondence to this office.

If you have any medical reports concerning the applicant, we request that you serve them on us at this time, and provide us with a copy of the attorney disclosure form as required by Labor Code Section 4906(e).

Also, please provide us with the applicant's Social Security Number, and the names of all treating doctors for any prior workers' compensation cases the applicant has filed.

Thank you for your courtesy and cooperation in this matter.

Very truly yours,

[Attorney]

LETTER 1-37
LETTER OF REPRESENTATION TO TORTFEASOR

[Date]

[Tortfeasor's Name]
[Address]

Re: Name of Client: [Name]
Date of Accident: [Date]

Dear [Tortfeasors name]:

We represent [Client] in his claim for personal injuries sustained in the automobile collision of [Date]. [Add the following if the defendant driver is different from the defendant owner: [Driver] was driving a vehicle which you owned that was involved in this accident.]

This letter is to request that you contact our office within ten days with the name of your insurance carrier, or to advise us of your status of insurance at the time of the accident. Please notify your insurance company of this accident if you have not already done so. Please have a representative of your insurance company contact us as soon as possible but no later than thirty days from the date of this letter. This will eliminate the need for us to contact you further.

Thank you for your cooperation and assistance.

[Signature]

LETTER 1-38
LETTER TO DEFENDANT
REQUESTING AFFIDAVIT OF NO INSURANCE

[Date]

[Defendant's Name]
[Address]

Re: Client's Name: [Name]
Date of Accident: [Date]

Dear [Defendant]:

As you know, we represent [Client] in his claim for personal injuries and damages sustained from the accident of [Date]. To date we have not heard from you or your insurance company. We therefore assume that you had no insurance at the time of this collision. This letter is to request that you complete the enclosed affidavit stating that fact so that we may pursue a claim under our client's insurance policy. After you have signed this affidavit it will eliminate the need for us to contact you further. The affidavit must be signed before a notary public.

Your courtesy and cooperation are appreciated.

[Signature]

LETTER 1-39
LETTER TO DEFENDANT
WHEN NAME OF LIABILITY CARRIER IS UNKNOWN

[Date]

[Name]
[Address]

RE: [Name]
Date of Accident: [Date]

Dear [Name]:

Please be advised that this office represents [Name] for personal injuries sustained in an automobile accident with your vehicle in [Place] on [Date]. Please route this letter to your liability insurance carrier immediately so that we may discuss settlement with them.

All communications regarding this matter should be directed to our office and not to [Name].

Thank you for your cooperation in this matter.

Sincerely,

____

[ATTORNEY]

LETTER 1-40
LETTER TO TORTFEASOR'S INSURANCE CARRIER

[Date]

Re: Bodily Injury

[Insurance Carrier]
[Address]

Re: Your Insured: [Name of defendant driver/owner]
Claim Number (or Policy Number, if known): [Number]
Date of Loss: [Date]

Dear [Insurance Representative]:

Our office has been retained by [Client] with regard to injuries and damages he received as a result of an accident with your insured, [Name of insured], which occurred on [Date] at [Location].

[Client] also sustained property damage to his vehicle. This portion of the claim may be handled directly with my client. My client's address is [Address]. Enclosed is an estimate of the damage sustained to the vehicle in the amount of [Amount of estimate] from [Name of company providing estimate].

We will provide your office with medical documentation and bills as they become available to us. After the property damage has been settled, please direct all further correspondence and communication through our office.

If you have any questions or comments, please feel free to contact me.

[Signature]

LETTER 1-41
LETTER TO PROPERTY OWNER REQUESTING INSURANCE INFORMATION

[Date]

[Name]
[Address]

RE: [Name]
Date of Accident: [Date]

Dear Mr. Scott:

Please be advised that this office represents [Name] for injuries received when she slipped and fell in the lobby of the building located at [Address]. According to records which were available for inspection at the San Francisco City and County Assessor's Office, the property listed at that address is owned by you. Accordingly, we are routing this letter to your attention with the request that you give it to your liability insurance carrier and ask them to contact us immediately so that we may discuss settlement of this action.

All communications regarding this matter should be directed to our office and not to [Name].

Sincerely,

____
[Attorney]

LETTER 1-42
LETTER OF REPRESENTATION TO INSURANCE COMPANY

[Date]

[Insurance company office]
[Address]

RE: [Name]
Date of Accident: [Date]

Dear [Insurance company office]:

Please be advised that this office has been retained by [Name] with regard to personal injuries sustained on [Date], when she slipped and fell in the lobby area of a building at [Location]. We have been informed by the building supervisor, [Name], that the appropriate insurance carrier to contact is [Name of carrier] with reference to the building's insurance coverage for premises liability.

The floor where she slipped was unreasonably slippery, not covered by area rugs, and the cause of numerous other slip and fall accidents.

[Name] reported the incident to a security guard stationed in the lobby, who made a report of the incident.

She has been under constant treatment for a fracture of her right leg, and we are attempting to contact medical care providers to obtain records and billing information.

I would appreciate your having a claims representative contact our office.

Sincerely,

____
[Attorney]

LETTER 1-43
LETTER TO INSURANCE ADJUSTER

[Date]

[Name]
[Insurance company office]
[Address]

Re: Our Client: [Name]
Claim No.: [Number]
Your Insured: [Name]
Date of Accident: [Date]

Dear [Name]:

Thank you very much for speaking with me on [Date]. This will confirm that [Name] has liability coverage through [Insurance company] and that the policy limits are [Amount]. [Name] is still under care and treatment for the injuries she received in this accident. Records have been requested from medical care providers. As soon as we are advised that she has been released from care and have obtained records from all treating medical care providers as well as bills, we will forward them to you in a settlement demand package. We will also forward any other material that you desire. We look forward to working with you to settle this matter in an expedient and equitable fashion.

Sincerely,

____

[Attorney]

LETTER 1-44
LETTER TO TORTFEASOR'S CARRIER WHEN CLIENT UNINSURED

[Date]

[Carrier]
[Address]

Re: Your Insured: [Name]
Our Client: [Name]
Date of Loss: [Date]

Dear [Representative]:

Our office has been retained by [Client] with regard to injuries and damages he received as a result of the negligence of your insured, [Name of insured], which occurred on [Date] at [Location].

We have requested medical records and bills from all health care providers and will forward the documentation to you as it becomes available.

We request that you provide us with a statement of the following information with regard to each known policy of liability insurance of your insured, including excess or umbrella insurance:

1. name of the insurer,
2. name of each insured, and
3. limits of liability coverage.

We further request that you provide us with a copy of all applicable insurance policies with the declaration sheets. Please forward all information to all other insurers. I would also appreciate your forwarding copies of any and all statements you have which were made by our client. Thank you for your cooperation and courtesy.

[Signature]

LETTER 1-45
DEMAND THAT LIABILITY CARRIER ASSUME OR PARTICIPATE IN DEFENSE

[Date]

[Insurance company]
[Address]

Re: [Case name]
Our Client : [Name]
Our File : [Number]
Date/Loss : [Date]
Insurance Policy No.: [Number]

Dear Sir/Madam:

Please be advised that I represent [Name] in the above referenced lawsuit. Our initial investigation indicates that the date of manifestation of damages being claimed in this lawsuit is uncertain. Our investigation also indicates that the insurance policy referenced above provided liability coverage for [Name] for the policy period during which damages may have been manifested.

For that reason, I hereby demand that you agree to assume or participate in the defense of [Name]. I sincerely appreciate your anticipated cooperation in handling this matter. I invite you to call me at your earliest convenience so that we may discuss this situation in detail.

Very truly yours,

[Attorney]

LETTER 1-46
LETTER TO INSURER RECENTLY BROUGHT INTO CASE ADVISING IT OF STATUS OF CASE

[Date]

[Name]
[Insurance company]
[Address]

Re: [Case name]
Our Client : [Name]
Our File : [Number]
Date/Loss : [Date]

Dear [Name]:

Thank you for your telephone call of [Date], wherein you advised me that [Insurance company] will be sharing in the defense costs on a 50/50 basis in the above referenced case. Enclosed with this letter, please find for your convenience copies of the original Complaint, the Cross-Complaint against our client, our Answer to Cross-Complaint, our Cross-Complaint and the Answer to our Cross-Complaint.

As I advised you on the telephone, discovery is underway in this case, there are many parties and the issues appear to be many and complex. As discovery responses come in and more information becomes available, we will be formulating further discovery strategies. To date, our focus has been to determine precisely the nature and extent of the damages allegedly caused by the insured.

I understand that you will be contacting [Insurance company] to coordinate with them concerning the cost sharing on this file. Please advise me of your preference concerning communication and reporting. Absent hearing from you, I will assume that you will be satisfied with copies of reports to Travelers.

The claims supervisor in charge of this file is [Name]. I advised him of your agreement to participate. Once you have discussed the case with him, please advise me of any questions, instructions or comments you may have. In the interim, I will advise you of any new developments.

Very truly yours,

[Attorney]

CHAPTER 2

PRELIMINARY INVESTIGATION OF CASE

Letter 2-27	**Request for Medical Records from Physician 2**
Letter 2-28	**Request for Medical Records from Physician 3**
Letter 2-29	**Request for Medical Records from Physician Citing Administrative Code**
Letter 2-30	**Request to Physician for Narrative Report and Disability Rating**
Letter 2-31	**Letter to Defendant's Carrier Enclosing Medical Information**
Letter 2-32	**Medical Records Summary Letter**
Letter 2-33	**Letter to Employer about Wages 1**
Letter 2-34	**Letter to Employer about Wages 2**
Letter 2-35	**Request to Insurance Company for Workers' Compensation File**
Letter 2-36	**Transmittal of Summary of Payments Made by Workers' Compensation Carrier**
Letter 2-37	**Letter to Client's No-Fault Carrier Re: Benefits Paid**
Letter 2-38	**Sample Letter to School Board for Information**
Letter 2-39	**Request for Forwarding Address from Postmaster**
Letter 2-40	**Transmittal of Memorandum Detailing Investigative Work Required**
Letter 2-41	**Witness Initial Contact Letter 1**
Letter 2-42	**Witness Initial Contact Letter 2**
Letter 2-43	**Witness Initial Contact Letter 3**
Letter 2-44	**Transmittal of Declaration for Witness to Sign**
Letter 2-45	**Witness Statement Confirmation Letter**
Letter 2-46	**Witness Initial Contact Letter and Witness Statement Form**
Letter 2-47	**Expert Witness Engagement Letter**
Letter 2-48	**Letter to Proposed Expert Witness Asking for Evaluation of Case**
Letter 2-49	**Transmittal of Miscellaneous Investigation Items**
Letter 2-50	**Request for Payment of Proportional Share of Expert's Fee**
Letter 2-51	**Notification of Designation of Expert Economist**

LETTER 2-1
LETTER TO CLIENT REQUESTING DOCUMENTATION

[Name]
[Company name]
[Address]

Re: [Case name]

Dear [Name]:

As you know, [Name] has been sued by [Name]. [Name] has made several claims against [Name], but they relate primarily to electrical, elevator, window framing, and timing problems. It is important that we are fully informed about what occurred on the site, what transpired at early design meetings, any verbal agreements that may have been reached that were not documented in any contract or amendment, and what occurred between Allied and the subcontractors.

We ask that you temporarily suspend your normal document retention policies, as documented in [Name]'s Policy 3.50-A (rev'd 1/91). This means that any documents that may relate to the [Name] project and the claims in the lawsuit, including drafts of documents, accounting records, and the like must be retained by you and your staff. I realize you have limited storage space. If the retention of documents presents a problem, please contact me so we can arrange to have the documents moved to another location.

We will need your staff's help to determine what documents [Name] has in its custody and control. This exercise is not only for our investigation but also to prepare for discovery efforts by [Name]. If there are any categories of documents that you feel are confidential or sensitive, please call me so that we can discuss the handling of those materials.

Specifically, we will need all design drawings, blueprints, design specs, field orders, change orders, certificates, meeting notes, all contracts and amendments relating to the [Name] project, accounting records reflecting billing and payment for services related to the [Name] project, and correspondence with [Name], the architects, and the subcontractors. There may be other categories that we will identify as our investigation continues.

I would like to arrange to have our paralegal, [Name] (ext. [Number]) contact the appropriate person on your staff who has the most extensive knowledge about the documents. Please let me know who that person is, and I will ask Susan to call him or her to coordinate a visit to your offices. Please call me if you have any questions or concerns about these procedures and this phase of the litigation.

Sincerely,

[Attorney]

cc: [Names]

LETTER 2-2
POST-VISIT LETTER TO CLIENT

[Name]
[Address]

Re: [Case Name]

Dear [Name]:

Thank you very much for taking the time yesterday to meet with me and show me around [Name]'s offices. I especially appreciated your answering my many questions about window framing. I now better understand those issues in the case.

As we discussed, when I left the offices I took with me two boxes of files and several design drawings. I am enclosing an index of the file titles and the design drawings that I removed to our offices. We will keep these files until the end of the litigation, but please call me if you need something from the files. For your information, I have labeled each of the files so that the label indicates the file cabinet and drawer from which they were pulled. (The label code is also reflected on the enclosed index.) We will make a working copy of the documents. The originals will be stored safely in our workroom for this case. If you have any specific concerns about the documents that we have not already discussed, I will be happy to address them.

You agreed to have the accounting records copied for us, because the originals of those records need to be given to [Name's] accountant for preparation of tax returns. If there are any questions about duplicating those records, please give me a call.

Again, thank you for your help. I am sure we will be speaking again soon.

Sincerely,

[Paralegal]

Enclosure: Index to files/drawings

cc: [Names]

LETTER 2-3
PRIVACY ACT REQUEST FOR ACCESS LETTER

Privacy Act Officer (or System of Records Manager)
[Name of Agency]
[Address of Agency]

Re: Privacy Act Request for Access

Dear [Name]:

This is a request under the Privacy Act of 1974.

I request a copy of any records (or specifically named records) about me maintained at your agency.

(To assist you in locating my records, please note that I have had the following written contacts with your agency:)

(This request is made also under the Freedom of Information Act. If there are additional records which may be provided under this Act, please include them with my request.)

(Please supply the records to me without contacting me first if the fees do not exceed $________.)

Enclosed please find (identifying document) which will verify my identity.

Thank you for your consideration of this request.

Sincerely,

[Name]
[Address]

LETTER 2-4
COVER LETTER FOR REQUEST FOR MILITARY RECORDS

[Date]

[Name]
[Address]

Dear [Name]):

Our law firm represents the interest of [Military person's name], a [Rank] [on active duty/on retired status/now deceased] in [Branch of service]. [Person's name] [is posted / was last posted] at [Location]. The full name and social security number are

[Full name]
[Social security number]

Enclosed is a Request Pertaining to Military Records, which has been completed and signed by [Name].

Also enclosed is a certificate from [Name] for the release of [His/her/name's] records to this firm. Please send copies of [All / specify if limited] to this office as listed below:

[Your name]
[Your office address]

If any costs are involved, please send a request for payment to the same address. Thank you in advance for your assistance.

I have made a diligent search of the decedent's possessions and have been unable to find the documents requested.

[*Signature—full name*]

We certify that we are well acquainted with ________________ the above-listed person, who has presented a current Uniformed Services Identification and Privilege card (DD Form 1173) to verify identity. We further certify that the signature of above-listed person as affixed in our presence.

______________________	______________________
[*Signature of Witness*]	[*Signature of Witness*]
______________________	______________________
______________________	______________________
[*Address*]	[*Address*]

LETTER 2-5
LETTER TO SHERIFF REQUESTING PHOTOGRAPHS

[Date]

County Sheriff's Office
Attn: Records Department
[Address]

Re: Accident Report No. [Number]
Photo Reference No. [Number]
Accident Date: [Date]
Location: [Location]

Dear Sir or Madam:

Please send me a duplicate set of the photographs taken by the investigating Deputy Sheriff in conjunction with the above-referenced accident. I am enclosing a check in the amount of $3.00 to cover your fee for duplicating these photographs in the 4-x-6-inch size. Also enclosed is a stamped return envelope for your convenience in returning these photographs to me.

I believe the information above is sufficient for you to locate the desired photographs. However, should you have any questions or need further information, please contact me at [Telephone number]. Thank you for your assistance.

Very truly yours,

[Paralegal]

Enclosures

LETTER 2-6
LETTER REQUESTING ACCIDENT REPORT

[Date]

[State Department of Motor Vehicles]
[Address]

Re: Date of Accident: [Date]
Location: [Location]
Drivers Involved: [Names]

To Whom It May Concern:

Enclosed is our check in the amount of [$__________] to provide this office with a copy of the traffic accident report involving the above-captioned parties. A self-addressed return envelope is enclosed for your convenience.

[Signature]

LETTER 2-7
LETTER TO OBTAIN PHOTOGRAPHS

[State Patrol]
[Address]

Re: Accident of: [Date]
Location: [Address]
Accident Report Number: [Number]

Dear [Contact Person]:

Please provide our office with information regarding any photographs you may have in your possession regarding the above referenced accident. Enclosed is our check in the amount of [$ ____________] so that you may comply with this request.

[Signature]

LETTER 2-8
LETTER TO OBTAIN STATEMENTS

[Investigative Officer]
[Address]

Re: Accident Report Number: [Number]
Date of Accident: [Date]
Location of Accident: [Address]

Dear [Investigative Officer]:

[Name] has requested that our office represent her in her claim for injuries arising from the automobile accident which occurred at [Location] on [Date]. For your information I have enclosed a copy of the accident report which you have prepared.

It is my understanding that [Name of defendant] who caused this collision to occur represented to you at the scene that [Nature of representation, e.g., "It was all my fault," "I was waving to a friend," "I never saw the car approaching," etc.]. If [Name of defendant] made such a statement, it is extremely relevant. Therefore, I request that you preserve your personal notes of the investigation and call me to advise of the existence and identity of any witnesses and any statements made by such persons.

(Optional paragraph: I request your assistance in obtaining the names and addresses of any witnesses who were present at the scene of the accident.)

Thank you for your courtesy and cooperation.

[Signature]

LETTER 2-9
LETTER REQUESTING DEFENDANT'S DRIVING RECORD

[Department of Motor Vehicles, Licensing Division]
[Address]

Re:	Driver's Name:	[Name]
	License Number:	[Number]
	Date of Birth:	[Date]

To Whom It May Concern:

Enclosed please find our check in the amount of [$__________] to cover the cost of providing our office with a copy of the driving record for the above-named driver.

A self-addressed, stamped return envelope is enclosed for your convenience.

[Signature]

LETTER 2-10
LETTER TO OBTAIN DEFENDANT'S PLEA

[Date]

[Clerk of the Court]
[Address]

Re: Name of Defendant: [Name]
Charge Against Defendant: [Charge]
Date of Accident: [Date]
Accident Report Number: [Number]

Dear [Clerk]:

Please provide this office with a certified copy of the plea made by the defendant, [Name of defendant], to the charge of [Charge against defendant] in accident report number [Report number] which occurred on [Date of accident].

Enclosed is our check in the amount of [$__________] for the charges so that you may comply with this request.

Thank you for your courtesy and cooperation.

[Signature]

LETTER 2-11
LETTER TO OBTAIN AFFIDAVIT OF LIABILITY

[Date]

Traffic Records Section
[Address]

Re: [Name of Minor]
Date of Birth: [Month/Day/Year]

Dear Records:

Please provide us with a copy of the Affidavit of Liability signed by [Name of minor]'s parent or guardian at the time [Name of minor] received his driver's license.

I have enclosed a check for [$ __________] so that you may comply with this request.

Thank you for your courtesy and cooperation.

[Signature]

LETTER 2-12
LETTER REQUESTING PATENT INFORMATION

[Date]

U.S. Patent and Trademark Office
P.O. Box 9
Washington, D.C. 20231

Gentlemen:

My law firm is presently involved in litigation in which the product [Name] is involved. Therefore, I am interested in receiving a copy of U.S. Patent No. [Number]. I have enclosed a check for $2.50 as required to cover the costs of receiving this document. Please forward the patent to my attention at the above address at your earliest convenience. If there are any problems in obtaining the patent I have requested, I would appreciate your notification by telephone. My direct office number is [Telephone].

I thank you for your assistance.

Very truly yours,

[Legal Assistant]

LETTER 2-13
LETTER REQUESTING COPY OF PRODUCT STANDARDS

[Date]

[Name Appropriate Agency]
[Address]

Gentlemen:

I would like to request a copy of your product standards for the following product:

1) [Name of product]
2) [Name of manufacturer]
3) [Specified performance for the product]
4) [Material product is made of]
5) [Any other helpful identification information]

I am also interested in learning if the standards for this product developed by your agency are statutorily binding on the manufacturer.

I understand that you will contact me to let me know the fee for the copying charges related to this request. I may be reached by phone at [Telephone] or by mail at the above letterhead address.

Thank you very much for your assistance in this matter.

Very truly yours,

[Paralegal]

LETTER 2-14
FREEDOM OF INFORMATION ACT REQUEST LETTER 1

[Date]

Custodian of Records
[Address]

RE: Freedom of Information Act Request

Dear Custodian of Records:

We hereby request disclosure of copies of materials available from your agency under the Freedom of Information Act 6, U.S.C. §552 et. seq., described as follows:

1. Each document which relates to [Subject].

2. Each document which evidences, refers, constitutes, or relates to [Subject] for the years 19___–19___.

We believe that all of the described documents will be found in your San Francisco office and/or your Washington office.

Under applicable law pertaining to the Freedom of Information Act, we believe that these documents are available to us and other members of the public. If any portion of this request is denied, we request a detailed statement of the reasons for the withholding and an index or similar statement of the nature of the documents withheld pursuant to the Freedom of Information Act. In accordance with the Act, we agree to pay reasonable charges incurred for the copying of these documents, upon presentation of an invoice, along with the finished documents. (If search and copying fees exceed $200.00, please telephone in advance at [Phone number]).

I look forward to hearing from you within the ten (10) days statutory period within which your agency must respond to this request.

Thank you for your anticipated cooperation in this matter.

Very truly yours,

[Attorney]

LETTER 2-15
FREEDOM OF INFORMATION ACT REQUEST LETTER 2

[Date]

[Agency Head]
[Agency Name]
[Address]

Re: Freedom of Information Act Request

Dear Sir or Madam:

In accordance with the Freedom of Information Act, 5 U.S.C. § 552, I am requesting that you send me information on [Subject].

Please let me know if there is any fee for searching or reproduction of this information and I will gladly send it to you by return mail.

If you deem it necessary to deny my request, please state the reason for your refusal and notify me of the appeal procedure.

I look forward to hearing from you within the next ten days. As you know, this is the time period stipulated by law for responses to requests such as mine. Thank you for your assistance.

Very truly yours,

[Paralegal]

LETTER 2-16
FREEDOM OF INFORMATION ACT REQUEST LETTER 3

[Date]

Freedom of Information Act Officer
[Department]
[Address]

Re: Freedom of Information Act Request

Dear Sir:

This request is made under the auspices of the Freedom of Information Act (5 U.S.C. §552 <u>et seq</u>).

I request that a copy of all documents generated by your department containing information relating to [Subject] be provided to me.

To assist in determining my status for the assessment of fees, you should know that I am affiliated with a law office that needs this information to prosecute an ongoing civil suit.

I am willing to pay for this request up to a maximum of $500. Please inform me if the fees will exceed this limit.

Thank you for your assistance with this request.

Very truly yours

[Attorney]

LETTER 2-17
FREEDOM OF INFORMATION ACT REQUEST LETTER 4

[Date]

[Agency Head (or FOIA Officer)]
[Name of Agency]
[Address]

Re: Freedom of Information Act Request

Dear [Name]:

Pursuant to the provisions of the Freedom of Information Act, 5 U.S.C. 552, I am requesting a copy of the following records:

[Identify the records with as much specificity as possible]

If any fees are to be incurred and assessed to me in the process of searching for information and filing this request, please contact me first. (or: . . . please supply the records without contacting me first as long as the fees do not exceed [$ ___________])

(I request a waiver of fees pertaining to this request as the information is to be used for a purpose primarily benefitting the public [Explain in detail] and will not be used for my commercial interest.)

Thank you for your consideration of my request.

Sincerely,

[Name]
[Address]

LETTER 2-18
FREEDOM OF INFORMATION ACT APPEAL LETTER

CERTIFIED MAIL
RETURN RECEIPT REQUESTED

[Date]
Custodian of Records
[Address]

ATTENTION: [Name]
Chief Department Head

Dear [Name]:

This is to advise you I have been denied access to the records contained in your office, specifically those documents which relate to [Subject] and those documents which relate to [Subject] for the years 19_–19_.

Attached hereto is a copy of the letter which we have received from [Name] of your office. We can see no reason why our request was denied. You will note that she cites no reasons in her letter. I have also included a copy of our original Federal Freedom of Information Act request letter, and call your attention to the third paragraph wherein we state "if any portion of this request is denied, we request a detailed statement of the reasons for the withholding and an index or similar statement of the nature of the documents withheld . . . ."

I trust that upon your investigation of this matter you will conclude that the information I am seeking should be disclosed.

As provided for in the Federal Freedom of Information Act, I will expect a reply from your office within twenty (20) days. Please be advised that if this appeal is not answered or if the information is not released, we will file an action in the U. S. District Court. We hope this legal action can be avoided.

If you have any further questions in this connection or wish to discuss the matter, please feel free to contact our office.

Very truly yours,

[Attorney]

Enclosures

(Enclosures include the original Federal Freedom of Information Act request letter and the denial letter.)

LETTER 2-19
REQUEST FOR MEDICAL RECORDS FROM HOSPITAL 1

[Date]

[Hospital]
[Address]

Attention: Medical Records Department

RE: [Patient name], D/O/B: [Date]

Dear Sir or Madam:

Would you please provide me with the complete records for admission (or abstract of the records for admission) of the above-named individual on [Date].

I am enclosing an authorization permitting you to release this information to us, and will forward you a check once you have advised me of the cost of reproducing the records requested.

Your prompt response would be greatly appreciated.

Very truly yours,

[Paralegal]

LETTER 2-20
REQUEST FOR MEDICAL RECORDS FROM HOSPITAL 2

[Date]

[Hospital]
[Address]

Attention: Medical Records Department

Re: Your Patient: [Name]
Accident Date: [Date]
Date of Admission: [Date]
Date of Release: [Date]
Your Patient Number: [Number]
Your Patient SS Number: [Number]

Gentlemen:

This firm represents [Name], date of birth [Date], social security [Number], who was admitted to [Hospital] on [Date] and released on [Date] for injuries sustained in an [Accident] in [City]. The purpose of this letter is to request one copy of [Name]'s entire medical records for the above-referenced stay, including all progress notes, nurses' notes, emergency room records, physical therapy records, etc.

Enclosed is a medical authorization duly executed by [Name], requesting your cooperation with our request. Any charges for photocopying will be paid at the statutory rate promptly upon receipt of your billing for same.

If you have any questions or need further information, please do not hesitate to contact me.

Very truly yours,

[Legal Assistant]

Enclosure

LETTER 2-21
REQUEST FOR MEDICAL RECORDS FROM HOSPITAL 3

[Date]

[Hospital]
[Address]

Re: [Name]
Date of Birth: [Month/Day/Year]
[Date of Service]

Dear [Records Custodian]:

We represent [Name] in a claim for damages and injuries arising out of an accident which occurred on [Date].

We have been advised by our client that [he/she] was examined and treated at your hospital after this accident. We are enclosing the medical authorization form signed by our client and request that you forward to us a complete copy of the hospital records including, but not limited to, the following:

1. X-ray reports
2. Summary of charges
3. Operation Log, if any
4. Emergency Log
5. Medical photographs, if any
6. All doctors' orders
7. Nurses' Sheet showing names of nurses
8. Physical Therapy Records
9. All Outpatient Records
10. Emergency Room Record
11. Incident Reports

This office hereby revokes any and all prior medical authorizations issued by our client. We request that before our client's medical reports are given to any other person or company, this office be consulted. Information can be furnished to unauthorized persons only pursuant to a subpoena.

Thank you for your cooperation.

[Signature]

LETTER 2-22
REQUEST FOR MEDICAL RECORDS FROM HOSPITAL 4

[Date]

[Name]
[Address]

RE: [Client name] Date of Accident [Date]

ENCLOSED PLEASE FIND: Our request for medical records to [Hospital], their response referring our office to you to obtain those records.

____ FOR YOUR INFORMATION.

____ IN ACCORDANCE WITH YOUR REQUEST.

____ FOR YOUR REVIEW AND COMMENTS.

____ PLEASE SIGN WHERE INDICATED AND RETURN.

____ FOR YOUR FILE.

____ SELF-ADDRESSED, STAMPED RETURN ENVELOPE ENCLOSED.

____ OTHER: Please forward medical records to our office.

[Signature]

LETTER 2-23
REQUEST FOR MEDICAL RECORDS FROM HOSPITAL CITING GOVERNING LAW

[Date]

[Hosptial]
[Address]

Attention: Hospital Administrator

RE: [Patient]

Date of Admission: [Date]
Date of Discharge: [Date]

Date of Request & Authorization: [Date]
Follow-up Request: [Date]

Dear Sir or Madam:

On the above date, an authorization and check were sent to your hospital concerning our client named above, requesting copies of your records relating to that person.

As you know, pursuant to [State Statute], we, as the legal representative of the above named, are entitled to these records. Also, pursuant to the [State] Department of Health Manual of Standards for Hospital Facilities, [Number], all records for discharged patients must be completed within 15 days following discharge.

If you fail to immediately provide us with the records requested, we will be forced to institute proceedings in the Courts and through the appropriate State Agencies.

Very truly yours,

[Attorney]

Certified Mail, Return Receipt Requested

cc: Custodian of Records

LETTER 2-24
REQUEST FOR MEDICAL RECORDS AND CHARGES (WITH CONSENT TO RELEASE INFORMATION)

[Date]

[Hospital]
[Address]

Attention: Medical Records/Billing

RE: My Client/Your Patient: [Name]
Date of Service: [Date]
Date of Loss: [Date]

We represent the above-named patient and for our information and guidance in negotiating a settlement on behalf of our client, we request that you provide us with COPIES OF YOUR RECORDS together with an ITEMIZED STATEMENT OF YOUR CHARGES, without showing credit for any payments made on account.

Your earliest attention to this request will be appreciated since your records will greatly assist us in our efforts to obtain a proper recovery for our client.

I am enclosing a medical authorization, signed by your patient, to enable you to release the requested information to our office.

Sincerely,

[Attorney]

Enclosures

CONSENT TO RELEASE INFORMATION

ALL PRIOR INFORMATION RELEASE AUTHORIZATIONS (IF ANY) ARE HEREBY CANCELLED.

TO : ______________________________

You are authorized and requested to permit my attorney, [Name], or his duly authorized agent or representative, to review and make copies or photocopies of any and all medical reports, x-rays, charts, records and other data in your possession or control relative to my injuries, physical condition, treatment and/or care.

You are also authorized to discuss with them injuries, physical condition, treatment and care, and to furnish them with a written report regarding same. A photostatic copy of this authorization shall be as valid as the original. I am aware of my right to receive a copy of this authorization.

TO ANY EMPLOYER:

You are authorized and requested to furnish my attorney, [Name], or his duly authorized representative with any and all information which they request regarding my employment, and to permit them to inspect and/or copy my personnel and payroll records.

Dated: ______________________ [Signature]______________

EXPIRATION DATE: ______________

DATE OF BIRTH: ______________

EVIDENCE CODE SECTION 1158

"Failure to make such records available during business hours, within five days after the presentation of the written authorization, may subject the person or entity having custody and control of the records to liability for all reasonable expenses, including attorneys' fees, incurred in any proceeding to enforce the provisions of this section."

LETTER 2-25
LETTER REQUESTING HOSPITAL BILL

[Date]

[Hospital]
[Address]

Attention: Business Office

Re: Your Patient: [Name]
Accident Date: [Date]
Date of Admission: [Date]
Date of Release: [Date]
Your Patient Number: [Number]
Your Patient SS Number: [Number]

Gentlemen:

This firm represents [Name], date of birth [Date], social security [Number], who was admitted to [Hospital] on [Date] and released on [Date] for injuries sustained in an [Accident] in [City]. The purpose of this letter is to request one copy of [Name]'s entire hospital bill for the above-referenced stay. A medical authorization, duly executed by [Name], requesting your cooperation with our request, has already been forwarded to your Medical Records Department. A copy is enclosed for your reference. Any charges for photocopying will be paid at the statutory rate promptly upon receipt of your billing for same.

If you have any questions or desire further information, please do not hesitate to contact me.

Very truly yours,

[Legal Assistant]

Enclosure

LETTER 2-26
REQUEST FOR MEDICAL RECORDS FROM PHYSICIAN 1

[Date]

[Doctor]
[Address]

RE: [Name]

Dear [Doctor]:

I am enclosing a duly executed medical authorization of your patient, our client, permitting you to release confidential and privileged information to our office, only, as attorneys.

Please forward me a copy of your office records relative to this individual from the inception of her treatment with you. If you do not have any record of treating this individual or wish to refer us to another source to obtain her records, kindly advise us by return mail.

We would be pleased to pay a reasonable fee for the reproduction of these documents upon request.

Thank you for your anticipated cooperation.

Very truly yours,

[Paralegal]

LETTER 2-27
REQUEST FOR MEDICAL RECORDS FROM PHYSICIAN 2

[Date]

[Doctor]
[Address]

Re: Your Patient: [Name]
Accident Date: [Date]

Dear [Doctor]

This firm represents J[Name] , who was injured in an [Accident] on [Date], in [City], and was subsequently admitted to [Hospital]. It is our understanding that he was seen by you in [Hospital] and treated subsequently in your office.

The purpose of this letter is to request a written report reflecting [Name] 's diagnosis, treatment and prognosis, along with a copy of your current bill. Enclosed is a medical authorization, duly executed by [Name], requesting your cooperation with our request. If there is a charge for this request, please include an invoice with the report, and we will remit payment forthwith.

If you have any questions or desire further information, please do not hesitate to contact me.

Very truly yours,

[Signature]

Enclosure

LETTER 2-28
REQUEST FOR MEDICAL RECORDS FROM PHYSICIAN 3

[Date]

[Doctor]
[Address]

Re: [Name]
[Date of Accident]

Dear [Doctor]:

This firm represents [Name] in processing a claim for injuries and damages.

Enclosed is a medical authorization which authorizes you to send to us *any and all* records you have concerning the care and treatment of [Name], including patient information sheets, office notes, hospital records, and any other correspondence and/or reports. Also, *please include billing statements.* Any statements for copying charges may be sent directly to this office. If you require payment in advance please notify me and I will see that a check is promptly forthcoming.

Should you have any questions, please do not hesitate to call our office. Thank you for your courtesy and cooperation.

[Signature]

LETTER 2-29
REQUEST FOR MEDICAL RECORDS FROM PHYSICIAN CITING ADMINISTRATIVE CODE

[Date]

[Doctor]
[Address]

RE: [Name]

Dear [Doctor]:

I have not heard from you in response to my letter of [Date] requesting a copy of your office record regarding the above named individual.

I should like to call to your attention [State statute], which requires physicians to release a copy of the medical record of a patient or his representative (attorney) within thirty days of the written request with an authorization .

I would appreciate receiving [Name]'s record within the next two weeks so as to avoid my having to contact the Board of Medical Examiners.

As was indicated in my prior letter, if you require payment in advance for the copy, please advise and we will forward a check.

Very truly yours,

[Attorney]

LETTER 2-30
REQUEST TO PHYSICIAN FOR NARRATIVE REPORT AND DISABILITY RATING

[Date]

[Doctor]
[Address]

Re: [Name]

Dear [Doctor]:

As you know, this firm represents [Name] in his claim for personal injuries sustained in an accident which occurred on [Date].

In order for us to make a proper and precise evaluation of this matter, it is necessary for us to be familiar with all the medical facts concerning our client. Please provide us with the following information:

1. A history of your patient's treatment,

2. your diagnosis,

3. your prognosis,

4. amount of medical expenses incurred, and

5. your opinion regarding permanency of his injuries.

Opinions of experts must be framed in terms of reasonable probabilities as opposed to "possibilities." The courts have established that "probable" means "more likely than not." When equated to a percentage, "probable" means to a degree of certainty of at least 51 percent. Therefore, please express your opinion as to permanent disability, if any, in terms of probability.

If I can provide you with any further information, please feel free to contact me.

[Signature]

LETTER 2-31
LETTER TO DEFENDANT'S CARRIER ENCLOSING MEDICAL INFORMATION

[Date]

[Defendant's Carrier]
[Address]

Re: Your Insured: [Name of Defendant or a name under which the defendant is insured, e.g., the owner of the vehicle.]
Your Claim Number: [Number]
Date of Accident: [Date]
Our Client: [Name]

Dear [Defendant Insurance Carrier]:

As you are aware, our firm represents [Name] in his claim for damages and injuries sustained as a result of the above-referenced accident.

Enclosed for your review are copies of the following medical records: [List in detail]

Also enclosed is a copy of the PIP ledger (or in the alternative, a list of the medical bills which includes a total of medical expenses to date).

I shall continue to update you with medical information as it is received. Thank you for your courtesy and cooperation.

[Signature]

LETTER 2-32
MEDICAL RECORDS SUMMARY LETTER

[Date]
[Client]
[Address]

Dear [Client]:

The following is a summary of medical records regarding Plaintiff as of [Date].

HOSPITAL "A"

4/1/9_: Plaintiff was assaulted at a bus stop by an assailant wearing a stocking over his head. He hit her on her right eyebrow with a baseball bat. She had no loss of consciousness but experienced headaches when seen in the e.r. on 4/11/9_. On examination, she was alert and oriented but had a tender right forehead and superficial cuts on her right malar area. Facial and orbital x-rays were negative.

6/8/9_: Plaintiff was pulling a sofa when it stuck on the carpet, causing her to twist her left knee. In the e.r. she complained of pain on the lateral aspect of her knee and physical examination revealed no bruises or effusion. She denied a previous problem.

9/10/9_: Plaintiff went to the e.r., stating that she slipped on ice in the front yard and fell on her back. She complained of moderate to severe pain in her mid- to lower back. She denied a previous problem. Lumbosacral spine x-rays were normal, but a transitional lower lumbar segment was noted.

HOSPITAL "B"

10/23/9_: Plaintiff was seen in the outpatient clinic with a diagnosis of acute lumbar strain as a result of a slip and fall on 9/10/9_. Her reflexes were intact. She complained of numbness and weakness on the posterior aspect of the left lower extremity down into the calf area. She received physical therapy on 10/25/9_ and 10/28/9_.

11/17/9_: Lumbar spine x-rays normal. A CAT scan showed moderate disc protrusion at L4-L5, slightly more prominent on the right. A lumbar myelogram was performed on 11/19/9_, in which Metrizamide, a contrast, was injected. The impression was a central disc protrusion at L4-L5, which was compatible with the CAT scan findings.

COMMENTS: We plan to retrieve the CAT scan and x-rays taken at Hospital "B" and send them to Expert M.D. for evaluation. I also plan to obtain records from Plaintiff's physicians who treated her before 199_. If you have suggestions or questions, please do not hesitate to contact our office.

Very truly yours

[Attorney]

LETTER 2-33
LETTER TO EMPLOYER ABOUT WAGES 1

[Date]

[Company]
[Address]

Attention: Personnel Department

Re: Your Employee: [Name]
Accident Date: [Date]
Accident Location: [City]

Gentlemen:

This law firm represents [Name] for damages and injuries sustained in an [Accident] on [Date] in [City]. It is our understanding that as of this date, [Name] was employed by [Company] as a [Job title]. In this regard, would you please be good enough to provide us with the following information at your earliest convenience:

1. Please confirm [Name]'s occupation and job title as of [Date].

2. As of that date, what was [Name]'s normal hourly wage?

3. How many hours per week did [Name] normally work?

4. Did [Name] work overtime? If so, please state how many overtime hours, on the average, he worked per week.

5. If the answer to Question 4 is in the affirmative, please indicate whether his overtime was routine (i.e., every week, every two weeks, etc.) or sporadic (i.e., as needed for a particular project). Also, what was his overtime rate?

6. From [Date] to the present, how many hours (both regular and overtime) has [Name] lost from work?

7. Has he returned to work on a regular basis? If so, when did he return?

8. If [Name] is not now working his regular hours, please state how many hours per week he is working and when it is anticipated that he will return to his normal schedule.

9. Is [Name] now doing the same type of work he was as of [Date]? If not, please describe his new duties and, if applicable, his new hourly rate.

10. Finally, what is [Name]'s total loss of wages, including any applicable overtime, from [Date] to the present?

You may provide the requested information directly on this letter if you so desire. In any event, please provide the full name and title of the person providing the information and a telephone number where this person may be reached for further information.

I am enclosing an authorization signed by [Name] specifically requesting that you release the requested information to us for purposes of this litigation.

If you have any questions, or desire further information, please do not hesitate to contact me.

Very truly yours,

[Attorney]

Enclosure

LETTER 2-34
LETTER TO EMPLOYER ABOUT WAGES 2

[Date]

[Company]
[Address]

Attention: Personnel Department

Re: [Name]—Social Security Number: [Number]
Date of Accident: [Date]

Dear Sir or Madam:

This office represents your above-named employee who was injured on [Date]. The information sought was authorized to be released by your employee and is important to proper representation.

Very truly yours,

[Paralegal]

[Client Signature]

You are authorized to supply the information requested.

1. Date first employed:

2. Present position:

3. Gross pay—hourly and weekly:

4. First day lost after accident, if any:

5. Subsequent loss of time:

6. Total wages that would have been paid during absence:

7. Specify any other benefits (lost vacation, sick time, etc.):

Employer's signature	Title	Date

LETTER 2-35
REQUEST TO INSURANCE COMPANY FOR WORKERS' COMPENSATION FILE

[Date]

[Insurance Company]
[Address]

Re: [Name]—Your File No. [Number]

Dear Sir or Madam:

Would you please provide our office with a copy of the worker's compensation file (including a printout of all payments made or canceled checks), and a breakdown of the lien on the above referenced matter. In particular, I would appreciate copies of any and all medical bills.

Counsel fees, costs for medical examinations, stenographic costs, etc., should not be included in your lien.

Thank you in advance for your anticipated cooperation in this matter.

Very truly yours,

[Paralegal]

LETTER 2-36
TRANSMITTAL OF SUMMARY OF PAYMENTS MADE BY WORKERS' COMPENSATION CARRIER

[Date]

[Attorney]
[Address]

Re: [Case Name]
OCSC Case No.: [Number]
Date of Loss : [Date]
Employer : [Name]
Our File No. : [Number]

Dear [Attorney]:

Enclosed is a copy of the Payment Summary breakdown of the lien amount. The following amounts have been paid:

Temporary Disability ....[ ]
Permanent Partial Disability ....[ ]
Vocational Rehabilitation ....[ ]
Medical Expenses ....[ ]

TOTAL [ ]

If you require any further information, please do not hesitate to contact me.

Very truly yours,

[Signature]

Enclosure: Payment Summary

LETTER 2-37
LETTER TO CLIENT'S NO-FAULT CARRIER
RE: BENEFITS PAID

[Date]

[Insurance Carrier]
[Address]

Re: Your Insured [Name]
Claim Number: [Number]
Date of Loss: [Date]

Dear [Insurance carrier]:

As you are aware, our firm represents [Name] in processing a claim for injuries and damages suffered as a result of the above-referenced incident. Please provide us with a complete copy of your PIP ledger together with a copy of all bills you have paid as a result of this claim. I have enclosed a release authorization so that you may comply with this request. Please also include your ledger and any worksheets you have showing the amount of lost wages that you have paid for on behalf of our client.

If you require prepayment for copying, please advise me and I will have a check promptly sent to you.

If you have any questions, please do not hesitate to contact me. Thank you for your cooperation and courtesy.

[Signature]

LETTER 2-38
SAMPLE LETTER TO SCHOOL BOARD FOR INFORMATION

[Date]

Board of Education
[Address]

Re: [Name]—Date of Birth: [Date]

Dear Sir or Madam:

Please be advised that this office represents the above-named individual for injuries sustained in an accident unrelated to your school. It is our understanding that [Name] is presently a student at [School] in your school district.

In order to particularly protect our client's interests in a pending lawsuit against the culpable party, I would appreciate your forwarding the following information:

1. The name and address of teacher at the time of the accident;
2. A profile of the student, including any psychological, neurological or medical examinations, evaluations and testings on the student;
3. School attendance records;
4. Any other copies of pertinent data, including "achievement, attendance and progress evaluations."

I am enclosing an authorization permitting you to release this information to us. If there is any charge for this information, please advise and I shall be happy to forward our check to cover the costs.

Very truly yours,

[Paralegal]

LETTER 2-39
REQUEST FOR FORWARDING ADDRESS FROM POSTMASTER

[Date]

Postmaster
[City, State, Zip]

(Remember to send letter to the zip code of the last known address. Use the national zip code directory to make certain you have the zip code correct.)

RE: Address Search, [Name]

Dear Sir or Madam:

In accordance with Section 262.7, U.S. Postal Service Manual, I have enclosed our check in the amount of $1.00 to cover reasonable search and copy charges. I request, pursuant to the Federal Freedom of Information Act, the forwarding address of [Name]. She was last known to have resided at [Address].

A stamped, self-addressed envelope is provided for your convenience, and a space is left at the bottom of this letter for your reply. Thank you for your courtesy and cooperation in this matter.

Sincerely,

[Legal Assistant]

FOR POST OFFICE USE ONLY

(   ) Address unchanged, still receiving mail.
(   ) Forwarding address filed on __(Date)__
Address: ______________________
____

LETTER 2-40
TRANSMITTAL OF MEMORANDUM DETAILING INVESTIGATIVE WORK REQUIRED

[Date]

[Name]
[Address]

Re: [Case Name]
O/client : [Name]
Our File : [Number]
Date/Loss: [Date]

Gentlemen:

Enclosed please find a memo detailing the investigative work required in the above-captioned matter. I have also included the police report of this incident for your reference.

Please advise if you require any further information.

Thank you for your cooperation in this regard.

Very truly yours,

[Signature]

LETTER 2-41
WITNESS INITIAL CONTACT LETTER 1

[Date]

[Name]
[Address]

Dear [Name]:

This law firm represents [Name], who was severely injured in an automobile accident early on the morning of [Date], at the intersection of [Location], when his vehicle impacted with that driven by [Name] of [Address].

It is our understanding from [Name] and the police report filed after this accident that you were an eyewitness to the accident. As I have thus far been unable to reach you by telephone, I would appreciate your contacting me at your earliest convenience, either by telephone or in writing, so that we may discuss this matter in greater detail.

I look forward to hearing from you in the near future.

Very truly yours,

[Legal Assistant]

LETTER 2-42
WITNESS INITIAL CONTACT LETTER 2

[Date]

[Name]
[Address]

RE: Accident of [Date]
Intersection of [Location]
Our Client: [Name]

Dear [Name]:

This office represents [Name] who was injured on [Date] in an accident at the intersection of [Location]. According to the police report, this accident occurred when (a 1976 Chevrolet Nova operated by [Name] hit the brown Mercury operated by [Name], causing it to strike a lamp pole and come to rest on the southwest corner of Webster Street). According to the police report, you gave a statement to the investigating officers.

I would like to have an opportunity to discuss this matter with you. Please contact our office so that we can make an appointment for a convenient time to discuss this further. If it is inconvenient for you to come into our office, please call [(area code)-(phone number)] between the hours of 9:30 – 5:30, and we can have a discussion over the phone.

On behalf of [Name], thank you very much for your anticipated cooperation.

Sincerely,

[Legal Assistant]

LETTER 2-43
WITNESS INITIAL CONTACT LETTER 3

[Date]

[Name]
[Address]

IN RE: Witness Statement
Our Client: [Name]
Date of Accident: [Date]

Dear [Name]:

I am writing to request your assistance in representing my client who was injured in an accident that you witnessed. I am attempting to recover my client's economic losses and damages as a result of this accident.

I have enclosed a form for information concerning the facts you observed on the day of the accident. I also have enclosed a self-addressed envelope for your use.

If, for any reason, filling out this form will be difficult or inconvenient, please feel free to call me, and my office will be glad to take your statement over the phone.

Thank you for taking the time to tell us the facts of this incident. Without your information, this matter may not be resolved justly.

If I can be any assistance, please feel free to call.

Very truly yours,

[Attorney]

LETTER 2-44
TRANSMITTAL OF DECLARATION FOR WITNESS TO SIGN

[Date]

[Name]
[Address]

Re: [Case Name]
O/client : [Name]
Our File : [Number]
Date/Loss : [Date]

Dear [Name]:

It was a pleasure speaking with you on the telephone on [Date]. Thank you very much for the information you provided during our telephone conversation.

Pursuant to our discussion, I enclose a Declaration for your signature. Please review the Declaration carefully and sign it only if it is accurate. If you wish to change any of the language, please call me collect at [Telephone number] so that I may accomplish the change.

You may return the executed declaration in the enclosed stamped self-addressed envelope. Thank you again for your assistance in this matter.

Very truly yours,

[Signature]

LETTER 2-45
WITNESS STATEMENT CONFIRMATION LETTER

[Date]

[Name]
[Address]

Dear [Name]:

Following our meeting of [Date], I have enclosed a summary of your description of the automobile accident to which you were a witness early [Date]. Please review this summary carefully and make any additions, deletions or other corrections necessary and return it to me as soon as possible in the envelope provided. Your cooperation is greatly appreciated.

Very truly yours,

[Legal Assistant]

LETTER 2-46
WITNESS INITIAL CONTACT LETTER AND WITNESS STATEMENT FORM

[Date]

[Name]
[Address]

Re: Our Client: [Name]
Date/Time of Accident: [Date/Time]
Location of Accident: [Address/Description]:

Dear [Name]:

Please be advised that this office represents [Name], who was involved in the above-referenced accident which you may have witnessed. (Include a physical description of the client or a general description of the incident if the potential witness may not know the client or remember the incident.) Please complete the enclosed Witness Statement in as much detail as possible and return it to this office in the enclosed self-addressed, stamped envelope, which has been provided for your convenience.

As time is of the essence, we ask that you return this within three days of receiving it. We understand that you may not wish to include all personal information, but please let us assure you that such information will remain confidential. We will use it only to contact you if we have more questions. Thank you in advance for your courtesy and cooperation.

WITNESS STATEMENT

ACCIDENT LOCATION: ______________________________
ACCIDENT DATE AND TIME: ______________________________
OUR CLIENT: ______________________________
YOUR LOCATION AT TIME OF INCIDENT: ______________________________

1. What is your full name?
2. What is your residence telephone? (____) _________-______________
3. What is your work telephone? (____) _________-______________
4. What are your work days and hours? ______________________________
5. What is your home address?______________________________
6. What is your work address? ______________________________
7. Please identify someone who will always know how to reach you if you move or go on vacation. Name and relationship: ____________________
   Address: ______________________________
   Telephone numbers: ______________________________

8. Did you see this accident? Yes _______ No _______
9. Please identify anyone else who might have seen this accident.
   Name(s): ______________________________
   Address(es): ______________________________
   Telephone number(s): ______________________________
10. Where were you and what were you doing before this accident occurred? ______________________________
11. What did you see and hear before this accident occurred?

____

____

12. Where were you and what were you doing at the time of this accident?

____

13. What did you see and hear at the time of this accident?

____

____

14. What did you do immediately after the accident occurred?

____

____

15. What did you see and hear immediately after the accident occurred?

____

____

____

16. At any time after this accident, did you hear anything said by:
    A. Any person involved in this accident? Yes _______ No _______
Name or Description ____________________ Date/Time ____________
Name or Description ____________________ Date/Time ____________
    B. Any witness to this accident? Yes _______ No _______
Name or Description ____________________ Date/Time ____________
Name or Description ____________________ Date/Time ____________
    C. Investigator (Police, Fire, Other)? Yes _______ No _______
Name or Description ____________________ Date/Time ____________
Name or Description ____________________ Date/Time ____________
    D. Anyone who arrived after the accident? Yes _______ No _______
Name or Description ____________________ Date/Time ____________
Name or Description ____________________ Date/Time ____________
    E. Anyone else? Yes _______ No _______
Name or Description ____________________ Date/Time ____________
Name or Description ____________________ Date/Time ____________

17. For each person identified in number 16 above, please tell us the substance of the statement and the identity of anyone else who might have heard the same statement:

____

____

____

____

____

____

____

I DECLARE THAT THE INFORMATION CONTAINED IN THIS STATEMENT IS TRUE AND CORRECT TO THE BEST OF MY KNOWLEDGE.

DATE ______________ SIGNATURE __________________________________

LETTER 2-47
EXPERT WITNESS ENGAGEMENT LETTER

[Date]

[Name]
[Address]

Re: [Case Name]
[Court] Case No. [Number]

Dear [Name]:

This letter will confirm our telephone conference of [Date], in connection with retaining your services as an accident reconstruction expert on the above-referenced case. As we discussed, I would like you to evaluate this case to determine the following:

(1) the pre-skid speed of the [Name] vehicle;

(2) to compare the time from [Name]'s first reaction to the [Name] vehicle as a hazard to

the interval of time that the [Name] vehicle was on Route 66 before impact; and

(3) whether the presence of a guardrail on the south edge of Route 66 could have lessened the severity of the impact and resulting injuries.

I am enclosing a check for $500.00 representing your retainer for work on this case. It is my understanding that, should the work be completed or stopped for any reason before using up the amount of the retainer, the balance will be refunded. It is my further understanding that your normal fee schedule for this type of work is as follows:

Preparation Time $50/hour

(Includes: background review, site visit, field work, engineering analysis, reports, meetings, depositions, travel time)

Court Time . . . . $400/8-hour day or part thereof

All Expenses (Includes air fare, tolls, lodging, meals, mileage, film, prints, aerial photography, etc.)

Under separate cover, I am forwarding a packet of background materials on this case for your review. You may feel free to contact my client, [Name], at

[Telephone] if you need any information directly from him. I would ask that you not prepare a written report of your findings until I request it at a later date. Please note that the trial of this case has been scheduled for [Date].

[Name] is the paralegal in my office who will be assisting me on this case. Please feel free to contact either of us if you have questions. If the terms outlined above comport with your understanding of your engagement on this case, please so indicate by signing the enclosed copy of this letter and return it to me in the envelope provided.

Very truly yours,

[Attorney]

LETTER 2-48
LETTER TO PROPOSED EXPERT WITNESS ASKING FOR EVALUATION OF CASE

[Date]

[Name]
[Address]

Re: [Name]. by her Executor, [Name]

Dear [Name]:

As we discussed this afternoon, we have been retained by [Name] to investigate a potential malpractice claim on her sister's behalf. The decedent, a 29-year-old woman, saw Dr. [Name] in his office with complaints of chest pain. Based solely on his physical examination, the doctor told the patient that she had indigestion and gave her an antacid for comfort. Approximately two hours later, the patient suffered a massive heart attack and died. I would like a report from you indicating whether you feel that there was a deviation from the accepted standards of medical practice and whether that deviation was the proximate cause of the decedent's death.

In order to facilitate your evaluation, we are enclosing copies of the following records:

1) Dr. [Name]'s office records dated [Date];

2) [Name] Township Emergency Squad Records;

3) Records from the Emergency Room of [Name]'s Medical Center; and

4) Autopsy records.

Kindly telephone me once you have reviewed these records to advise whether or not you feel this is a case that merits pursuit.

Thank you for your assistance.

Very truly yours,

[Attorney]

LETTER 2-49
TRANSMITTAL OF MISCELLANEOUS INVESTIGATION ITEMS

[Date]

[Name]
[Address]

Re: [Case Name]
Insured : [Name]
Our File : [Number]
Date/Loss : [Date]

Dear [Name]:

Enclosed herewith, please find the following documents for your review/file:

1. Deposition transcripts, volumes 1 and 2 of [Name];

2. Your Personal Injury Information Form;

3. Plaintiffs 1040 Tax Forms; and

4. Dr. [Name]'s report.

Should you have any questions or comments, please feel free to contact me.

Very truly yours,

[Signature]

LETTER 2-50
REQUEST FOR PAYMENT OF PROPORTIONAL SHARE OF EXPERT'S FEE

[Date]

[Name]
[Address]

Re: [Case Name]
Our Client: [Name]
Our File : [Number]
Date/Loss : [Date]

Dear [Name]:

Enclosed, please find a copy of billing received to date from [Name], our shared economics expert in the above referenced case. Pursuant to our agreement, my client has paid [Name] directly, and I request that you reimburse us for one-third of the costs by mailing to my attention a check made payable to [Name]. I sincerely appreciate your professional courtesy, cooperation, and assistance. Should you have any questions or comments, please do not hesitate to call.

Very truly yours,

[Signature]

LETTER 2-51
NOTIFICATION OF DESIGNATION OF EXPERT ECONOMIST

[Date]

[Name]
[Company]
[Address]

Re: [Case Name]
Our Client : [Name]
Our File : [Number]
Date/Loss : [Date]

Dear [Name]:

As you know, three separate law firms representing three separate Defendants are sharing the costs associated with your company's involvement in this lawsuit. Expert witness designation has been made, and my firm designated [Company] as the expert economist. However, all Defendants understood that [Name] will be handling the file, and two Defendants have specifically designated you as the expert economist. I would therefore request that you [Name] be familiar with the file and be prepared to testify at deposition and trial in this case.

I sincerely appreciate your professional courtesy and cooperation. Should you have any questions or comments, please do not hesitate to call.

Very truly yours,

[Signature]

CHAPTER 3

COMMENCING SUIT

Letter 3-1	**Notice of Claim Enclosure Letter Against Governmental Entity**
Letter 3-2	**Notification to Governmental Authority of Intent to Sue**
Letter 3-3	**Letter to Clerk of Court Enclosing Complaint**
Letter 3-4	**Cover Letter to Process Server 1**
Letter 3-5	**Cover Letter to Process Server 2**
Letter 3-6	**Transmittal of Proof of Service of Summons and Declaration (with Declaration Attached)**
Letter 3-7	**Transmittal of Resubmitted Answer to Cross-Complaint**
Letter 3-8	**Transmittal to Opposing Party of Copy of Stipulation and Amended Answer**
Letter 3-9	**Transmittal to Opposing Party of Stipulation and Order Regarding Amended Answer**
Letter 3-10	**Transmittal of Summons and Complaint in Interpleader**
Letter 3-11	**Grant of Open Extension of Time for Response to Complaint in Interpleader**
Letter 3-12	**Transmittal of Copy of Complaint**

LETTER 3-1
NOTICE OF CLAIM ENCLOSURE LETTER AGAINST GOVERNMENTAL ENTITY

CERTIFIED MAIL #

[Date]

[Name]
[Address]

RE: [Case name]

Dear Sir:

Enclosed please find the original and one copy of a Claim Against the [Name] on Behalf of [Name].

Please acknowledge receipt of this claim by completing and returning the additional copy of this letter to our office. The enclosed envelope is for your convenience.

If you have any questions, do not hesitate to call.

Very truly yours,

____
[Name]
Legal Assistant

Enclosure—claim

Receipt of the above-referenced claim is hereby acknowledged.

Dated: __________.

____
Name

____
Title

LETTER 3-2
NOTIFICATION TO
GOVERNMENTAL AUTHORITY OF INTENT TO SUE

Re: Intent to Sue

[Governmental Entity]
[Address]

Re: Notice of Claim Pursuant to [Local Statute]

Dear [Representative]:

The following notice of claim and injury is given pursuant to the requirements of [Local statute]. Pursuant to this statute, the following information is provided:

1. The claimant's name and address are:

[Client's name and address]

2. Claimant is represented by counsel whose name and address are:

[Attorney's name and address]

3. The event occurred on [Date] at [Time of day] at [Location]. [State basis of claim. Example: While attending a physical education class at [Name of high school], claimant was struck by a baseball bat. The claimant had not been provided with any protective gear. The injuries that the claimant sustained resulted from the fact that he was not provided with such protective gear. At the time of the incident the claimant was under the supervision of his physical education teacher, [Name of teacher], who together with the school district, [Name of school district], failed to provide proper supervision for the claimant.]

4. The name and address of the public employee involved are:

[Name and address of employee]

5. [State nature and extent of injury. Example: The claimant has suffered a head injury resulting in deterioration of his intellectual functioning and memory. The exact extent and nature of his injuries is currently being evaluated and assessed.]

6. The amount of monetary damages claimed herein is [amount]. [*OR* The monetary damages that will be sought by the claimant are uncertain and cannot be determined at this time. For purposes of this notice only, the claimant states the monetary damages will not exceed [Amount].]

We respectfully request that a copy of this notice be sent to the insurance carrier or appropriate provider with the request that the said carrier or provider contact us regarding this claim so that we may submit supporting medical records, bills and other information pertaining to this accident.

Thank you for your cooperation and courtesy.

[Signature]

LETTER 3-3
LETTER TO CLERK OF COURT ENCLOSING COMPLAINT

[Clerk's Name]
[Court]
[Address]

Dear [Clerk]:

Enclosed please find for filing the original and [Number of copies required by local laws] copies of plaintiff's complaint, together with our check in the amount of $[ ]. [Check local court fee schedule.] Please date stamp and return one copy to me in the enclosed self-addressed envelope.

[Signature]

LETTER 3-4
COVER LETTER TO PROCESS SERVER 1

[Process Server or Sheriff]
[Address]

RE: [Name of case]

Dear Sir:

Enclosed please find the following:

1. Original and copy of Summons

2. Copy of Complaint

Please serve the Defendant [name of defendant] at the address on the Summons and forward your return of service to this office.

Thank you for your assistance.

[Signature]

Enc.

LETTER 3-5
COVER LETTER TO PROCESS SERVER 2

[Date]

[County name] County Sheriff's Office
[Address]

Re: [Case name]
[Court file number]

Dear Sir/Madam:

Enclosed please find documents which need to be served on defendant Pierce Enterprises. Said documents are as follows:

1. Plaintiff's Complaint;

2. Plaintiff's First Amended Complaint;

3. Cross-Complaint of [Name];

4. Cross-Complaint of [Name]; and

5. Cross-Complaint of [Name].

Kindly effect service on:

[Name]
[Address]

Also enclosed is a check in the amount of $20.00 to cover the service fee. Should you have any questions or comments, please do not hesitate to call me.

Very truly yours,

[Attorney]

LETTER 3-6
TRANSMITTAL OF PROOF OF SERVICE OF SUMMONS AND DECLARATION (WITH DECLARATION ATTACHED)

[Date]

[Name]
[Address]

Re: [Case name]
Our Client: [Name]
Our File No.: [Number]
Date of Loss: [Date]

Dear [Name]:

This envelope contains three sets of documents with individual yellow post-its to alert you as to the type of action needed.

1. **Proof of Service:** Please have the person delivering this package fill out and sign the enclosed **Proof of Service.**

2. **Declaration:** Please review the **Declaration** carefully and sign it only if it is accurate. If you wish to change any of the language, please change it with a pen.

3. **For your file:** These documents are for your information.

IMPORTANT: Please place the **Proof of Service** and your **Declaration** into the return envelope, and give it to the delivery person.

Thank you again for your assistance in this matter.

Very truly yours,

[Name]

DECLARATION OF [Name]

I, [Name], declare:

I am [Identity]. I reside at [Address].

I make this declaration of my own personal knowledge and could competently testify to the within facts if called upon to do so.

On or about [Date], I received the summons and complaint in interpleader, that were filed by [Name], by first class mail, certified, return receipt requested, which receipt was signed by [Name], on or about [Date].

I declare under penalty of perjury under the laws of the State of California that the foregoing is true and correct, and that this Declaration was executed in [Place] on [Date].

____

[Name]

LETTER 3-7
TRANSMITTAL OF
RESUBMITTED ANSWER TO CROSS-COMPLAINT

[Date]

[Name]
[Law firm]
[Address]

Re: [Case name]

Dear [Name]:

Enclosed please find another copy of my client's Answer to Cross-Complaint of [Name] in the above-referenced matter. The court rejected the original answer, therefore we resubmitted the answer as to [Name].

If you have any questions regarding this matter, please do not hesitate to contact me.

Very truly yours,

[Attorney]

cc: All Counsel of Record

LETTER 3-8
TRANSMITTAL TO OPPOSING PARTY OF COPY OF STIPULATION AND AMENDED ANSWER

[Date]

[Name]
[Law firm]
[Address]

Re: [Case name]
OCSC Case No. : [Number]
Our File No. : [Number]

Dear [Name]:

You will recall that prior to transfer of the case to Municipal Court, we agreed to an amendment of my client's Answer to your client's Complaint. We executed a stipulation to that effect.

Because of the transfer to Municipal Court, the amended Answer was never filed. Now that the case is back in Superior Court, I will file the amended Answer. Enclosed for your file is a copy of the executed stipulation and amended Answer.

Thank you for your assistance.

VERY TRULY YOURS,

[Name]

LETTER 3-9
TRANSMITTAL TO OPPOSING PARTY OF STIPULATION AND ORDER REGARDING AMENDED ANSWER

[Date]

[Name]
[Law firm]
[Address]

Re: [Case name]
Our client : [Name]
Our File : [Name]
Date/Loss : [Date]

Dear [Name]:

The deposition testimony of your client has disclosed that our answer to your complaint should be amended to include affirmative defenses regarding mitigation of damages and assumption of the risk. Because case law allows for liberal amendment of pleadings, it seems it would be a waste of time and money for all parties to bring or oppose a noticed motion regarding the amendment. Therefore, I have prepared a stipulation and order regarding the filing of the amended answer.

If you will agree to the answer amendment without the necessity of a noticed motion, please sign the stipulation and return it to our office by [Date].

Thank you for your assistance.

Very truly yours,

[Attorney]

Enclosures

LETTER 3-10
TRANSMITTAL OF
SUMMONS AND COMPLAINT IN INTERPLEADER

[Date]

<u>**CERTIFIED MAIL RETURN RECEIPT REQUESTED**</u>

[Name]
[Address]

Re: [Case name]
Our client : [Name]
Our File : [Number]
Date/Loss : [Date]

Dear [Name]:

In accordance with Section [Number] [State] Code of Civil Procedure, you are hereby served with Summons and Complaint in Interpleader as the closest living relative of [Name].

Service of the Complaint is deemed to be completed within ten (10) days after this letter is mailed. Thereafter, you will have thirty (30) days to respond to the Complaint. Your failure to respond within the thirty (30) days could subject you to having a default judgment taken against you.

Please call me if you have any questions.

Very truly yours,

[Name]

LETTER 3-11
GRANT OF OPEN EXTENSION OF
TIME FOR RESPONSE TO COMPLAINT IN INTERPLEADER

[Date]

[Name]
[Law firm]
[Address]

Re: [Case name]
Our client : [Name]
Our File : [Number]
Date/Loss : [Date]

Dear [Name]:

This will confirm our telephone conversation on [Date], during which I granted an open extension of time in which [Name] may respond to the complaint in interpleader, subject to a 30-day written notice of the revocation of such an extension.

I hope that all the parties can agree on an equitable distribution of the funds available so that may finally resolve this matter. If I can be of any assistance in such a resolution, please let me know.

Thank you for your assistance.

Very truly yours,

[Attorney]

LETTER 3-12
TRANSMITTAL OF COPY OF COMPLAINT

[Date]

[Name]
[Address]

Re: [Case name]
Our client : [Name]
Our File : [Name]
Date/Loss : [Date]

Dear [Name]:

Enclosed, per your request, please find a copy of [Name]'s initial Complaint. Please feel free to contact this office should you need further documents.

Very truly yours,

[Attorney]

Encl.

CHAPTER 4

SETTLEMENT

LETTER 4-1
TRANSMITTAL OF STIPULATION SETTLING A MOTION

[Date]

[Name]
[Address]

Re: [Case Name]
Our Client : [Name]
Our File : [Number]
Date/Loss : [Date]

Dear [Name]:

Pursuant to our discussion on [Date], I have prepared the enclosed stipulation. If you find it acceptable, please sign it where indicated and return it to me as soon as possible. Once I receive the stipulation with your signature, I will sign it myself, file it with the court and take our motion off calendar.

Should you have any questions or comments concerning the stipulation, please do not hesitate to call. I sincerely appreciate your courtesy and cooperation and look forward to hearing from you soon.

Very truly yours,

[Signature]

LETTER 4-2
SETTLEMENT DEMAND LETTER 1

[Date]

[Settlement attorney's name]
[Firm]
[Address]

Re: [Client name]; Cause/File No. [Number]

Dear [Name]:

I am submitting this letter and the enclosed material in an attempt to present the facts of this claim on behalf of my client, [Name]. Sufficient information has been obtained allowing us to give meaningful evaluation to the above-referenced damage claim. Photocopies of all documents pertinent to our evaluation are enclosed.

Special damages are currently in the amount of [$]. For convenience, those damages have been outlined on the attached Schedule of Special Damages.

Based on the enclosed information, we believe this claim has a fair settlement value of special damages in the amount of [$], plus general damages in the amount of [$], for a gross settlement of [$].

This letter and all of the enclosed material is, of course, submitted solely for the purpose of settlement negotiations and not by way of any admissions against interest. Therefore, I submit it only on the condition that this letter and all of the materials submitted with it are not to be used if this matter is tried in court.

Please review the enclosed information and then contact [Name], Legal Assistant of my office, to acknowledge your receipt of this demand package and to advise us when we can expect to receive your response to our settlement demand.

Thank you in advance for your prompt cooperation.

Sincerely,

[Attorney]

Enclosures

LETTER 4-3
SETTLEMENT DEMAND LETTER 2 (AUTO ACCIDENT)

[Date]

[Insurance adjuster]
[Insurance company]
[Address]

RE: [Client name]
Your Insured : [Name]
Date of Loss : [Date]
Claim No : [Number]

Dear [Insurance adjuster]:

The condition of my client, Marcus Goodwin, has now stabilized to the extent that we are able to make a settlement demand. Enclosed for your review are copies of Mr. Goodwin's medical records and bills from San Francisco General Hospital and Dr. John Green. We have also enclosed wage loss verifications from Mr. Goodwin's employers.

As you know, Marcus Goodwin suffered physical injuries to his lower back and neck in the accident which occurred on October 18, 19__, when he was a passenger in a vehicle driven by Natalie Warren.

FACTUAL SUMMARY

This accident occurred when Mr. Goodwin, who was sitting with his seat belt on in the front passenger seat, was injured when a vehicle driven by Mr. Reed pulled out unexpectedly, hitting the right front fender of the Warren vehicle. Mr. Goodwin was able to get out of the car without difficulty and noted no symptoms until the following morning, at which time he noted considerable stiffness of the lower back area with associated soreness and pain prompting him to seek treatment at San Francisco General Hospital's Emergency Department. Examination at that time revealed mild paracervical and upper trapezium tenderness in the neck area and a mild lumbar strain and tenderness, particularly in the lower back. Dr. Davis, the emergency room physician, prescribed heat, aspirin and rest as well as further examination by Mr. Goodwin's regular doctor if the pain persisted.

On October 28, 19__, Mr. Goodwin consulted Dr. John Green complaining of considerable stiffness in the lower back area. He also had been unable to return to work, since his job required carrying heavy objects. He also noted difficulty in sitting for long periods of time. Dr. Green's examination revealed considerable spasms of the lower lumbar muscles and limitation in forward bending, backward bending, and sideward bending with discomfort and tenderness on percussion over the lumbar spine area. Dr. Green's diagnosis was acute back strain and he applied tape for relief of the local pain and discomfort. Mr. Goodwin was advised to continue using the heating pad and aspirin and to remove the tape in about 5 days.

Treatment was continued with Dr.Green through November 18, 19__, at which time Mr. Goodwin was able to bend forward, backward and sidewards without limitation and had no residual muscle spasms in the lumbar region. At that time, Dr. Green released him to return to work.

Mr. Goodwin was advised to continue with caution to his back, and return on an as-needed basis for treatment. At this time, Mr. Goodwin appears to have recovered from the injuries suffered to his lower back.

DAMAGES

San Francisco General Hospital		$ 95.00
Dr. John Green		$ 123.00
	TOTAL	$ 218.00

WAGE LOSS

At the time of the accident, Mr. Goodwin was employed through The Service Corporation as a concessionaire at the Cow Palace selling beer and soft drinks. Because of the physical demands of this position, Mr. Goodwin was unable to work for a total of 15 days. A wage and salary verification form signed by Joan North for The Service Corporation establishes the wage loss Mr. Goodwin suffered as a result of injuries received in this accident at $1,628.00.

Mr. Goodwin also worked at a temporary position through Certified Temp Staff as a demonstrator. At the time of the accident, his wages were $7.40 per hour. As a result of the accident, he was unable to work from November 13 through November 22, 19__ and lost a total of 43 hours, or $307.10 in wages. This amount is verified by the wage verification signed by the assistant service supervisor of Certified Temp Staff.

In addition to the medical expenses previously itemized, Mr. Goodwin's damages consist of a total wage loss in the amount of $1,935.10.

LIABILITY

It is clear that the cause of this accident was the inattentiveness of the driver of the Reed vehicle who was a 16-year-old minor driving on a license he had for three weeks. At the time of the accident he told Mr. Goodwin he was driving his mother's car and simply "didn't see you guys." At the time of the accident, the Warren vehicle, in which Mr. Goodwin was a passenger, was proceeding at approximately 30 miles per hour on O'Shaunessey, going west. As the vehicle travelled up the hill to make a turn at Bosworth and O'Shaunessey, the Reed vehicle driven by the 16-year-old minor failed to stop at O'Shaunessey and proceeded to come out of Bosworth Street and attempt a left turn. The Reed vehicle instead turned diagonally, almost hitting the Warren vehicle head on. The left front of the Reed vehicle hit the right front of the Warren vehicle causing extensive damage to the right front of the car, the frame, the left fender, and the left door. It does not appear that a police report was made concerning this accident, however, Mr. Goodwin gave a statement recounting the accident to CSAA.

My client has authorized me to demand $5,000.00 in full settlement of this case. I look forward to your prompt reply to this settlement demand.

Very truly yours,

[Attorney]

LETTER 4-4
SETTLEMENT DEMAND LETTER 3 (AUTO ACCIDENT)

CERTIFIED MAIL
RETURN RECEIPT REQUESTED,
REGULAR MAIL and
HAND DELIVERY

[Date]

[Name]
[Address]

Re: Accident Date: [Date]; Your Client [Name]

Dear [Name]:

We have been retained by [Name] to represent him/her concerning injuries and damages he/she has incurred as a result of an accident which involved your client [Name].

On [Date], at approximately [Time] our client was driving his/her vehicle in a ________ direction on ________ Avenue in the vicinity of its intersection with ________ Drive. Your client failed to stop his/her vehicle at the stop sign located at said intersection and drove his/her automobile into the intersection with wanton disregard for the approach of the vehicle driven by our client, thereby causing his/her vehicle to collide with that of our client.

As a result, our client was hospitalized with severe internal injuries for a period of two months and has suffered permanent and disabling injuries. Medical costs incurred to date total [$].

Our client has not been able to return to work since the time of the accident and has suffered additional monetary damages in the amount of [$] for wage and benefit loss.

In addition, our client's vehicle was deemed to be a total loss, and he/she has suffered [$] in property damages.

We are therefore making a demand upon your client to pay our client for the damages incurred, plus attorneys' fees. If no response is made to this letter within 30 days, we will be forced to serve you with a lawsuit.

Very truly yours,

[Attorney]

LETTER 4-5
SETTLEMENT DEMAND LETTER 4 (AUTO ACCIDENT)

[Date]

[Name]
Senior Accounts Adjustor
[Insurance company]
[Address]

Re:	Our Client	:	[Name]
	Your Insured	:	[Name]
	Your Policy Number	:	[Number]
	Accident Date	:	[Date]

Dear [Name]:

As you are aware, both from my letter of representation of [Date] and from our subsequent telephone conversations, this firm represents [Name] for injuries and damages sustained in an automobile accident on [Date], when his vehicle was struck by the vehicle driven and owned by your insured, [Name] of [City]. [Name]'s medical expenses incurred as a result of this accident are as follows:

[Washington Hospital Center (1/1/87 to 2/17/87)	$28,787.60
Dr. Samuel L. Jones	775.00
Dr. Robert T. Smith	2,250.00
Capitol Area Ambulance Service	50.00
Radiology	300.00
Drug Fair	272.19
People's Drug	+ 37.95
TOTAL MEDICAL EXPENSES:	$32,472.74]

A copy of each of the above-referenced bills is enclosed. For your information, I am also enclosing copies of the Washington Hospital Center record in its entirety, and reports from Drs. Jones and Smith. As a result of this accident, [Name] suffered the following injuries:

[1. Fracture, left tibula (lower leg)

2. Fracture, left femur (upper leg)

3. Severe pain and discomfort throughout left leg

4. Residual pain and discomfort in left hip

5. Extreme difficulty sleeping

6. Inability to perform marital duty
7. Permanent limp in left leg
8. Fracture, left humerus (upper arm)
9. Residual pain and discomfort throughout left arm and shoulder
10. Temporary loss of use of left arm
11. Cervical spine sprain
12. Inability to turn or move head without pain
13. Residual pain in neck area
14. Severe, recurring headaches
15. 4″ Laceration on left upper arm, requiring sutures
16. Large abrasion, left temple
17. Multiple contusions over face and body
18. Extremely nervous and upset
19. Inability to drive or ride in car, due to nerves

Due to the injuries sustained in this accident, [Name] was forced to remain in traction for the majority of his hospital stay, and after returning home, required complete bed rest for nearly another month. He wore a cervical collar for approximately three weeks, and casts on both his left upper arm and shoulder and left leg for approximately ten weeks. [Name] now walks with a permanent limp and often has to use a cane to support himself. His sutured laceration has left a permanent scar. He has residual pain and stiffness in his neck and upper back, and has been told by his physician that he will continue to suffer from same for an as yet undetermined period of time.

At the time of this accident, [Name] was employed as a Mechanical Engineer at Westinghouse Electric Corporation. In this capacity, he was earning $15.00 per hour for a 40-hour work week. In addition, [Name] regularly worked a minimum of 5 hours of overtime per week, for which he was paid time and a half, or $22.50 per hour.

Due to the severe injuries in this accident, [Name] was off from work from [Date] to and through [Date], at which time he returned to work on a part-time basis, working a maximum of 20 hours per week. He returned to his regular work schedule, including overtime, on [Date]. He has not lost time from work due to this accident since that date. Westinghouse Electric Corporation has computed his loss of wages as follows:

[Total regular hours lost from work:	896.00	
Regular hourly rate:	x $ 15.00	
Total regular loss of wages:		$13,440.00
Total overtime hours lost:	148.00	
Overtime hourly rate:	x $ 22.50	
Total overtime loss of wages:		+ $ 3,330.00
Total loss of wages:		$16,770.00]

A letter from the Personnel Department of Westinghouse Electric Corporation, dated November 16, 1987 is enclosed for your information.

At the time of this accident, [Name] was driving a 1984 Oldsmobile Cutlass, which he owned. Enclosed are statements from three repair garages, including an Oldsmobile dealership, as well as your own independent examination, estimating damages between $5,627.63 and $7,047.56. The car's current Blue Book value is $9,500. [Name] has not yet had the car repaired.

In view of all of the above, and recognizing that it is to our clients' mutual benefit to settle this litigation promptly, I have been authorized by, and do hereby make a sincere offer on behalf of, my client to settle this case for $500,000.00, for [Name]'s medical expenses, bodily disability, severe pain and suffering, and property damage.

If you have any questions, or wish to discuss this matter further, please do not hesitate to contact me.

Very truly yours,

[Attorney]

Enclosures

LETTER 4-6
SETTLEMENT DEMAND LETTER 5 (AUTO ACCIDENT)

[Letterhead]
[Date]

[Insurance company]
[Address]

Attention: [Name]
Claims Adjuster

RE: Your Client: [Name]
Date of Loss: [Date]
Your File #: [Number]

Dear [Name]:

This is in response to your letter of [Date] and our interim telephone conversations regarding the damages and injuries sustained by Mr. [Client] and Mrs. [Client] in an automobile accident caused by your insured, [Name], on [Date].

Accompanying this letter in a 3-ring binder is a prepared synopsis containing documentation of those damages and injuries and a recapitulation of the aggregate damages incurred. You will note that the automobile collision damage alone was only slightly less than [$]. Even at that cost, the structural and mechanical damage was so massive (please note copies of photos) that the vehicle was, in fact, not wholly repairable. On [Date], only days after the [Clients] had retrieved the car from your insurance mandated repair garage, an uncorrected/undetected engine surge problem caused the engine to rev uncontrollably in reverse, dragging the brake-locked front tires nearly 35 feet backward before Mr. [Client] could switch off the ignition, further endangering the [Clients] (again, note 2nd page of photos of skid marks, etc).

When the [Clients] finally managed to sell the car the next month, the collision damage repairs has caused a loss of resale value of the vehicle of an additional [$] in damages, which was anticipated by [Expert] (see affidavit in Lost Value section of binder). This loss did not take into consideration the additional devaluation which would have occurred upon detection of the undetected and uncorrected defects.

Mr. and Mrs. [Client] also lost [$] in income due to the collision: Mrs. [Client] missed a week's work due to her injuries, and Mr. [Client] lost 8 days' income, engendered by coping with the problems and aggravations of estimates, repair garages, tow-trucks, repeat visits to repair garages, etc.

Mrs. [Client] was under a physician's care for more than a month as a result of her injuries, which were so severe as to cause her, as previously noted, to miss a week's work. Dr. [Name] prescribed multiple medications to combat the pain and the muscle spasms (which are, in themselves, additionally extremely painful). While the doctor and Mrs. [Client] both believe that she has now reached maximum healing, this does *not* mean "full" healing. Even through the holiday season, Mrs. [Client] continued her home neck and shoulder exercises (as ordered, see medical records) in order to alleviate the pain and to regain Range Of Motion in her neck and shoulders.

To this day, Mrs. [Client] continues to experience a couple of episodes of pain per week, which are intensified by her desk job if they occur during the work week, which is most usually the case. She attempts to relieve the pain by getting up from her desk and moving around, performing stretching maneuvers, and continuing the use of her prescription drugs. When she is "fortunate" enough to experience a pain episode while at home, she attempts to relieve the pain further thorough heat applications. There is little likelihood that these pain episodes will abate, and she expects that they will exacerbate.

Mrs. [Client] has pursued both medical pain management and activity modification to the extent that either she or her doctor are able to do so. She is quite concerned, and rightly so, about the probability that the muscle strain and injury will, with age and use, subject her to post-traumatic chronic myofacial irritation and increase dysfunction and pain.

In view of the [Client]'s monetary damages in excess of [$], and based upon the foregoing damages, please consider this letter a demand for compensation for both [Clients]' monetary damages and Mrs. [Client]'s personal injuries and her pain and suffering, past and future, in the sum of [$].

Please respond.

Very truly yours,

[Attorney]

LETTER 4-7
SETTLEMENT DEMAND LETTER 6 (AUTO ACCIDENT)

[Letterhead]

[Date]

[Name], Claims Adjuster
[Insurance company]
[Address]

Re: Your Claim No.: [Number]
Your Insured: [Name]
Claimant: [Name]

Dear [Name]:

This is in response to your letter of [Date], regarding the injuries suffered by [Name] in an automobile accident caused by your insured, [Name], on [Date].

Attached are medical records and invoices for [Name] incurred subsequent to my [Date] letter to [Independent adjuster] and a recapitulation of her total medical bills incurred.

As stated in my letter to [Independent adjuster], [Name]'s left arm and elbow still continue to suffer numbness and tingling, muscular weakness, and pain, because of the accident. This problem is compounded by the physical requirements of her profession. As a hairdresser, it is necessary that her wrists, hands and arms be constantly raised, extended and repeatedly flexed. By the end of her work day, the injured arm is weak, painful and extremely fatigued.

As I discussed in my previous letter, [Name] has already effected significant unpleasant and restrictive modifications to her lifestyle. Although she is unable to avoid the pain caused by her profession or housework, she no longer plays racquetball or participates in her aerobic classes; she knows she will have to resign from her organized softball team.

Since there were no further lifestyle modifications available to her, she recently revisited [Doctor] in an attempt to achieve improved pain management. [Doctor] scheduled her for an electromyogram in order to rule out nerve damage. As I'm sure you are aware, the test itself is not only time consuming, but extremely painful. The test did, however, confirm [Doctor]'s original diagnosis of chronic tendonitis and epicondylitis. He is therefore unable to offer her any respite from the pain other than drugs or inactivity. The analgesic which [Name] was taking was no longer effective; it became necessary for [Doctor] to once again prescribe an anti-inflammatory drug, despite the gastrointestinal upset that this drug causes.

[Doctor] continues to feel that, although the problem was caused by the accident, it is aggravated somewhat by the type of work she does and it would be similarly aggravated by any other occupation involving similar activity. Despite the continuing pain, [Name] is resistant to the idea of a change of profession. She has already invested considerable time, effort and finances in completing the necessary schooling, training hours, testing and licensure procedures in order to enter her chosen profession, which she enjoys immensely. She has likewise invested four years of work in pursuit of success in her profession, toward her ultimate goal of owning her own shop.

[Name] has pursued both pain management and lifestyle modification to the extent that either she or her physician are able to do so. She is quite concerned about the probability that the epicondylitis will, as she ages, subject her to post-traumatic arthritic problems and increased dysfunction and pain.

Based upon the foregoing, this letter is a demand for compensation for the personal injuries, and past and future pain and suffering of [Name] in the amount of [$]. I look forward to hearing from you regarding this.

Very truly yours,

[Signature]

Enclosures

LETTER 4-8
SETTLEMENT DEMAND LETTER 7 (ACCIDENT)

[Date]

[Carrier's name]
[Address]

Re: Our Client : [Name]
Your Insured : [Name]
Date of Loss : [Date]
Your Claim No. : [Number]

Dear [Adjustor]:

I have reviewed this matter with my client and propose the following settlement. My client [Name] has asserted claims [Describe claim] due to damages and injuries sustained in the accident of [Date].

A summary of the client's medical treatment following the accident is as follows: [Summarize treatment, employment and financial aspects as well].

We believe that a probable jury verdict in this case would not be less than [$] and a probable verdict would be approximately [$]. In an effort to avoid the expenses and costs of trial, we are willing to accept an offer in the sum of [$] in exchange for a full and final release from our client.

I look forward to hearing from you regarding our settlement proposal by [Date].

Sincerely,

[Signature]

LETTER 4-9
SETTLEMENT DEMAND LETTER 8 (CLEAR LIABILITY)

[Date]

[Carrier's name]
[Address]

Re: Our Client : [Name]
Your Insured : [Name]
Date of Loss : [Date]
Your Claim No. : Number]

Dear [Insurer]:

I have reviewed this matter with my client and propose the following settlement. As you know, my client [Name] has asserted claims for [Describe claims] due to the injuries that she sustained in the automobile accident with your insured. My review of the file indicates that liability is clear. At the time of the collision [Describe client's action], your insured [Describe defendant vehicle's action, for example, was driving under the influence of alcohol]. The force of the collision was severe and my client sustained [Describe injuries].

I would be willing to recommend to my client a settlement in the amount of [$].

I look forward to hearing from you with regard to our settlement proposal within the near future.

Sincerely,

[Signature]

LETTER 4-10
SETTLEMENT DEMAND LETTER 9 (EXCESS LIABILITY)

[Date]
[Carrier's name]
[Address]

Re: Our Client : [Name]
Your Insured : [Name]
Date of Loss : [Date]
Your Claim No. : [Number]

Dear [Insurer]:

This is a demand for full and final settlement of this case for the policy limit amount of [$]. Liability is clear in this case. As you know, the actual damages alone will be greater than the [$] coverage by the time of trial if one considers only the medical expenses and lost wages already accumulated by my client as a result of this accident.

Pursuant to the information disclosed in discovery, discovery clearly shows the severity of the injuries of [Client], including [Describe injuries]. My client has lost over [$] in wages during recovery after the accident as well as [$] which she would have received had she been able to accept a supervisory position with her company. These facts alone demonstrate that the case is valued at more than [$], had your insured obtained adequate insurance. Inasmuch as there may be some question as to the ability of your insured to pay a claim or judgment in excess of this policy, I have been authorized to submit an offer of settlement on behalf of [Client] for the full sum of [Total amount of policy limits].

I also believe that this case is an excellent punitive damage case, because [Disclose any facts which may aggravate or suggest a punitive damage claim].

I suggest that you act upon this offer on or before [Date]. Thank you for your consideration.

Sincerely,

[Signature]

LETTER 4-11
SETTLEMENT DEMAND LETTER 10
(EXTENDED COURSE OF TREATMENT)

[Date]

[Adjuster]
[Insurance company]
[Address]

Re:	Your Insured:	[Name]
	My Client:	[Name]
	Claim No .:	[Number]
	D/A:	[Date]

Dear [Adjuster]:

Today I met with [Client] to review his personal injury case with him and to discuss the damages which he incurred, and continues to incur, due to the negligence of your insured on [Date].

I have been informed that on said day, at approximately [Time], [Driver] was driving a [1980 Dodge eastbound on Florida Avenue at its intersection with New York Avenue]. The owner of that vehicle is your insured, [Name]. I have further been informed that on said day, [Driver] was inattentive, and ran through a red light at that intersection, and struck [Client]'s vehicle on the driver's side, causing it to spin out of control. An officer came to the scene and determined that [Driver] had failed to yield to a traffic signal. Further, the officer concluded that [Client] did no improper driving.

As a result of your insured's negligence, significant property damages were incurred. More importantly, as a result of your insured's negligence, and the violent impact, [Client] suffered multiple and serious physical injuries as described in the enclosed medical reports.

Prior to the time of the accident, [Client] was a healthy, happy twenty-seven (27)-year-old male. However, subsequent to the accident, and as a direct result thereof, [Client]'s life has been drastically altered, and the quality of his life has greatly deteriorated.

Upon impact, [Client]'s body was tossed around his vehicle. The force of said collision caused his right shoulder to be thrown into the passenger door. As a result, [Client] developed painful injuries to his right shoulder, back, and neck. Further, he developed migraine-type headaches.

Since the above described symptoms caused so much discomfort and distress for [Client], and were getting worse instead of better, [Client] scheduled an appointment and met with Dr. Dan Chiro, D.C., on [Date] for consultation, evaluation, and treatment. After examining [Client], Dr. Chiro diagnosed his injuries as: "Post-traumatic cervical strain-sprain complex, post-traumatic sub-deltoid bursitis, and post-traumatic separation of the rt. A-C joint." Further, said doctor noted that the x-rays taken revealed abnormal deviations.

Due to the severity of [Client]'s injuries, he was referred to Dr. Bill Lewis, a doctor who specializes in orthopedic and traumatic surgery. After examining [Client], Dr. Lewis confirmed Dr. Chiro's findings. Further, he recommended that [Client] continue with his therapy with Dr. Chiro, have hydrocollator packs applied to his neck and right shoulder, have intermittent spinal traction, take Naprosyn, consider injections of the right sub-deltoid, and have x-rays taken of both shoulders.

After reviewing the x-rays, Dr. Lewis noted in his [Date] report that [Client] had incurred a separation of the right acromioclavicular joint. He therefore placed [Client] in a sling. [Client] saw Dr. Lewis six times in all.

On [Date], [Client] met with Dr. John Oland regarding his shoulder pain. Upon examination, Dr. Oland concluded that [Client] incurred a right shoulder separation with ligamentitis tendonitis. He recommended anti-inflammatory agents and trigger point injections. [Client] treated with Dr. Oland up until [Date].

On [Date], [Client] met with Dr. A.H. Bones, an orthopedic surgeon. After examining [Client], Dr. Bones's impressions were (1) acromioclavicular joint separation, and (2) possible rotator cuff tear (doubtful). Dr. Bones recommended that [Client] have a right shoulder arthrogram, an excision of the distal clavicle, and that he take Naprosyn. [Client] was, accordingly, scheduled for an arthrogram at [Hospital].

On [Date], [Client] had the arthrogram at [Hospital]. Said test confirmed that [Client] had suffered injury to his right shoulder. Further, said test ruled out the possibility of a rotator cuff tear of the right shoulder.

[Client]'s shoulder pain persisted. On [Date], Dr. Bones stated in a letter to me that: "Without surgical intervention, [Client] will not recover from his degenerative changes in the acromio-clavicular joint." The cost of his fee for such surgery would be approximately $3,000.

On [Date], Dr. Randall diagnosed [Client]'s injury as: "painful first-degree chronic AC separation, right shoulder." He operated on said shoulder at [Hospital]. A detailed description of said operation can be found in the [Hospital] notes enclosed herein, dated [Date].

Dr. Randall took the sutures out on [Date]. On [Date], Dr. Randall noted in his report that [Client] was still recovering. He further noted that [Client] did not yet have the ability to throw. As a result of said accident, [Client] is now left with permanent scarring. Enclosed please find a picture depicting such.

In addition to the medical expenses incurred to date, in the sum of [$], [Client] has been damaged in numerous other ways. At the time of the accident, [Client] was between jobs. Obviously, the accident prevented him from seeking employment, as he was unable to perform physical labor. As a result, [Client] was unemployed until [Date] at which time he gained employment.

In addition to the pain and suffering which [Client] has had to endure, he has been greatly inconvenienced as a result of the accident. Having to go in for numerous treatments proved to be terribly inconvenient for him.

Additionally, as a result of his injuries, [Client] has had to forego participation in various recreational activities. Prior to the accident, he actively participated in horseback riding, archery, and softball. However, [Client]'s injuries have prevented him from participating in such activities and this has caused him to become quite depressed.

Further, it has proven to be very inconvenient for [Client] to engage in home physical therapy each night for 15-30 minutes per night. These exercises, and his injuries in general, have created a damper on his social and sexual life.

Additionally, as a result of the accident, [Client] finds himself to be more tense, irritable, and unfriendly. Under the circumstances, this is understandable. Moreover, his irritability and crabbiness caused considerable friction between him and his wife.

At the present time, [Client]'s major complaint is that his shoulder is still not as strong as before, and he is left with a visible, ugly, permanent scar on his shoulder.

Without belaboring the obvious, it is clear that [Client] has suffered greatly, and continues to suffer, due to his injuries. In a good-faith attempt to presently resolve [Client]'s case, I have been authorized to settle this matter for the total sum of [$]. Based upon the facts and circumstances of this case, I sincerely believe that this offer is exceedingly reasonable.

I look forward to hearing from you, and I thank you for your anticipated cooperation in this matter.

Very truly yours,

[Attorney]

LETTER 4-12
SETTLEMENT DEMAND LETTER 11 (PROMISSORY NOTE)

[Date]

CERTIFIED MAIL
RETURN RECEIPT REQUESTED,
REGULAR MAIL and
HAND DELIVERY

[Name]
[Address]

Re: [Describe Promissory Note]

Dear [Name]:

Please be advised that the above-referenced Promissory Note ("Note") became due and payable on [Date], and is presently due and owing.

We have been requested by [Name] ("Lender"), the holder of the Note, to make this demand on you for Payment in full of all amounts currently owing on and under the Note. You may contact Mr./Mrs./Ms. [Name] at [Bank], [Address], [Phone number] to obtain the exact amount now due and payable on and under the Note. All payments on the Note should be made to Lender at the foregoing address.

If payment is not received from you of all sums now due and payable on the Note on or before [Time], [Date], Lender will exercise its right to accelerate the entire amount due and owing along with the accrued, earned and unpaid interest as of the date of acceleration pursuant to the terms and conditions of the Note.

Should you continue to ignore your obligations, Lender will institute and prosecute litigation designed to enforce your obligations under the Note. You are hereby specifically notified that your failure to pay your obligations herein will result in increased liability by way of attorneys' fees and costs of Court incurred by Lender in the institution and prosecution of litigation designed to enforce such obligations.

Nothing herein shall be deemed a waiver of any other defaults, whether matured or unmatured, and whether enumerated above or not, existing or hereafter arising under the Note or any other agreement, instrument or document executed in connection with or as security for the Note, or a waiver or abandonment of any rights or remedies available to Lender (whether against you or any other person or any property) each of which rights or remedies is hereby specifically reserved (including, without limitation, the right to seek judgment and/or to proceed against personal property).

Very truly yours,

[Firm name]
[Signature]

LETTER 4-13
SETTLEMENT DEMAND LETTER 12
(DECEPTIVE TRADE PRACTICES)

CERTIFIED MAIL
RETURN RECEIPT REQUESTED,
REGULAR MAIL and
HAND DELIVERY

[Date]

[Name]
[Address]

Re: Violations of [Texas] Deceptive Trade Practices Act.

Dear [Name]:

Pursuant to Section 17.50A, Deceptive Trade Practices—Consumer Protection Act, Tex. Bus. & Com. Code Ann. (Supp. 1980) ("DTPA"), ABC Corporation, hereby gives you notice that Mr. Y, his agents, servants, or employees have breached certain provisions of the DTPA directly affecting ABC Corporation's lease of property situated in Houston, Harris County, Texas, commonly known as 110 Main, and more particularly described as follows:

> The south 25 feet of lot No. 25 in block No. 25 in the City of Houston, Harris County, Texas, on the south side of Buffalo Bayou and the improvements thereon consisting of a 3-story and basement masonry stone building, known as 110 Main Street, in said City of Houston.

Section 17.45, DTPA defines "consumer" as follows: "'Consumer' means an individual, partnership, corporation, or governmental entity who seeks or acquires by purchase *or lease*, any goods or services." (emphasis added). The same section defines "goods" as follows: "'Goods' means tangible chattles or *real property* purchased or *leased for use*." (emphasis added). The Act therefore applies to Mr. Y as the landlord of 110 Main, being the successor in interest of Mrs. W, the original owner of the above-described premises.

Section 17.50(a) DTPA provides, in pertinent part, the following:

> A consumer may maintain an action where any of the following constitute a producing cause of actual damages:
>
> 1. The use or employment by any person of a false, misleading, or deceptive act or practice that is specifically enumerated in a subdivision of Subsection (b) of Section 17.46 of this subchapter;
>
> 2. Any unconscionable action or course of action by any person . . .

Section 17.46(b) DTPA, provides, in pertinent part, the following:

> Except as provided in subsection (d) of this section, the term "false, misleading, or deceptive acts or practices" includes, but is not limited to, the following acts:
>
> * * *
>
> (12) Representing that an agreement confers or involves rights, remedies, or obligations which it does not have or involve, or which are prohibited by law;
>
> (13) Knowingly making false or misleading statements of fact concerning the need for parts, replacement, or repair service...

The specific complaints which are alleged to be in violation of the DTPA are as follows:

(1) Mr. Y has violated express and implied warranties. The lease itself provides the express warranty that "the lessee shall and may peaceably and quietly have, hold and enjoy possession of the Premises for and during the full term of the lease." This warranty has been violated. Further, Mr. Y has violated the implied warranty of quiet enjoyment. Mr. Y has violated these implied and expressed warranties of quiet enjoyment and peaceable possession by pursuing an appeal of the case *Mr. Y v. ABC Corporation,* No. 222, 222, Justice Court, Precinct 1, Harris County, Texas, which was tried on July 15–16, 19__. Judgment was rendered unanimously in favor of ABC Corporation by a six-member jury panel. After only a ten-minute deliberation, the jury returned, finding that grounds for forfeiture did not exist and that Y's suit was frivolous. To further pursue this cause after such a decisive verdict amounts to a breach of expressed and implied warranties in violation of DTPA § 17.50(a)(2). Further, by tortuously interfering with contractual relations under the lease, Mr. Y has broken implied warranties that he would not so interfere. Further, to continue to pursue this case after the clear verdict in the case above cited amounts to malicious prosecution which breaches implied warranties under the DTPA.

(2) Through letters from Mr. Y, his agents, servants or employees, and via Plaintiff's Original Petition in the case above cited, representations have been made that the lease confers rights, and remedies upon Y to allow a present right to have the lease forfeited. The continued pursuit during the pendency of this appeal demonstrates that Mr. Y continues to represent to ABC Corporation that the lease agreement confers a present right and remedy of forfeiture, when, in fact, the lease does not confer nor involve such a present right, and this is a violation of DTPA § 1746(b)(12).

(3) Further, Mr. Y has knowingly made false or misleading statements of fact concerning the need for replacement or repair to the glass in the showcase windows of the leased premises, and continues to make such claim by pursuing an appeal of this cause all of which are in violation of DTPA § 1746(b)(13).

(4) Continuing to attempt to evict Defendant when no grounds for eviction are present is an "unconscionable action or course of action" in violation of DTPA § 17.50(a)(3).

All conduct of Mr. Y, as described herein, was committed "knowingly." All such actions of Mr. Y have been a producing cause of damages to ABC Corporation.

ABC Corporation hereby gives notice that from the date of the appeal of the above cited case, it has been damaged in the amount of $100,000.00 actual damages (for settlement purposes), in addition to expenses, including attorneys' fees reasonably incurred in asserting these claims against Mr. Y in a current amount of $5,000.00.

ABC Corporation hereby formally makes demand upon Mr. Y for payment of its damages as described herein and notifies Y that failure to do so within thirty (30) days after receipt of this letter might result in trebling of some or all of the damages plus an award of expenses, court costs and attorneys' fees adjudged against Y, if a claim under the DTPA were successfully asserted by ABC Corporation against Mr. Y.

Your prompt attention to this matter will be appreciated.

Very truly yours,

[Firm name]
[Attorney]

LETTER 4-14
LETTER TO CLIENT RE: SETTLEMENT OFFER

Date]

[Client's name]
[Address]

Re: [Case name]

Dear [Client]:

We have received an offer of settlement from [Defendant's insurance company].

Please contact our office so that we may discuss in detail whether or not you would like to accept this settlement offer. We would like to discuss with you the advantages and disadvantages of accepting the offer and your options at this time.

We look forward to hearing from you in the near future.

[Signature]

LETTER 4-15
NOTICE OF TIME OF SETTLEMENT CONFERENCE

[Date]

[Name]
[Address]

Re: [Case name]
Our File : [Number]
Date/Loss : [Date]

Dear [Name]:

Please be advised that a Mandatory Settlement Conference has been scheduled in the above entitled matter for [Date] at [Time], in [Department Number] of the [County] Superior Court, located at [Address].

I will, of course, be present for the conference as well as a representative from [Insurance company]. Please meet us in [Department] at [Time] on the above mentioned date. Please contact me with any questions or comments regarding this matter.

Thank you for your courtesy and cooperation.

Very truly yours,

[Signature]

cc: [Insurance company]

LETTER 4-16
NOTIFICATION OF SCHEDULING OF ARBITRATION

[Date]

[Attorney]
[Firm]
[Address]

Re: [Case name]
OCSC Case No.: [Number]
Date of Loss : [Date]
Our File No. : [Number]

Dear [Attorney]:

The arbitration in our case has been set to take place in your office on [Date] at [Time].

My estimate for the hearing is two (2) hours.

Should you have any questions, please do not hesitate to contact me.

Very truly yours,

[Signature]

LETTER 4-17
POST-ARBITRATION REPORT TO CLIENT'S INSURER

[Date]

[Name]
[Insurance company]
[Address]

Re: [Case name]
Insured : [Name]
Claim No. : [Number]
Our File : [Number]
Date/Loss : [Date]

POST-ARBITRATION REPORT

Dear [Name]:

The arbitration in this matter took place on [Date]. Plaintiff [Name] testified at the arbitration. Defendants submitted evidence by way of declarations.

Plaintiff's testimony at the arbitration was consistent with his deposition testimony. He stated that about one and one-half hours after getting into the car, he felt an excruciating pain in his buttocks. He continued to have this pain during the remaining two-hour drive home. When he arrived home, he did not wash the area or seek medical assistance. Instead, he went to bed. When he woke up the next morning, he was still in excruciating pain. He did not wash the area that day or seek medical treatment. Not until his mother told him one or two days later to see a doctor did he seek medical treatment.

Plaintiff testified that he still has daily pain and itching at the scar sight. Future scar revision surgery will be necessary to minimize the appearance of the scar.

Plaintiff's counsel argued throughout the arbitration that strict liability applies to this case and that the battery leakage caused his client substantial harm. In response, I argued that there was no product defect, and, therefore, there is no strict liability.

I submitted the declaration of [Name] which set out the technical aspects of our defense. I pointed out that the battery contained a state-of-the-art safety device which operated properly after plaintiff inserted at least two of the batteries backwards. I also submitted copies of photographs from the plaintiff's expert's report, clearly showing that at least two of the batteries were installed backwards.

After making my liability arguments, I also asserted plaintiff's failure to mitigate his damages. When he initially felt the pain, he did not immediately seek medical attention or attempt to wash the area during his two-hour ride home. When he arrived home, he did not wash the area or seek medical attention. Instead, he went to bed. When he woke up the next day, he again did not attempt to wash the area or seek medical care. These inactions of plaintiff substantially increased his injuries. I submitted the declaration of [Name], M.D., who stated that time is of essence, and that the area should be washed as soon as possible to avoid serious burns.

During the arbitration, plaintiff's counsel identified medical expenses totalling $1,557.60. The cost of future surgery was alleged to be $12,000.00. At the close of final arguments, plaintiff made a demand of $224,997.00. This demand includes past pain and suffering and $10.00 per day for the rest of plaintiff's life for future pain and suffering.

At the close of my final argument, I asked the arbitrator for a defense award. I believe that we will probably receive a defense award, unless the arbitrator wants to use his award as a settlement tool and award a relatively small amount so that plaintiff doesn't de novo the award. If we do receive a defense award, plaintiff's counsel has thirty days from the service of the award within which to request a trial.

Following the arbitration, plaintiff's counsel asked me if there was any way we could resolve this case. He seemed to be fishing for information regarding whether or not Eveready would be willing to pay a small amount to resolve this case.

At this time, I recommend that we wait for the arbitrator's award and then discuss the pros and cons of a nominal settlement.

I will, of course, promptly notify you when the arbitration award is received. Should you have any questions in the interim, please do not hesitate to contact me.

Very truly yours,

[Signature]

cc: [Names]

LETTER 4-18
NOTIFICATION TO CLIENT'S INSURER OF OPPOSING PARTY'S REJECTION OF ARBITRATION AWARD

[Date]

[Name]
[Insurance company]
[Address]

Re: [Case name]
Insured : [Name]
Claim No. : [Number]
Our File : [Number]
Date/Loss : [Date]

Dear [Name]:

As expected, we have received plaintiff's rejection of the arbitration award (Trial de Novo).

A Mandatory Settlement Conference and/or trial date will now be set.

I will continue to keep you informed.

Very truly yours,

[Signature]

cc: [Names]

LETTER 4-19
LETTER TO CLIENT'S INSURER CONFIRMING TELEPHONE CONVERSATION REGARDING BINDING ARBITRATION

[Date]

[Name]
[Insurance company]
[Address]

Re: [Case name]
Insured : [Name]
Claim No. : [Number]
Date of Loss : [Date]
Our File No.: [Number]

Dear [Name]:

This will confirm our telephone conversation in which we discussed plaintiff's offer to have a binding arbitration with a $50,000.00 high and a $1,000.00 low. As I mentioned, I believe that plaintiff's counsel is flexible as to the high and low figures for purposes of negotiation.

If we can find a strong arbitrator who would be willing to give a defense award if the evidence justifies it, I believe that a binding arbitration would be a good idea. It would be less costly than a jury trial and there would be a benefit to having a specific date set for the arbitration. As you know, with trials we are never sure when the trial will actually begin. This will make it difficult for our expert, who works in [State], to schedule trial testimony.

I understand that you will contact [Insured] to discuss the possibility of a binding arbitration. Once you have done this, please contact me so that we may discuss this matter further.

Very truly yours,

[Signature]

cc: [Name]

LETTER 4-20
TRANSMITTAL OF STIPULATION REGARDING ARBITRATION FOR VARIOUS PARTIES' SIGNATURES

[Date]

[Attorney]
[Firm]
[Address]

Re: [Case name]
Our File No.: [Number]

Dear [Attorney]:

Pursuant to the telephone conversation of [Date], enclosed please find the original Stipulation Regarding Arbitration and Waiver of 90 Rule that I have prepared in the above-referenced matter. This letter will also confirm that the original date of [Date] was not available on your calendar and at that time we chose the date of [Date]. Please execute where indicated, forwarding same on to [Mr. Qualls] for signature. It is at that time requested that [Mr. Qualls] send the stipulation to [Mr. Feld]. [Mr. Feld] is then requested to send the fully executed Stipulation on to [Mr. Moore]. [Mr. Moore] is then requested to file the original Stipulation and attached Declaration with the court.

I look forward to seeing you all at the Arbitration presently set for [Date] at [Time].

Thank you for your courtesy and cooperation in this matter.

Very truly yours,

[Signature]

cc: [Names]

LETTER 4-21
PRE-ARBITRATION REPORT TO INSURER

[Date]

[Name]
[Insurance company]
[Address]

Re: [Case name]
Insured : [Name]
Claim No. : [Number]
Our File : [Number]

Dear [Name]:

PRE-ARBITRATION REPORT

Suddenly, and without the usual warning such as a Status Conference, this case has been assigned to Arbitration in [Location]. Our Arbitration hearing date is [Date] at [Time] before Attorney [Name]. I know nothing about [Name]'s expertise or whether he is favorably disposed toward realtors. This is my pre-arbitration report.

JURISDICTION

Unchanged from prior report.

FACTS

To refresh your recollection, this lawsuit began as an action to recover $11,000.00 owed to Town Square Realtors, our clients, under a promissory note, filed in Municipal Court. However, the Teeles responded to that complaint with a cross-complaint alleging breach of contract, negligence, intentional misrepresentation, suppression of facts, negligent misrepresentation, rescission based on fraud, declaratory relief and indemnity. The basis for the cross-complaint is that the property the Teeles bought, using our client's services as dual agents, has a water problem and a problem with ongoing cracking in the slabs for the house and garage, about which, the Teeles contend, our clients either knew or should have known and disclosed.

In January 1985 the cross-complainants began looking for a house to buy in Redlands, after having first rejected the idea of adding onto their existing house in Redlands because it would over-improve that house for the neighborhood. The Teeles asked Carolyn Schumacher, who was then an agent with Town Square Realtors, to assist them in finding a new home, although they also looked with other agents. The Teeles were acquaintances of Carolyn's from

School Board Campaigns and their children's sports activities. The Teeles wanted a large, one-story house, with either a pool or room for one, in the same school area as their prior house, thus limiting the inventory they could consider.

After viewing about a dozen homes with Carolyn, and at Carolyn's suggestion, the Teeles agreed to meet with Mr. Dwight Rutherford who had purchased the subject lot, known as 1605 Crestview Road, Redlands, California, 92374, some years earlier through Town Square Realtors, and who had plans to build a house on it for spec purposes to be sold through Town Square Realtors. Plaintiffs were interested in the plans, which were presented by the architect and Mr. Rutherford at Rutherford's home. Plaintiffs also toured Rutherford's home, which Mr. Rutherford had constructed, in order to assess Mr. Rutherford's workmanship. According to Mr. Teele's testimony at the deposition, he and his wife spent some time at the bare lot and spent quite a bit of time meeting with Rutherford, looking at other properties, and discussing the idea of buying the bare lot from Mr. Rutherford and entering into a construction agreement for Mr. Rutherford to build the house on the lot, before making any final decisions to purchase.

As you know, Mr. Rutherford had originally purchased this lot from C Y Development. From what I can gleen from plaintiffs' testimony, the C in C Y Development must stand for Mr. Coffin, as Mr. Coffin was later brought to plaintiffs' attention when the damages started showing up, as the person who prepared the lot for sale before Mr. Rutherford obtained it. As you know, C Y Development sold the lot to the Rutherfords on July 12, 1984, for $34,500.00, with one of the conditions of their contract being a provision that the seller, (C Y Development in that case) guarantee approval of a soils report by the City of Redlands. Ms. Perrie Mundy of Town Square Realtors, who had had prior dealings with Rutherford, had agreed to market the property for Rutherford prior to Carolyn Schumacher becoming aware that the property was available for sale. It should be noted that, although our file contains a report from C H J Laboratories which was prepared in April of 1979 and filed with the City of Redlands referring to dry density tests prepared for the lot, I do not have any information to indicate whether our client had possession of this document until after a lawsuit was filed and the issue was investigated.

Back to this transaction, as you know, after Mrs. Schumacher brought the plaintiffs' inability to find a suitable home to the attention of Ms. Mundy, Ms. Mundy suggested that they might be interested in the home that Mr. Rutherford intended to build on the subject lot, which was how Mrs. Schumacher came to introduce plaintiffs to Mr. Rutherford.

Once the plaintiffs determined that they wanted to purchase the property, they found out they could not obtain construction financing unless they already owned the lot. Thus, it was agreed that the plaintiffs would purchase the bare lot from Mr. Rutherford as buyer, and would, as soon as they owned the lot, execute a construction agreement with Mr. Rutherford for him to be the contractor to build the house. The lot was sold to the Teeles for $46,000.00.

The plaintiffs obtained a first trust deed for the property in the amount of $75,000.00, which is the limit of the Veteran's Administration Financing. Plaintiffs believed they could not stretch themselves beyond $190,000.00 to $200,000.00 total consideration for the property, including of course the structure on top on the lot. Their intention was to take out a home equity loan on their existing property in Redlands to finance the construction, and then to sell their home in Redlands once the subject property was close to completion, so that they would not move out of their existing home in Redlands until the subject property was ready for occupancy.

Construction started on the subject property in approximately June of 1985, with the official contract to purchase the lot being executed in April of 1985. According to Carolyn Schumacher, plaintiffs were going to have difficulty obtaining the necessary financing, and in lieu of agreeing to pay a commission on the sale of the bare land, it was agreed that plaintiffs would execute a promissory note in the amount of $11,000.00 as part of the construction agreement, to be paid to Town Square Realtors as soon as construction was completed. Mr. Teele testified that he did agree to sign the promissory note, and that construction was indeed totally completed by June of 1986, and was substantially completed by December of 1985, when the Teeles took occupancy of the house. Evidently, the driveway was troublesome to be completed, but the main house was pretty much finished by December of 1985. In spite of problems encountered during construction, the Teeles also admit Mr. Rutherford was fully compensated according to the construction contract, even though no monies were paid under the promissory note.

According to Mr. Teele and Mrs. Teele's depositions, problems were discovered on the subject property in late Summer or early Fall of 1985. The initial problems discovered were cracks in three places in the house: the kitchen, living room, and a guest bedroom. Plaintiffs were at the construction site on a regular basis just to observe the process, while they still lived at their old property, and they brought the cracking to the attention of Mr. Rutherford. Mr. Rutherford explained that the cracks were due to normal concrete shrinkage, and he assured them he would fill in those cracks prior to completion of the structure, probably after framing was completed but before carpeting was installed. While at first both plaintiffs testified that this filling in process was not completed, they later qualified their response by indicating that although the cracks were filled in with some sort of putty-like material, they did not believe that the cracks were filled in deeply enough to correct the problem, whatever that problem was, because they had since experienced difficulty with ants infesting those same cracks.

The second, and more troublesome problem the plaintiffs discovered during construction was the ponding problem on the property. Both plaintiffs seem to believe the ponding was discovered around October of 1985 and that actually it was Mr. Rutherford who first brought the ponding to their attention. The area of ponding started out somewhat small, but according to both plaintiffs had grown to some 30 by 20 feet in the back of their yard. Mr. Rutherford admitted to plaintiffs that while he had owned the property (which I believe was only a one-year time frame) he had observed an area in the northeastern corner of the property in which water would pond and take a long time to be absorbed into the ground. Mr. Rutherford told plaintiffs that he had believed it was a minor problem, but that during the construction of plaintiffs' house, he had become aware that the water seemed to sit for a longer period of time than he had anticipated. Plaintiffs asked Mr. Rutherford to take care of the water problem, to which he responded "I am only the contractor; it is your problem because it is your property." Mr. Rutherford was not entirely uncooperative, in that he did refer plaintiff to Mr. Coffin, the party from whom Mr. Rutherford had purchased the bare lot, and Mr. Rutherford also referred plaintiffs to a John Byerly, of Byerly Engineering, who quoted a figure of $1,200.00 simply to do an evaluation of the problem.

Mr. Rutherford stated he could not complete construction of the residence, or the garage, until after this problem with inadequate drainage was corrected. Hence, plaintiffs hired Leija Engineering to evaluate the problem. They also had officials from the City of Redlands check the lot to see whether the water was sewage water or due to some old leak or over-irrigation from the residence that was on the property to the back of their lot uphill approximately 35 feet from the level at which their house was going to be located.

Although Mrs. Leija did not identify the source of the water, she recommended that french drains and a sump pump be installed, which plaintiffs did do. There was also a second recommendation regarding a retaining wall. Plaintiffs elected instead to install the swimming pool, and had surface drains located around the pool to channel water away from the pool so that it would not float when emptied due to the high-water table, if indeed that is what the problem is.

Insofar as I can tell, the Teeles have not to date isolated the exact cause of the water intrusion problem, although the french drains and surface drains have largely, though not completely remedied it. The Teeles allegedly still are claiming that the cracking to their slab, and especially the garage slab, is a continuing problem.

According to both of the Teeles, the reason they named Town Square Realtors in their cross-complaint, and the reason they did not pay Town Square Realtors the money owed on the promissory note, was that they believed that Town Square Realtors either knew or should have known about this water intrusion problem and warned them to obtain a soils or geotechnical report prior to entering into this transaction. The reason for the suspicion concerning Town Square Realtors is based on two different factors:

1. The mere fact that Town Square Realtors acted as a dual agency. While both Teeles admit they understood that a dual representation was being carried out throughout this transaction, both felt that Perrie Mundy was acting more for

Rutherford and that Carolyn Schumacher was acting more for the Teeles and that, at some point during the construction, Ms. Schumacher's role seemed to change and she seemed to act more as if she were Rutherford's agent. In short, the distinction in her roles was not made clear to the Teeles from the beginning. Both Teeles expressed skepticism as to whether any realtor representing both sides of a transaction could do a decent job of fully representing the interests of either one of their clients.

2. Both Teeles testified to a conversation with Carolyn Schumacher in December of 1985, after they had already moved onto the property but before the promissory note would have been due. In the conversation Carolyn indicated that Town Square Realtors had been previously involved in a transaction in which they represented a developer where a water intrusion problem was discovered, and Town Square Realtors was sued or threatened to be sued for nondisclosure. In that conversation, Carolyn Schumacher allegedly told both of the Teeles that there was apparently a water intrusion problem in the subject property which should have been disclosed and, to protect Town Square from any potential liability, she was now going to disclose it. Mrs. Teele appeared to be more suspicious in her deposition than Mr. Teele as to the motive behind this disclosure. Whereas Mr. Teele believes that Carolyn made the disclosure more out of guilt, and was not necessarily admitting that she had any prior awareness of the water problem, Mrs. Teele seems to think that it was implied by Mrs. Schumacher's tone of voice that she was aware of a prior water intrusion problem and that she had failed to disclose it previously.

Both Teeles admit in their depositions that Mr. Rutherford admitted to having previously seen some ponding in one corner of the lot and that Mr. Rutherford never indicated that he had disclosed this to anyone at Town Square Realtors.

Based on the documentation in the file, it appears that the Teeles have spent approximately $7,000.00 for french drains, a sump pump, and additional surface drains which had to be added around the swimming pool that were not services connected to the installation of the pool itself. Further, according to Mr. Teele, he has been told that it would cost another $11,000.00 to completely correct this problem of water intrusion on the property. But he has not yet spent this $11,000.00, and the majority of the water ponding problem seems to have been corrected by the steps already taken.

As you know, Perrie Mundy had previously met with Nancy Kerr, the original attorney handling this file, and informed her that as far as Ms. Mundy was concerned, the area in which the subject property is located does not have a reputation for having any sort of water problems. Yet both of the Teeles testified that their neighbors, both uphill and next door, suffered similar water drainage problems and have all been forced to install french drains, surface drains, and sump pumps. Admittedly, though, the Teeles testified that these neighbors did not engage in this work until after the Teeles had already had their drainage problems relieved.

LIABILITY

Liability remains questionable, but is partly going to hinge on credibility. Both of the Teeles recognize that Carolyn denies any memory of belatedly disclosing this water intrusion problem in December of 1985 in conversations they had after they refused to pay the $11,000.00 on the promissory note. Thus, plaintiffs recognize that in any hearing, should Ms. Schumacher be asked to testify, there will be straight liar's contest as between the Teeles and Schumacher as to whether she made any such statement. Further, even if she were to admit to having made the statement, she clearly will not admit that it was with the implication that the Teeles wished to give to it, that she had previously known about the water intrusion problem and was now confessing to it. Instead, I am quite certain that she would testify that if she said anything at all it would be to the effect that her firm had indeed been involved in a water intrusion problem involving a developer in the past and she regretted that it was coming up again but that it was a problem of which she had no prior knowledge. It is my understanding from the impression of the witnesses which Mr. Tasoff had when he took the Teeles' depositions that both Teeles make good witnesses on their own behalf.

Other than the possibility that an Arbitrator or other fact finder would agree with Mrs. Teele's suspicion that Carolyn Schumacher did indeed make a late disclosure of information she was aware of prior to December of 1985, I believe liability is remote, unless plaintiffs produce at the Arbitration several witnesses, such as their neighbors, who can allege that this water intrusion problem was well known in the area, such that a realtor farming in that area should have been on notice. The C H J soils report which was on file with the City of Redlands and received City approval prior to the lot being developed, says nothing about an excessive water intrusion problem or any special steps that need to be taken prior to construction. Assuming our clients had access to the C H J report, and assuming they would have had a duty to be able to interpret it, there would not have been any thing in the contents of that report to put them on notice of a potential problem. Although Mr. Rutherford apparently was aware of some ponding prior to selling the lot, there is no evidence that he was aware that the problem was anywhere near as extensive as it allegedly turned out to be, or any evidence that he passed this information on to anyone associated with Town Square Realtors. Assuming there are no neighbors or other locals who can testify on behalf of the Teeles that there were people from Town Square Realtors present on the lot when the drainage problem was uncovered prior to the Teeles entry into the contract to purchase this lot, liability should remain remote.

It should also be noted that in cases involving brand new construction, the builder usually has strict liability for any defects. If the Teeles can indeed support their contention that the land itself was defective for construction, the liability would be strict liability presumably on Mr. Rutherford because although he was not the owner of the land at the time the construction was being performed, he was the owner of the land who sold it to the Teeles. It would have been his responsibility to have the land properly prepared for the construction which he had proposed to do as part of this sale. Hence, if anyone does have liability to the Teeles, primary liability should fall on Mr. Rutherford. As you know, we are not filing any cross-action against Mr. Rutherford because he has an ongoing relationship with our client, and we would prefer to maintain a united defense against the Teeles' cross-complaint in any event, so as not to lend any further credence to their contentions.

DAMAGES

As noted above, the Teeles are claiming approximately $7,000.00 in out-of-pocket damages and, arguably, an additional $11,000.00 in future costs necessitated by this water intrusion problem and cracked slab problems, which they say have not entirely been corrected to date. Those numbers should represent the absolute outside limits of our liability on the cross-complaint. It should be noted that normally, in a real estate transaction, the real estate agent does not forfeit his commission simply because he has committed some sort of negligence in the performance of his duties. Normally, a real estate agent only forfeits the commission or will be compelled to disgorge benefits obtained if the real estate agent can be shown to have committed fraud in the transaction which fraudulently induced the buyer and/or seller to execute the contract to purchase in the first place.

This is not a case in which I see any realistic likelihood that our clients could be held accountable or could be found liable for fraud sufficient to deprive them of their right to a commission. Further, since our clients have sued under a promissory note, it is really irrelevant whether the note is characterized as a commission or loan, since Mr. Teele acknowledges in his deposition that he did agree to this promissory note and that the conditions under the note were fulfilled by our client and that none of the monies owed under the note have been paid to our client.

Incidentally, Mr. Teele also testified that in the sale of their existing home, Mr. Teele sold by owner. You will recall that Ms. Schumacher indicated previously that she assisted the Teeles in the sale of their existing home and received no compensation for her assistance. That information may not be legally relevant, but it may have some bearing on what an Arbitrator feels would be an equitable award.

LITIGATION PLAN

1. We are serving the Teeles with a request to produce documentation in support of their liability and damage contentions.

2. We are scheduling a property site inspection by a geotechnical expert to determine whether the steps taken by the Teeles thus far have been reasonable and necessary to correct the water intrusion problem. Additionally, we will check the public records from the City of Redlands to determine whether Mr.

Rutherford and/or Town Square Realtors should have been on notice from the records available prior to construction that a potential water intrusion problem existed which should have been disclosed prior to the sale.

Since the Teeles' alleged damages are not extensive, I will not send an appraiser to this site inspection to determine whether there is any difference between the fair market value of the property and structures at the time they were purchased and the combined price the Teeles paid for such structures. However, if we are not satisfied with the Arbitrator's Award, we always have the option of requesting a second site inspection to be attended by an appraiser for this purpose.

3. I will prepare a 20-day notice of intention, and, pursuant to the Arbitrator's request, will prepare an arbitration brief to be submitted no later than five days prior to the hearing.

4. I will be in touch with Perrie Mundy and, unless she is no longer available, with Carolyn Schumacher to prepare both of them to testify at the Arbitration hearing, since neither of them had a deposition taken and it will be the Teeles' word against theirs if we do not have our clients testify on their own behalf.

Let me know if you have any additional suggestions for further handling.

Thank you for your courtesy and cooperation in this matter.

Very truly yours,

[Signature]

cc: [Names]

LETTER 4-22
TRANSMITTAL OF ORIGINAL STIPULATION TO CONTINUE ARBITRATION FOR SIGNATURES OF VARIOUS PERSONS

[Date]

[Attorney]
[Firm]
[Address]

RE: [Case name]:
Our File No.: [Number]

Dear [Attorney]:

Please find enclosed the original Stipulation to continue Arbitration Hearing in the above-entitled matter. It is requested that you execute same and forward the stipulation on to [Mr. Qualls]' office for his signature. It is further requested that [Mr. Qualls] execute the stipulation and forward it on to [Mr. Feld] for his signature. It is then finally requested that the stipulation be forwarded to the Arbitrator for signature.

When all signatures have been obtained, it is requested that the stipulation be returned to this office for filing with the court.

Thank you for your courtesy and cooperation in this matter.

Should you have any questions, please feel free to contact the undersigned.

Very truly yours,

[Signature]

cc: [Names]

LETTER 4-23
NOTIFICATION TO INSURER OF OPPOSING PARTY'S REQUEST FOR TRIAL DE NOVO AFTER ARBITRATION

[Date]

[Name]
[Insurance company]
[Address]

Re: [Case name]
Insured : [Name]
Claim No. : [Number]
Our File : [Number]

Dear [Name]:

Enclosed, please find a copy of the Arbitrator's Award in the above-referenced case. As you will note, the arbitrator awarded $21,000.00 to Town Square Realtors, Inc. The arbitrator awarded nothing to the Teeles, as against Town Square on the Teeles' cross-complaint. However, I fully expect that the Teeles will request a trial de novo.

I will continue to keep you advised of new developments. In the interim, should you have any questions or comments, please do not hesitate to call.

Very truly yours,

[Signature]

LETTER 4-24
NOTIFICATION TO WITNESS OF OPPOSING PARTY'S REQUEST FOR TRIAL DE NOVO AFTER ARBITRATION

[Date]

[Name]
[Address]

Re: [Case name]
Our Client : [Name]
Our File : [Number]

Dear [Name]:

Please be advised that defendants in the above referenced case have requested a trial de novo in the Superior Court, following an arbitration award in our favor. I therefore anticipate that we will need your assistance in preparing this case for trial.

Consequently, I am enclosing for your review copies of the following documents:

[1. Deposition transcript of Name 1;

2. Deposition transcript of Name 2;

3. Deposition transcript of Name 3; and

4. Our arbitration brief, summarizing the facts and issues.]

Our client, Town Square, was never deposed. It is alleged we had knowledge prior to sale of a drainage problem, which we deny. Note the [Name]'s testimony concerning their conversations with Carolyn Schumacher, our agent.

I would ask that you review these transcripts at your discretion. We do not presently have a trial date set, so there are no immediate deadlines for completion of this task. I would also ask that you refrain from preparing a written report at this time. Simply call me when you have completed your review so that we may discuss the issues and any opinions you may have based on your review of the transcripts.

I sincerely appreciate your courtesy, cooperation and professional assistance. Should you have any questions or comments, please do not hesitate to call.

Very truly yours,

[Signature]

Encls.

LETTER 4-25
NOTIFICATION OF CONTINUANCE OF ARBITRATION

[Date]

[Name]
[Insurance company]
[Address]

Re: [Case name]
Insured : [Name]
Our File : [Number]
Claim No. : [Number]
Date/Loss : [Date]

Dear [Name]:

Please be advised that the arbitrator in the above referenced case continued the arbitration until [Date]. Our Summary Judgment Motion hearing has been continued until [Date]. If the arbitrator enters an award with which we disagree, we have until well after the date set for Summary Judgment Motion hearing to request a Trial de Novo.

I will advise you of any new developments. In the interim, should you have any questions or comments, please do not hesitate to call.

Very truly yours,

[Signature]

LETTER 4-26
POST-ARBITRATION STATUS REPORT TO INSURER

[Date]

[Name]
[Insurance company]
[Address]

Re: [Case name]
Insured : [Name]
Our File : [Number]
Claim No. : [Number]
Date/Loss : [Date]

Post-Arbitration Status Report

Dear [Name]:

Enclosed, please find a copy of the Arbitrator's Award in the above referenced case. As you will note, the arbitrator awarded $100,000.00 in damages to Plaintiff [Name], and $5,000.00 for loss of consortium to her husband, [Name]. However, the arbitrator assigned zero liability to [Insured]. We are obviously very pleased with this result.

We cannot be certain of the complete basis underlying the arbitrator's award. However, my feeling is that he probably agreed with our arguments concerning the patent nature of the balcony railing, [Insured]'s lack of knowledge concerning the pebbles and any hazard associated with the pebbles, and therefore concluded our clients had no duty to the Plaintiffs.

I cannot be sure exactly what gross value the arbitrator may have placed on the Plaintiffs' claim. All Defendants argued strenuously that Plaintiffs should be saddled with substantial comparative fault. I believe that Plaintiffs' damages were realistically worth in excess of $100,000.00. I therefore believe the arbitrator must have assigned some comparative fault to the Plaintiff, possibly as much as 50 percent.

I anticipate a Request for Trial de Novo from one of the other Defendants, or possibly from the Plaintiff. I expect the Court will then set a Mandatory Settlement Conference before trial. As you know from our many prior discussions, I believe we have strong arguments on both the legal and factual issues. However, if this case goes before a jury, we would have some exposure simply because our clients rebuilt the balcony railing, leaving out most of the support members. A jury could possibly see this as culpable, although the arbitrator did not.

As noted in earlier correspondence, this case has been set for a prospective trial date on [Date], in [County] Superior Court, [City], Department [Number]. We have a Post-Arbitration Status Conference set for [Date]. I will report all further developments to you. In the interim, should you have any questions or comments, please do not hesitate to call.

Very truly yours,

[Signature]

Encl.
cc: [Insured]

LETTER 4-27
TRANSMITTAL OF SIGNATURE CONCERNING VOLUNTARY SETTLEMENT CONFERENCE

[Date]

[Attorney]
[Firm]
[Address]

Re: [Case name]
Our Client : [Name]
Our File : [Number]
Date/Loss : [Date]

Dear [Attorney]:

Enclosed, please find my signature concerning the proposed Voluntary Settlement Conference in this case. Thank you for your professional courtesy, cooperation and skill in arranging this Settlement Conference.

Also enclosed, please find a copy of the billing received to date from Brinton Economics for their services in this case. Please see that my principal, [Insurance company] is reimbursed by forwarding to my attention a check made payable to "[Name] Insurance Company" for one-third of the total due.

Should you have any questions or comments, please do not hesitate to call.

Very truly yours,

[Signature]

LETTER 4-28
REPORT TO CLIENTS OF PROGRESS OF CASE TOWARD POSSIBLE SETTLEMENT

[Date]

[Name]
[Address]

Re: [Case name]
Our File : [Number]
Date/Loss : [Date]

Dear [Name]:

On [Date], I attended a Voluntary Settlement Conference in the above referenced case. I was accompanied by [Name] of [Insurance company], your liability insurance carrier in this case. All other parties also appeared at the settlement conference.

Despite extensive negotiations, the case was not resolved. It remains scheduled for trial on [Date] at [Time] in Department [Number] of [County] Superior Court, [City]. The Courthouse is located at [Address].

The other parties to this action appear motivated to settle and I therefore feel there is still a strong chance of pretrial resolution. Even if the case is not resolved prior to trial, we cannot be certain that trial will commence on [Date]. Even if trial does commence on [Date], your testimony may not be needed until later in the week. However, I would ask again that you arrange to be available, if needed, on [Date] and for the ensuing two weeks.

Naturally, if the case should settle, I will notify you immediately. Otherwise, I will need to meet personally with you sometime prior to the date of trial to discuss our strategy and your possible testimony. I understand you will be in [City] on [Date] and will be available to meet with me at about 2:30–3:00 p.m. at the [Location]. I will ring your room before coming over. I look forward to meeting you.

Very truly yours,

[Signature]

LETTER 4-29
LETTER TO CLIENT REPORTING SETTLEMENT OF CASE

[Date]

[Name]
[Address]

Re: [Case name]
Our File : [Number]
Date/Loss : [Date]

Dear [Name]:

Please be advised that the above-referenced case has been settled by your liability insurance carrier. [Insurance company] agreed to pay the Plaintiffs a total of $49,500.00 for release and dismissal of the entire action. As you may recall, the other Defendants had paid a total of $115,000.00 among them.

While we felt we had good arguments on liability, the Plaintiff had suffered substantial injuries and we had projected her total gross damages to be in the $225,000.00 range. We also had projected trial and trial preparation costs in excess of $35,000.00. In light of these projected costs and the total exposure, [Insurance company] viewed settlement as the most economically practical resolution.

I have sincerely appreciated your courtesy and cooperation throughout the course of this lawsuit. It has been my pleasure to have represented your interests in connection with this matter. Should you have any additional questions, please do not hesitate to call.

Very truly yours,

[Signature]

LETTER 4-30
NOTIFICATION TO WITNESS OF SETTLEMENT OF CASE

[Date]

[Name]
[Address]

Re: [Case name]
Our Client : [Name]
Our File : [Number]
Date/Loss : [Date]

Dear [Name]:

Please be advised that the above-referenced matter has settled. Therefore your testimony at the [Date] trial is not necessary. Thank you for your assistance, courtesy and cooperation. Should you have any questions, please feel free to contact this office.

Very truly yours,

[Signature]

LETTER 4-31
NOTIFICATION TO CONSULTANTS OF SETTLEMENT OF CASE

[Date]

[Name]
[Company]
[Address]

[Name]
[Company]
[Address]

Re: [Case name]
Our Client : [Name]
Our File : [Number]
Date/Loss : [Date]

Gentlemen:

Please be advised that the above-referenced matter has settled. Thank you for your assistance, professional courtesy and cooperation in this matter. Should you have any questions or comments, please do not hesitate to call.

Very truly yours,

[Signature]

LETTER 4-32
REQUEST TO COURT FOR REFUND OF JURY FEES POST-SETTLEMENT

[Date]

Auditor/Controller
[County] Superior Court
[Address]

Re: [Case name]
OCSC Case No.: [Number]
Trial Date : [Date]

Dear Sir/Madam:

Please be advised that the above-referenced matter has settled. Please be further advised that this office posted jury fees on or about [Date] (receipt [#]) in the amount of $150.00. Request is hereby made for an immediate refund of said fees.

Should you have any questions, please do not hesitate to contact this office.

Very truly yours,

[Signature]

LETTER 4-33
NOTIFICATION TO OPPOSING PARTY OF TIME OF EVALUATION CONFERENCE

[Date]

[Name]
[Address]

Re: [Case name]
Our Client : [Name]
Our File : [Number]
Date/Loss : [Date]

Dear [Name]:

Please be advised that the court has set an Evaluation Conference for [Date], at [Time], Department [Number], of the [County] Superior Court located at [Address]. Please advise your attorney of this date so he can make arrangements to attend.

Should you have any questions regarding this matter, please feel free to contact me.

Very truly yours,

[Signature]

LETTER 4-34
NOTIFICATION OF MANDATORY SETTLEMENT CONFERENCE

[Date]

[Name]
[Insurance company]
[Address]

Re: [Case name]
Your Claim No.: [Number]
Insured : [Name]
Date/Loss : [Date]
Our File No. : [Number]

Dear [Name]:

On [Date] I attended the Evaluation Conference in this action. The Court ordered that a Mandatory Settlement Conference take place on [Date] at [Time] in Department [Number] of the [County] Superior Court.

The appearance of a representative from your office will be required at the MSC.

In order that settlement negotiations may begin, plaintiff's counsel has asked for a current breakdown of the lien. Please provide this to me.

Thank you for your assistance.

Very truly yours,

[Signature]

LETTER 4-35
NOTIFICATION TO JUDGE OF DATES UNAVAILABLE FOR MANDATORY SETTLEMENT CONFERENCE

[Date]

Honorable [Name]
SUPERIOR COURT, [County]
[Address]

Re: [Case name]
OCSC Case No.: [Name]
Date of Loss : [Date]
Our File No. : [Number]
Current MSC Hearing Date: [Date]

Re: Continuance of Mandatory Settlement Conference

Dear Judge [Name]:

In an attempt to schedule the Mandatory Settlement Conference for a date convenient for the Court and all involved parties, the following list of unavailable dates (due to trials/arbitrations) is provided on behalf of [Names]:

[September 20–24, 1993; September 30, 1993; October 5, 1993; October 14–15, 1993; October 18–22, 1993; October 26–29, 1993; November 15–19, 1993.]

Thank you for your assistance. If there are any questions, please contact our office.

Very truly yours,

[Signature]

cc: [Names]

LETTER 4-36
FAX COVER SHEET FOR COPY OF SIGNED STIPULATION AND ORDER CONTINUING MANDATORY SETTLEMENT CONFERENCE

TO: ____
NAME LOCATION

FROM: ____
SENDER'S NAME

RE: ____
CASE NAME

****

DOCUMENT: Copy of Signed Stipulation and Order Continuing [DATE] MSC

MESSAGE : Notice of Continuance to follow in mail

****

NUMBER OF PAGES (INCLUDING THIS SHEET): 4

DATE: ______________________ TIME: ____________

IF YOU HAVE ANY QUESTIONS OR PROBLEMS WITH THIS TRANSMISSION, PLEASE CALL [Telephone]

LETTER 4-37
TRANSMITTAL OF COPY OF REQUEST FOR DISMISSAL 1

[Date]

[Attorney]
[Firm]
[Address]

Re: [Case name]
Our Client : [Name]
Our File : [Number]
Date/Loss : [Date]

Dear [Name]:

Enclosed with this letter, please find a copy of the Request for Dismissal which I have filed with respect to my Cross-Complaint against [Name] in the above-referenced case. I will see that you receive a copy of the conformed dismissal once it is returned by our attorney service from the court.

Should you have any questions or comments, please do not hesitate to call.

Very truly yours,

[Signature]

LETTER 4-38
TRANSMITTAL OF COPY OF REQUEST FOR DISMISSAL 2

[Date]

[Name]
[Address]

Re: [Case name]
Our File : [Number]
Date/Loss : [Date]

Dear [Name]:

Enclosed herewith, please find a copy of the conformed Request for Dismissal dismissing the above-referenced case. This office will be closing our file. It has been a pleasure representing your interest in this matter. Should you have any questions, please do not hesitate to call.

Very truly yours,

[Signature]

LETTER 4-39
TRANSMITTAL OF CONFORMED COPY OF ACKNOWLEDGMENT OF SATISFACTION OF JUDGMENT

[Date]

[Name]
[Firm]
[Address]

Re: [Case name]
Our Clients : [Names]
Our File No : [Number]
Date/Loss : [Date]

Dear [Name]:

Enclosed herewith, please find a conformed copy of the Acknowledgment of Satisfaction of Judgment. We are now closing this file. It has been a pleasure representing you in this matter. Should you have any questions, please do not hesitate to call.

Very truly yours,

[Signature]

LETTER 4-40
TRANSMITTAL OF SETTLEMENT CHECK ENCLOSING REQUEST FOR DISMISSAL AND RELEASE OF ALL CLAIMS

[Date]

CERTIFIED MAIL—RETURN RECEIPT REQUESTED
[Attorney]
[Address]

Re: [Case name]
SBSC Case No. : [Number]
Our File : [Number]
Date/Loss : [Date]

Dear [Name]:

Enclosed please find a check in the amount of [$], made payable to [Name] and one in the amount of [$] made payable to [Name] representing full and final settlement of the above-entitled matter. You are authorized to cash this check upon receipt by this office of the executed Request for Dismissal and Release of All Claims-Individual, which are enclosed for your signature and that of your client, respectively.

Your courtesy and cooperation in the settlement of this matter is appreciated.

Very truly yours,

[Signature]

Enclosures: Request for Dismissal
Release of All Claims

cc: [Insurance company] {without enclosures}

LETTER 4-41
TRANSMITTAL OF SATISFACTION OF JUDGMENT CHECK TO BE HELD IN TRUST UNTIL SATISFACTION OF JUDGMENT IS SIGNED

[Date]

[Attorney]
[Address]

Re: [Case name]
Our Client : [Name]
Our File : [Number]
Date/Loss : [Date]

Dear [Name]:

I enclose our check for [$] representing full satisfaction of our portion of the judgment; the costs of all parties having been waived by agreement (our motion has been taken off calendar).

You are to hold this check in trust and are authorized to negotiate same only after you have signed the enclosed Satisfaction of Judgment. To avoid confusion, the Satisfaction is a full Satisfaction of Judgment including [Name] so you will want to wait until you receive their check.

Please forward the signed Satisfaction to me. I will file same and return conformed copies to all. Should you have any questions or comments, please do not hesitate to call.

Very truly yours,

[Signature]

LETTER 4-42
TRANSMITTAL LETTER TO OPPOSING PARTY REQUESTING EXECUTION OF SETTLEMENT PAPERS

[Date]

[Name]
[Address]

RE: Cause No. ____________, In the ___________
Judicial District Court in and for ____________
County, _________, ___________________
v. ______________________________

Dear ______________:

I enclose an original and _________ [copy/copies] of a [final judgment in this cause / ______________________________________], together with _________ multiple original releases and [a] settlement draft[s] in the agreed amount of $ ______________________________.

Please make arrangements for the execution and return to me of the original and _______ [copy/copies] of [the final judgment /_________] and ___________ original release[s]. Please hold the draft[s] until [the judgment has been filed and has been signed by the Court / ______________________________. The draft[s] will not be accepted for payment until that time.

Thank you for your courtesy and cooperation in this matter.

Very truly yours,

[Signature]

_____/_____
Enclosures

LETTER 4-43
LETTER TO SUBROGATED HEALTH CARE PROVIDER ANNOUNCING SETTLEMENT AND ENCLOSING CHECK

[Date]

[Name]
[Company]
[Address]

Re:	Patient	:	[Client name]
	Responsible Party	:	[Parent if client is a minor]
	Account #	:	[Number]
	Date of Services	:	[Date]
	Balance	:	[Amount]

Dear [Name]:

This office represents the above-named client in litigation and settlement negotiations arising from injuries received in a motor vehicle accident which occurred on [Date]. We have now reached a settlement of this matter, and we are happy to enclose our disbursement Check [Number] in the amount of [$] in full payment of the balance due on the account indicated above.

We would appreciate it if you would acknowledge payment of this account in full by signing the enclosed receipt and returning it to us for our records in the envelope provided.

Thank you on behalf of our client for your patience and cooperation in withholding collection proceedings on this account. If you should have any questions regarding the enclosed payment, please contact the undersigned.

Very truly yours,

[Signature]

Enclosures

LETTER 4-44
THANK-YOU LETTER FOLLOWING OUT-OF-COURT-SETTLEMENT

[Date]

[Name]
[Address]

Re: [Case name]

Dear [Name]:

As Burgess told you on the phone earlier today the accident case of our client, [Client], against [Name] of [City] settled recently, for a fair and deserved amount. We believe this favorable settlement was largely due to your excellent testimony at deposition, when you stated unequivocally that you, like [Client], had a green light at the intersection. By so doing, you made clear that [Name] was at error by running a red light, causing her to strike [Client]'s vehicle. Your assistance and cooperation, particularly in taking the time off from work to testify, was invaluable, and we do appreciate it greatly.

If you have any questions, or if my colleagues or I can be of future assistance to you, please do not hesitate to contact me.

Best personal regards.

Sincerely,

[Signature]

CHAPTER 5

DISCOVERY—PRODUCTION OF DOCUMENTS

LETTER 5-1
LETTER REQUESTING ACCESS TO FILES

[Date]

[Name]
[Address]

Re: [Case name]

Dear Counselor,

As you know I represent [Name] in the above captioned matter. The discovery process we are about to undertake should, I hope, be amicable and adhere to the rules of procedure. In light of the spirit of the rules, please advise when my office can review the following files: [describe]

[Closing]

[Attorney]

LETTER 5-2
TRANSMITTAL OF REQUEST FOR PRODUCTION OF DOCUMENTS AND THINGS

[Date]

[Name]
[Insurance Company]
[Address]

Re: [Case name]
Insured : [Name]
Our File : [Number]
Claim No. : [Number]
Date/Loss : [Date]

Dear [Name]:

Enclosed please find defendant-in-intervention's first Request for Production of Documents and Things. Kindly provide this office with any documents in your possession or control listed in Exhibit "A."

Thank you for your courtesy and cooperation. Should you have any questions or comments, please feel free to contact me.

Very truly yours,

[Attorney]

LETTER 5-3
LETTER TO CUSTODIAN OF RECORDS REQUESTING PRODUCTION

[Date]

[Name]
[Address]

Dear Custodian of Records:

Enclosed is the subpoena served upon Federal Bank for the records pertaining to accounts of [Name], as well as various business entities of which [Name] is an officer, director, partner or controlling person. Please note that you do not need to make a personal appearance to satisfy the requirements of this subpoena. You may choose to execute the enclosed Declaration in compliance with Evidence Code § [Number].

To comply with the Subpoena Duces Tecum for business records, copies of the records designated in Exhibit A should be separately enclosed in an inner envelope sealed with the title and number of the action (Case No: [Number] [Case name]) inscribed upon the envelope. That sealed envelope shall then be enclosed in an outer envelope, sealed, and mailed to:

Name and address of
Deposition Officer

You must mail the records requested within fifteen days after your receipt of this subpoena.

The enclosed check is the witness fee authorized by Evidence Code § [Number]. If there are additional photocopying or reproduction charges, you may claim reimbursement for reasonable fees by submitting an invoice directly to the deposition officer.

If you have any questions regarding compliance with this subpoena or execution of the enclosed declaration, please do not hesitate to call me.

Sincerely,

____

[Legal Assistant]

LETTER 5-4
LETTER NOTIFYING CUSTODIAN OF RECORDS THAT PRODUCTION OF DOCUMENTS WILL SATISFY SUBPOENA DUCES TECUM

[Date]

Custodian of Records for
[Name]
[Address]

Re: [Case name]

Dear Custodian:

Served with this letter is a Notice of Deposition, a Subpoena Duces Tecum, an Authorization for release of records, and a Proof of Service/Notice to Patient. We do not intend to take testimony. We merely wish to obtain the designated records. Thus, you may comply with the Subpoena by simply forwarding copies of the items listed on the Subpoena to me at the above address prior to the subpoena date. Please use the attached witness fee check for any charges incurred in copying these records. Any additional photocopy charges will be paid at the statutory rate, promptly upon receipt of your billing for the same. It is not necessary to contact me unless you need an extension of time in which to gather the records.

Thank you for your anticipated cooperation and assistance.

PLEASE DIRECT YOUR RESPONSIVE DOCUMENTS TO THE ATTENTION OF THE UNDERSIGNED.

Sincerely,

[Legal Assistant]

LETTER 5-5
LETTER TRANSMITTING DOCUMENT REQUEST TO CLIENT 1

[Date]

[Name]
[Address]

Re: [Case name]

Dear [Name]:

Enclosed for your review is a request to produce documents which has been propounded by counsel for the defendant, [Name] Corporation, to plaintiff, [Name]. The date scheduled for production of these documents is [Date]. We must submit a written response to this document production 10 days before the actual date of production, [Date]. In our written response, we may assert privilege claims for document(s) which are responsive to any of the requests but should be protected by the attorney/client, attorney work product, or trade secret confidential information privilege.

You have provided our office with a great deal of documentation over the past few months to assist us in preparing the complaint in this action and responding to defendant's first set of interrogatories, and we will review those documents to see if they are responsive to any of the categories of this request. However, you will note that this document request addresses not only those documents within the possession, custody, and control of [Name] Corporation, but those documents which [Name] Corporation has access to through their agents, employees, subsidiaries, and other individuals who may have worked for [Name]Corporation as independent contractors. It will be necessary for you to review each and every request and make a due and diligent search for all documentation responsive to that request. If there are documents which you will need to retrieve from storage or other corporate facilities, please make arrangements to do so immediately. If you anticipate any problem or delay in obtaining any of these documents, please notify us immediately so that we may seek an extension of time within which to respond to this document request.

[Name], my legal assistant, whom you met when we were preparing responses to your interrogatories, is available to assist you in gathering the "universe of documents" necessary to respond fully and completely to this document request. [Name] will be contacting your secretary to make an appointment to visit your offices and assist your staff in gathering all of the documents needed to respond to this request.

We need to receive documents in our office no later than [Date], in order to allow adequate time for screening, reviewing, and indexing them prior to production. We will also want to Bates stamp each and every document to establish its identification in this action. Stamping will be done in the lower left hand corner, and will not alter or destroy the document in any fashion. We highly recommend stamping original documents, as we have found this is the best way to preserve the integrity of the document and avoid evidentiary problems at time of trial. Should you have any questions about this numbering procedure, please do not hesitate to contact [Name].

Thank you for your courtesy and cooperation.

Sincerely,

[Attorney]

LETTER 5-6
LETTER TRANSMITTING DOCUMENT REQUEST TO CLIENT 2

[Date]

[Name]
[Address]

Dear [Name]:

On [Date], received a set of requests for production of documents from [name of opposing counsel]. These requests for production must be answered fully and under oath within (the appropriate number of days) from the date of their receipt. A request for production of documents is a form of discovery which is allowed by the rules of civil procedure and which either side may use to obtain information and documents about the other side's case.

The rules of discovery are strict. If this request is not responded to, the other side can move for an order compelling you to respond to it or they may seek attorney's fees and other actions, including the dismissal of the lawsuit.

Please respond to these questions and obtain the necessary documents requested. Please contact me immediately to arrange for an appointment so that you may come in and I can assist you in preparing your responses. Some of the documents may already be a part of our file and need not be duplicated by you. We may also object to some of the documents which they request but you should provide us with all of the information and your attorney will determine which request, if any, she will object to.

I look forward to hearing from you soon.

Sincerely,

[Legal assistant to [Attorney]]

LETTER 5-7
LETTER TRANSMITTING DOCUMENT REQUEST TO CLIENT 3

[Date]

[Name]
[Address]

Dear [Client]:

Enclosed is a copy of the following document served on us recently by [Name] in this matter:

Defendant [Name] First Request for Production of Documents from Plaintiff; Exhibit A.

With respect to the request for documents, under the applicable Rules, we are also required to produce the documents requested. With certain exceptions, we should comply as fully and completely as possible. Therefore, please locate <u>all</u> the documents that could possibly fit within the scope of [Name]'s request. After you have gathered the documents, please contact [Name], the paralegal assisting me in this case. She will arrange for delivery of them to our office. The documents requested include all documents located in your control, possession, or custody. I would prefer that you be over-inclusive in providing me with the documents requested. I will review them and delete those that are not within the scope of the request.

The response to the request for documents must be filed in court no later than [Date], therefore we ask that you provide them to us no later than [Date], so we will have time to review and produce them.

Thank you for your cooperation in this matter. If you have any questions or comments, please do not hesitate to contact me.

Sincerely,

[Attorney]

LETTER 5-8
TRANSMITTAL OF REQUESTED DOCUMENTS 1

[Date]

[Attorney]
[Law firm]
[Address]

Re: [Case name]
Our Client : [Name]
Our File : [Number]
Date/Loss : [Date]

Dear [Attorney]:

I enclose the documents you requested. Should you have any questions or comments, please feel free to contact me.

Very truly yours,

[Attorney]

LETTER 5-9
TRANSMITTAL OF REQUESTED DOCUMENTS 2

[Date]

[Name]
[Address]

Dear Opposing Counsel:

Plaintiff, [Name], responds to defendant [Name]'s Request for Inspection and Production of Documents by enclosing documents numbered 0010 through 0549. These documents represent all documents which have been found to be responsive to the categories of items detailed in [Name]'s Request for Production of Documents served on [Name] on [Date]. Photocopies of these documents amount to [Number] pages and comprise one Bekins box, which has been hand delivered to your office on this date by [Name], legal assistant to [Name] attorney for [Name].

Please examine these documents at your earliest convenience to confirm that you have received all numbered pages indicated in this transmittal letter, and that all numbered pages are legible and complete.

Thank you for your cooperation.

Sincerely,

[Legal Assistant]

LETTER 5-10
TRANSMITTAL OF ACCIDENT REPORT

[Date]

[Name]
[Address]

Re: [Case name]
Our Client : [Name]
Our File : [Number]
Date/Loss : [Date]

Dear [Name]:

Enclosed with this letter, please find a copy of the accident report which you requested when I spoke with you on the telephone on [Date]. Once you have had an opportunity to review the report, please call me so that we may discuss it further. I also understand that you will be checking your calendar to verify dates on which you may be available to give deposition testimony.

I sincerely appreciate your cooperation in this case. I look forward to hearing from you soon.

Very truly yours,

[Attorney]

LETTER 5-11
TRANSMITTAL OF COPY OF MEMORANDUM OF CONVERSATION DURING DOCUMENT SESSION

[Date]

[Name]
[Address]

Re: [Case name]
Our File No. : [Number]
Our Client : [Name]
Date of Loss : [Date]

Dear [Name]:

Enclosed is a memorandum to [Name] to summarize our conversation during our meeting on [Date]. Please contact me if there are any discrepancies in the information in the memorandum, or if you would like to add more information.

Thank you for going through the documents with me. It was very informative.

Very truly yours,

[Attorney]

LETTER 5-12
CONFIRMING LETTER FOR JOINT PRODUCTION

[Date]

[Name and address of each of
the other parties' attorneys]

Re: [Case name]

Dear Counsel:

As we confirmed today by telephone, the production of documents by [Your client's name] will take place at [Location of production] beginning [Day and date] at [Time]. All counsel have agreed to be present at the production or to send a representative, to review the documents, and to note at that time which of those documents they wish to have copied.

The production will continue on consecutive successive business days until all counsel have had a reasonable opportunity to complete their document review. We believe, however, that the review process can be accomplished in [Estimated number of days] days. Once you have seen the volume of documents that must be reviewed, if you believe this length of time is unreasonably short, please call me so that we can discuss it.

We will make arrangements to have suitable facilities within which you can work. We will have the documents you select for copying duplicated within a reasonable time period, billing you for the copy costs at a rate of [Amount] per page. We will send you our firm's invoice to reimburse us for the copying expense, or if you prefer, you can make arrangements in advance with the copy service to be billed directly by them. If you make arrangements directly with the copy service, your copies will be held there pending receipt of payment.

The person in our office who is coordinating this production is [paralegal's name]. [Paralegal] can be reached by phone at [Paralegal's direct dial number or extension] to answer any questions you may have prior to or during the production. [Paralegal] is not authorized, however, to reschedule or extend the production for any party's counsel.

If this letter does not reflect our agreement regarding the arrangements for this production, please call me directly. Thank you for your cooperation.

Sincerely,

[Attorney's name and signature]

LETTER 5-13
LETTER TRANSMITTING RELEASES TO OPPOSING COUNSEL

[Date]

[Counsel's name]
[Address]

Re: [Case name]

Dear [Counsel's Name]:

Enclosed are the releases executed by my client as follows:

Dr. [Name]
Dr. [Name]

These releases are submitted to you based upon our mutual understanding as to their use which is as follows:

1. The releases are for the purpose of record production only.

2. The releases do not permit or authorize ex parte communications between defense counsel or any representative defense counsel and any health care provider and no representation will be made that such authorization has been given.

3. All written correspondence to any health care provider will be copied to plaintiffs counsel. Cover letters requesting copies of medical records will note that [Law firm] is to receive copies of all material copied to defense counsel at our expense and will include our address.

4. In the event that defense counsel receives any written information from the health care provider which was not provided to plaintiff's counsel, copies will be forwarded to plaintiff's counsel by defense counsel within 10 days of their receipt.

5. No alterations will be made to the releases by defense counsel.

If the above does not reflect your understanding as to the terms under which these releases have been executed by my client, then you are not authorized to use the releases.

[Signature]

Enc.

LETTER 5-14
LETTER REQUESTING CLARIFICATION REGARDING PRIVILEGE OBJECTION TO REQUEST FOR PRODUCTION OF DOCUMENTS

[Date]

[Name of defendant's attorney]
[Address]
[City/State/ZIP]
Re: [Case name]

Dear [Name]:

I am writing to request some greater definition of the terms of your objections to Plaintiff's First Request for Production of Documents. You have claimed attorney/client or alternatively work product privilege in refusing to produce any statement of either the defendant or [Name], an eyewitness to the collision.

First of all, I would request that you identify by date, general subject matter, and name the persons giving those statements. Which of those statements do you believe are subject to the work product privilege or fall under the context of the attorney/client relationship? Did (Defendant) give a statement? If so, on what date, and to whom did she give the statement? Did (Witness) give a statement? If so, on what date, and to whom did she give that statement?

I direct your attention to the specific requirements of <u>National Farmers Union v. District Court</u>, 718 P.2d 1044 (Colo. 1986) and <u>Hawkins v. District Court</u>, 638 P.2d 1372 (Colo. 1982). Both of these Colorado Supreme Court cases make it abundantly clear that documents must be examined individually as to the claim of privilege. An insurance company's business is to investigate claims and it is presumed that such investigations are part of the normal business activities of the company. Such investigation records are "ordinary business records as distinguished from trial preparation materials." The burden is on the party claiming the privilege to prove that such document was specifically "prepared in contemplation of specific litigation."

If a basis does exist for your objection, I would appreciate receiving the particulars necessary to support such a claim. Otherwise, I look forward to receiving copies of these statements.

I look forward to your response to this letter within ten days. I would be happy to discuss this matter with you on the telephone or in any other fashion in order to attempt to resolve this discovery problem.

Very truly yours,

[Signature]

LETTER 5-15
REQUEST FOR DOCUMENTS NOT PRODUCED 1

[Date]

[Name]
[Address]

Dear [Name]:

At the production of documents in your office on (Date), several documents were either not produced or not produced legibly. Those documents are as follows:

File 2784: 2-pg ltr dated 5/2/88 to Party C regarding injury

File 3265: 6-pg warranty dated 1986 regarding product X

File 4711: Entire contents

Please send legible copies of those documents within 10 days of your receipt of this letter. Thank you for your cooperation.

Sincerely,

Legal Assistant

LETTER 5-16
REQUEST FOR DOCUMENTS NOT PRODUCED 2

[Date]

[Name]
[Address]

Dear (Opposing counsel):

Copies of documents produced by your firm for our review on (Date) have been received and reviewed. The following list indicates missing documents.

1.

2.

3.

Please either copy the above-listed documents and send them to us or contact the undersigned to arrange the same. A response by (Date) will be appreciated.

Thank you in advance for your courtesy and cooperation.

[Signature]

LETTER 5-17
REQUEST FOR DOCUMENT NOT PRODUCED 3

[Date]

[Name]
[Address]

Dear (Opposing counsel):

We have received the documents requested in the (Set number) request to produce which was propounded to your client, (Responding party's name), on (Date). Upon review, certain documents appear to be missing.

Please copy the documents listed/described on the attached sheet and send them to the undersigned. If you are unable to comply with this request by (Date), please call our office so other arrangements may be made.

Thank you in advance for your courtesy and cooperation.

(Signature)

LETTER 5-18
LETTER REQUESTING INSURANCE POLICY AND REGARDING OTHER MATTERS

[Date]

[Name]
[Law firm]
[Address]

Re: [Case name]
Our Client : [Name]
Our File : [Number]
Date/Loss : [Date]

Dear [Name]:

This will confirm our conversation that we have agreed to split the costs of the plaintiffs' depositions and [Name]'s Independent Medical Examination with Dr. [Name] on a 50/50 basis.

Given the discussion at the Mandatory Settlement Conference, I am attempting to get approval to go ahead and depose Dr. [Name] following the Independent Medical Examination.

In review of your response to my demand for documents you attached the declaration page rather than the insurance policy, which is fine. However, I need exemplar copies of [GE-C6808(0788), CL175(0286), CG0001(1188), GE-C6824(0289), GE-C6806(1088) and GE-C6828(0188)]. If my clients are additional insureds, please forward that document. I am particularly interested in whether the policy had a contractual liability endorsement. Please let me know as soon as possible.

Very truly yours,

[Attorney]

LETTER 5-19
DEMAND FOR RESPONSE TO REQUEST FOR PRODUCTION OF DOCUMENTS 1

[Date]

[(Opposing Attorney)]
[Address]

Re: [Case name]

Dear [Name]:

In reviewing my file I have determined that you have never responded to my First Request for Production of Documents in this case which was delivered to you on or about [Date]. Pursuant to applicable rule, please consider this an informal request for you to provide me with the responses to this request for production within 10 days.

Inasmuch as I have never been advised by you that there is any problem in obtaining the requested information and inasmuch as you have not asked me for any additional time, after the expiration of 10 days from this letter, I shall feel that I have no choice other than to file a motion to compel.

Sincerely,

[Attorney]

LETTER 5-20
DEMAND FOR RESPONSE TO REQUEST FOR PRODUCTION OF DOCUMENTS 2

[Date]

[Name]
[Address]

Re: [Case name]

Dear [Name]:

On [Date], Plaintiff [Name] served a Request for Production of Documents on your client, Defendant [Name], in the above-entitled matter, a response to which was due on [Date].

Our files indicate that we have not yet received a Response to our Request. We would appreciate receiving your response by [Date].

Please contact the paralegal assisting me in this matter, [Name], to arrange for a mutually convenient time for us to inspect your documents.

Thank you for your attention to this matter.

Sincerely,

[Attorney]

LETTER 5-21
SECOND DEMAND FOR RESPONSE TO REQUEST FOR PRODUCTION OF DOCUMENTS

[Date]

[Name]
[Address]

Dear [Name]:

On [Date], Plaintiff [Name] served a Request for Production of Documents on your client, Defendant [Name], in the above-entitled matter, a response to which was due on [Date].

On [Date], I wrote to you requesting that the documents be provided no later than [Date]. To date, we have not received a Response to our Request or the documents, nor have you contacted us with an explanation as to your failure to respond to this Request.

Please give our client's Request for Production of Documents your immediate attention. If we do not receive a proper Response to our Request by [Date], we will be forced to move the Court to compel production of documents pursuant to Rule 37(a) of the Federal Rules of Civil Procedure.

Thank you for your prompt attention to this matter.

Sincerely,

[Attorney]

LETTER 5-22
LETTER REGARDING INADEQUATE RESPONSE TO REQUEST FOR PRODUCTION OF DOCUMENTS

[Date]

[Name]
[Address]

Dear [Name]:

On or about [Date], we received your responses and objections to Defendant's First Request for Production of Documents to Plaintiffs. Upon reviewing the responses, we find that your objections to Request Nos. 4, 5, and 8 are unfounded and unacceptable. Each of your objections will be addressed more fully below.

Request Nos. 4 and 5 asked for documents relating to [Item]. You objected to these requests on that grounds that they are "vague and ambiguous." We fail to see how requests for documents concerning [Item] can be deemed vague and ambiguous. We believe the court would be equally unpersuaded by your objection, and we again request that you provide us with copies of documents responsive to these requests.

Request No. 8 asked for all documents relied upon by Plaintiff in support of the allegations contained in Plaintiff's Complaint. While we respect Plaintiff's right to object to the production of documents protected by the work-product and attorney-client privileges, we are unpersuaded that Plaintiff possesses no documents that should properly be produced in response to this request.

Defendant's Request for Production of Documents clearly and specifically sets forth the documents sought. Surely, Plaintiff must have in its possession the requested documents discussed above. For this reason, we ask that those documents be made available for inspection and copying. If they cannot be produced, we should be provided with an acceptable reason as to their unavailability. If you insist on objecting to the Requests and fail to produce those documents requested therein, we will have no alternative but to file a motion to compel.

Your prompt attention to this matter is appreciated.

Sincerely,

[Attorney]

LETTER 5-23
REQUEST FOR CLARIFICATION OF DOCUMENTS PRODUCED

[Date]

[Attorney]
[Law firm]
[Address]

Re: [Case name]
Our Client : [Name]
Our File : [Number]
Date/Loss : [Date]

Dear [Name]:

I have reviewed the documents which you produced on [Date], pursuant to our discovery request. A few questions remain, namely:

[1. Number 13 (13 pages - punch list of): Please verify whether the correct document order is, according to your numbering system, C-92, C-91, C-90, C-89, C-88, C-87, C-86, C-85, C-84, C-93, C-94, C-95, C-96], assuming the order is

2. Number 14 (3 pages - Add to Fix Up List from): Pages 2 and 3 are missing.

3. Number 14 (3 pages - Add to Fix Up List from): The handwritten notations are not legible. Will you please send a darker copy of each page?

4. Number 25 (Page 2 of letter from): This second page was not enclosed. Would you please send a copy of page 2 as well as the rest of the letter?]

Thank you in advance for your assistance. If you have any questions, please call me between [Hours].

Sincerely,

[Attorney]

LETTER 5-24
REQUEST OF THIRD PARTY FOR COPIES OF DOCUMENTS PRODUCED 1

[Date]

[Name]
[Law firm]
[Address]

Re: [Case name]
Our Client : [Name]
Our File : [Number]
Date/Loss : [Date]

Dear [Name]:

I have reviewed your responses to [Name]'s Request for Production of Documents, 1st Set, propounded to [Name]. Please provide me with copies of any documents produced in response to the request. Naturally, this firm will reimburse you for the cost of copying.

I sincerely appreciate your courtesy and cooperation. Should you have any questions or comments, please do not hesitate to call.

Very truly yours,

[Attorney]

LETTER 5-25
REQUEST OF THIRD PARTY FOR COPIES OF DOCUMENTS PRODUCED 2

[Date]

[Name]
[Attorney]
[Address]

Re: [Case name]
Our Client : [Name]
Our File : [Number]
Date/Loss : [Date]

Dear [Name]:

I have received defendant [Name]'s Demand to Identify and Produce Documents to plaintiff. I request that you supply me with copies of any documents produced in that demand. Naturally, I will be happy to reimburse you for the cost of copying such documents.

Should you have any questions or comments, please do not hesitate to call. I sincerely appreciate your courtesy and cooperation.

Very truly yours,

[Attorney]

LETTER 5-26
TRANSMITTAL OF RETURNED DOCUMENTS

[Date]

[Name]
[Address]

Re: [Case name]

Dear [Name]:

As you know, the lawsuit brought by [Name] has been settled. As I indicated when we removed files from your offices, I am returning those documents to you.

Enclosed for your reference is a copy of my letter to you dated [Date], including the file index that was enclosed. Please call me if you have any questions about the documents.

I have enjoyed working with you over the course of this case. Thank you for all of your help.

Sincerely,

[Paralegal]

Enclosure:

LETTER 5-27
TRANSMITTAL OF RETURNED PHOTOGRAPHS TO OPPOSING PARTY

[Date]

[Name]
[Law firm]
[Address]

Re: [Case name]
O/client : [Number]
Our File : [Number]
Date/Loss : [Date]

Dear [Name]:

Enclosed please find the twenty (20) original photographs you produced at the time of plaintiff's deposition, in response to our request for production.

Thank you for your cooperation in providing these photos. We have made duplicate prints of each.

Should you have any questions, please do not hesitate to contact me.

Very truly yours,

[Attorney]

LETTER 5-28
TRANSMITTAL OF RETURNED BLUEPRINTS

[Date]

[Name]
Attorney at Law
[Address]

Re: [Case name]
Our Client : [Name]
Our File : [Number]
Date/Loss : [Date]

Dear [Name]:

Enclosed please find the original blueprints you provided this office recently. Thank you for your courtesy and cooperation in this matter.

Very truly yours,

[Attorney]

CHAPTER 6

DISCOVERY—INTERROGATORIES

LETTER 6-1
TRANSMITTAL OF INTERROGATORIES TO CLIENT 1

[Date]

[Name]
[Address]

Dear [Name]:

On [Date], we received these Interrogatories from opposing counsel. By law, we must file answers to these questions by [Date]. Since that period of time can go by very quickly, we would like you to review these questions immediately and begin to jot down notes about the answers.

[Name], a paralegal in our firm, will be calling you in approximately one week to discuss the answers with you. If necessary, she will set up a meeting with you to go over the questions thoroughly. Once the answers have been prepared, it will be necessary for you to review them and sign them on sworn affidavit in front of a notary public. We will contact you as soon as they are ready.

In the meantime, if you have any questions about the Interrogatories, please call and speak with me or my paralegal.

Very truly yours,

[Attorney]

LETTER 6-2
TRANSMITTAL OF INTERROGATORIES TO CLIENT 2

[Date]

[Name]
[Address]

Dear [Name]:

Enclosed is a set of questions known as interrogatories. Please list your answers on a separate sheet of paper, numbering them to correspond to the appropriate questions.

[State] law provides only a limited time in which to respond to these interrogatories. With that in mind, please mail your answers back to us within the next week. We will put them in proper legal form and return them for your review along with a verification form for your signature.

Answer each question fully and completely. It will be more expeditious for us to leave out some information, if necessary, than to contact you for further responses.

If you have any questions relating to this matter, please do not hesitate to contact this office. Your prompt attention will be appreciated.

[Signature]

LETTER 6-3
TRANSMITTAL OF INTERROGATORIES TO CLIENT 3

[Date]

[Name]
[Address]

Dear [Name]:

Enclosed is a copy of [Defendant]'s First Set of Interrogatories and First Request for Production of Documents. These interrogatories and requests for production must be answered fully and under oath within thirty days from the day we received them. These documents are a form of discovery which is allowed by the Rules of Civil Procedure and which either side may use to obtain information and documents about the other side's case.

The rules of discovery are strict. If this request is not responded to, the other side can move for an order compelling you to respond to it or they may seek attorneys' fees and other actions, including the dismissal of the lawsuit.

Please respond to these questions and obtain the necessary documents requested. Please contact me immediately to arrange for an appointment so that you may come in and I can assist you in preparing your responses. Some of the documents may already be a part of our file and need not be duplicated by you. We may also object to some of the interrogatories and documents which they request, but you should provide us with all of the information and your attorney will determine which request, if any, he will object to.

I look forward to hearing from you soon.

Sincerely,

[Signature]

LETTER 6-4
TRANSMITTAL OF INTERROGATORIES TO CLIENT 4

[Date]

[Name]
[Address]

Dear [Name]:

Enclosed are the interrogatories recently received from the attorneys for the defendants in your case. Would you please read carefully through each interrogatory and answer each question to the best of your ability on a separate sheet of paper? You should return your answers to me in the envelope provided within the next ten (10) days. You must take great care to make your answers accurate and complete. Some of the requested information will be supplied from that contained in our file, and those questions which address legal contentions or theories will be answered by [Name], your attorney.

Some of these interrogatories may be confusing to you because of the language and style in which they are written. This is due to the fact that interrogatories are a formal legal document and are not drafted in everyday language. Please contact our office and we will be happy to assist you in interpreting the questions. I would also be happy to meet with you, if you prefer, to answer the questions in an interview session.

We are enclosing a verification form which you must sign, but do not date, and return along with your answers. The verification form is a legal requirement and it is necessary to attach it to the final version of your interrogatory answers.

We must submit final answers to the defendants no later than [Date]. If you find that you are unable to provide your answers to our office within the next ten (10) days, please contact me immediately so that I can attempt to arrange an extension of time within which to respond.

Thank you for your cooperation in this matter.

Sincerely,

[Legal Assistant]

LETTER 6-5
TRANSMITTAL OF INTERROGATORIES TO CLIENT 5 (CORPORATE CLIENT)

[Date]

[Name]
Chief Executive Officer
[Corporation]
[Address]

RE: [Case name]

Dear [Name]:

Enclosed are the interrogatories recently received from the attorney for the plaintiff in this action. Please go through and answer each question to the best of your ability on a separate sheet of paper, returning your answers to me in the envelope provided within ten days.

You will note that the interrogatories are addressed to the [Name] Corporation as a corporate entity. It is the obligation of [Name] Corporation, and you as its chief executive officer, to make a thorough investigation of all files maintained not only at this office but at corporate headquarters to obtain the information requested in the interrogatories. It is also your obligation to contact any officer, agent or employee of [Name] Corporation who is within your control and may have information relating to any of the interrogatories.

Some of the requested information can be supplied from that which is contained in our files or in documents you have previously provided to our office. Those Interrogatories directly addressed to pleadings on file in this action and legal contentions will be answered in that fashion.

A copy of these interrogatories has been sent to [Name], corporate counsel for [Name] Corporation, and we suggest that you coordinate your information gathering and preparation of responses with her office.

Enclosed is a verification form which must be signed by yourself, or any other corporate officer who has the power to bind the corporation to the responses provided.

If you have any questions or problems, please give my office a call. Thank you for your prompt cooperation in this matter. I look forward to receiving your responses within the next ten days. If you anticipate there will be a delay in the retrieval of information from corporate files, please contact me immediately and I will request an extension of time from opposing counsel. It is necessary that we request our extension of time prior to the expiration of the statutory time to provide responses, so that we may preserve our rights to enter objections to any of the interrogatories.

Sincerely,

[Legal Assistant]

LETTER 6-6
LETTER TO CLIENT ASKING FOR ANSWERS TO INTERROGATORIES

[Date]

[Name]
[Address]

Dear [Name]:

Enclosed for your review and further handling is a copy of Plantiff's First Request for Answers to Interrogatories to Defendant ("Interrogatories"), which was served on us on [Date].

Under the applicable rules of Federal Civil Procedure ("Rules"), we are required to answer the Interrogatories for the lawyers on the other side as fully and completely as possible, so please give us as much help as you can. While we have information that will allow us to answer some of the Interrogatories for you, we would like you to answer all of them, or as many as possible, in your own words. This will save you money and will help us be sure that we have not overlooked anything.

It may be that you will simply not be able to answer some of these questions. If so, please indicate that the answer is unknown to you. Also, some of the questions may be repetitious, and your answer to some of the later ones may be the same as for an earlier one. If so, simply indicate this. For example, if in answering Interrogatory no. 15, you believe that the answer has been previously provided in answer to Interrogatory no. 10, just indicate this by writing "see answer to Interrogatory no. 10."

You may write your answers directly on the face of the copy we have enclosed and return it to us in the enclosed return envelope. If you do not have sufficient room for your answer on the enclosed copy, use any plain piece of paper and number your answers consistently with the number of the question you are answering. No particular form is necessary, and do not be too concerned with the wording. All we want are simple, accurate, and complete answers, so far as you can provide them. We will revise the answers accordingly and raise legal objections where appropriate.

At this point, the answers to the Interrogatories must be served on their counsel no later than[Date]; therefore, we ask that you send us back your draft answers no later than [Date], so that we will have sufficient time to review and revise them.

It is permissible for the person signing the Interrogatories to ask others associated with him for information requested; however, it is preferred that only one person sign the Interrogatories. If the information provided in answering a particular question was provided to you from another person, simply indicate this in the answer by stating "according to Richard Garfield . . .," or words to that effect.

Once the Interrogatories are finalized, you will need to sign the last page of the Interrogatories in black ink and have your signature properly notarized.

Thank you for your cooperation in this matter. If you have any questions or comments, please do not hesitate to contact me or [Name], the paralegal assisting me with this matter.

[Signature]

LETTER 6-7
COVER LETTER TO CLIENT REGARDING FINAL ANSWERS TO INTERROGATORIES

[Date]

[Name]
[Address]

Dear [Name]:

Enclosed please find the revised answers to [Defendant's] Request for Answers to Interrogatories for your review. You will note that some of the information you provided to us has been withheld as privileged or irrelevant and outside the scope of discovery in this case.

We ask that you review the answers and, if they meet with your approval, please sign the verification page at the end of the document, before a notary, in black ink.

In particular, please verify the answer to Interrogatory [Number], regarding [Your prognosis]. If you feel there should be changes to this or any of the answers, please feel free to make the changes, corrections, or comments on the enclosed answers.

Once you have had the chance to make any changes or to sign the answers, please call our office. As the answers are due to be submitted to [Defendant's] attorney on or before [Date], your immediate attention is greatly appreciated.

If you should have any questions, please do not hesitate to call.

[Signature]

LETTER 6-8
FOLLOW-UP LETTER TO CLIENT RE INTERROGATORY ANSWERS

[Date]

[Name]
[Address]

RE: Answers to Plaintiff's First Set of Interrogatories

Dear [Name]:

On [Date], we forwarded to you a copy of Plaintiff's First Set of Interrogatories, along with a request that you begin to assimilate information for the preparation of the answers to those questions.

We have not yet received any material from you, and we are now concerned that we may not be able to file and serve the Answers to Interrogatories within the statutorily mandated time frame of the [State] Rules of Civil Procedure. Failure to respond to these interrogatories in a timely fashion can result in the court ordering sanctions against you in the form of monetary fines or the striking of any or all of your claims or defenses in this action.

It is imperative that you contact me immediately to arrange a time to finalize the answers to these interrogatories. Please recognize the urgency of this matter; it is vital to your legal representation. Thank you for your cooperation.

Respectfully yours,

[Name]
Legal Assistant to [Attorney]

LETTER 6-9
TRANSMITTAL OF DRAFT RESPONSES TO REQUEST FOR ADMISSIONS AND FORM INTERROGATORIES FOR CLIENT'S SIGNATURE

[Date]

[Name]
[Address]

Re: [Case name]
Our Client : [Name]
Our File : [Number]
Date/Loss : [Date]

Dear [Name]:

Enclosed with this letter, please find my draft responses to Request for Admissions and Form Interrogatories which were served on [Name] some time ago by two of the other parties to the above referenced lawsuit. For your convenience, I am also enclosing additional copies of the original requests.

Please review the requests carefully and, if you find them in order, sign the enclosed verifications, returning the verifications to me immediately.

Should you have any questions or comments concerning the draft responses, or the original requests, please do not hesitate to call. I sincerely appreciate your courtesy and cooperation and look forward to hearing from you soon.

Very truly yours,

[Signature]

LETTER 6-10
TRANSMITTAL OF VERIFICATION TO BE SIGNED FOR INCLUSION IN RESPONSES TO INTERROGATORIES

[Date]

[Name]
Chief Executive Officer
[Corporation]
[Address]

Re: [Case name]
Insured : [Name]
Our File : [Number]
Date/Loss : [Date]

Dear [Name]:

Enclosed with this letter, please find Form Interrogatories directed to you by defendant [Name]. If this case is not settled, it will be necessary for us to serve a response on counsel for [Name] no later than [Date]. I will prepare a written response from information which I already have in the file.

However, it will be necessary for you to verify the Response. I am enclosing with this letter a Verification form for your signature. Please sign it and return it to me as soon as possible. Once I have prepared draft responses, I will forward them for your review. Once you approve the draft responses, I will put them in final form and serve them on counsel for [Name] along with your Verification.

Should you have any questions or comments about this or any other aspect of the lawsuit, please do not hesitate to call. I sincerely appreciate your courtesy and cooperation and look forward to hearing from you soon.

Very truly yours,

[Signature]

LETTER 6-11
OBJECTION OF RESPONDING PARTY TO INTERROGATORIES

[Date]

[Name]
[Address]

Dear [Name]:

Please be advised that your [Number] set of interrogatories was received by [Client name] on [Date]. However, (state your problem, such as, said interrogatories are so numerous as to be burdensome, or my corporate client is out of state and not easily available). Therefore, we request that (make your request, such as, you either revise said interrogatories or select certain numbers for this party to respond to, or you allow thirty additional days in which to respond). Thank you in advance for your courtesy and cooperation.

[Signature]

LETTER 6-12
LETTER REGARDING INADEQUATE RESPONSE TO INTERROGATORY REQUEST 1

[Date]

[Name]
[Address]

Dear [Name]:

On [Date], we received your responses to Defendant's First Request for Answers to Interrogatories. Upon reviewing the responses, we find that your objections to request Nos. 5 and 7 are unfounded and unacceptable.

With respect to Interrogatory No. 5, Plaintiff objected to providing information relating to the diagnosis and treatment of the emotional distress and mental anguish which Plaintiff claims to have suffered as a result of Defendant's actions. The Interrogatory is directly related to Plaintiff's claim for damages in this matter, and therefore, we fail to see how you can object to it as being "irrelevant and not calculated to lead to the discovery of admissible evidence."

Request No. 7 asks for all facts in support of the allegations contained in Count 11 of Plaintiff's Complaint. Plaintiff objected because "some of the information requested is protected by the attorney-client privilege." We request that Plaintiff provide those facts which are not protected by this privilege.

[Attorney]

LETTER 6-13
LETTER REGARDING INADEQUATE RESPONSE TO INTERROGATORY REQUEST 2

[Date]

[Name]
[Address]

Dear [Name]:

On [Date], we received [Responding party's name]'s responses to [Client's name]'s [Number] set of interrogatories which were propounded on [Date]. However, certain of those (interrogatories remain unanswered) (responses are incomplete). Please (answer) (supplement) numbers [Specify numbers]. If you have difficulty understanding what information is requested by certain interrogatories, please do not hesitate to call this office for an explanation. Thank you in advance for your courtesy and cooperation.

[Signature]

LETTER 6-14
FOLLOW-UP LETTER REGARDING UNANSWERED INTERROGATORIES

[Date]

[Name]
[Address]

Dear [Name]:

On [Date], this office sent you a letter requesting (responses) (supplemental responses) to [Client's name]'s [Number] set of interrogatories. We have not received any responses nor has your office called to make other arrangements. If we do not receive responses or hear from you within ten (10) days of the date of this letter, it may be necessary to file a motion, at which time sanctions will be requested. Since discovery is important to the resolution of this matter, we would appreciate your full cooperation.

[Signature]

LETTER 6-15
LETTER RESPONDING TO OBJECTIONS TO INTERROGATORIES (MEET AND CONFER LETTER) 1

[Date]

Law Offices of
[Name]
[Address]

RE: [Case name]
[Number]

Dear [Name]

I have had an opportunity to review the first set of responses provided by defendant to plaintiff's first set of interrogatories which were received by this office on [Date]. We would appreciate further responses to several of the interrogatories.

In your response to interrogatory 3, you identify by name, address and policy number your insurance carrier; however, you fall to state the limits of coverage for each category of coverage contained in the policy. Clearly the amount of available insurance, both primary and excess, is relevant and discoverable.

With regard to your response to interrogatory 18, it is respectfully submitted that your objection on the grounds of privilege and legal conclusion is improper. In your answer to the complaint on file you assert as affirmative defenses the allegation that the negligence that proximately caused the injury to the plaintiff was that of third parties. In your second affirmative defense you allege that the injuries to the parties are the proximate result of independent third parties or their agents or employees. In your sixth affirmative defense you allege that the co-defendants so negligently, carelessly and recklessly conducted and maintained themselves as to proximately cause this incident and the alleged injuries and damage. Interrogatory 18 asks for the necessary information on which you are basing your affirmative defenses. Clearly this is not privileged information, nor does it call for legal conclusions. We respectfully request that you file further responses stating the name, address, employer and job title of each person you contend is in any way legally responsible for the injuries to plaintiff. We also respectfully request that you state the factual basis of the contentions and any information pertaining to writings which will support the factual basis of these contentions.

With respect to interrogatory 20, it is well-recognized that statements obtained by a party from non-parties are relevant and discoverable and not protected by attorney-client or work product privileges. Accordingly, request is hereby made that you provide the information sought in interrogatory 20 and its sub-parts including the name, address, phone number and Job title of the custodians of such statements.

I would greatly appreciate your forwarding to this office further responses to the above interrogatories within twenty (20) days. If you are unable to do so in that period of time and wish more time, I would be happy to extend further time to file responses, provided that you extend plaintiff's time to file a motion to compel further responses. Please contact me at your earliest convenience to discuss these matters in an attempt to resolve them without court intervention.

Sincerely,

[Attorney]

LETTER 6-16
LETTER RESPONDING TO OBJECTIONS TO INTERROGATORIES (MEET AND CONFER LETTER) 2

[Date]

[Attorney]
[Firm]
[Address]

RE: [Case name]

Dear [Attorney]:

This letter concerns the response that you, on behalf of your client, filed to Plaintiff's First Set of Interrogatories in the above-referenced action, on [Date].

As you are aware, if a dispute exists on the response to the interrogatories, the parties are under an obligation to "Meet and Confer" on the disputed responses. I have such a dispute on the response you made to Plaintiff's Fifth Interrogatory.

However, despite three telephone calls to your office ([Dates and Times]) and three messages left with your secretary, you have seen fit not to respond to my communications.

Therefore, please be advised that unless I hear from you prior to the close of business on [Date], I will have no alternative but to bring the appropriate motion before the court. In doing so, I will seek all appropriate sanctions from the court.

Very truly yours,

[Attorney]

LETTER 6-17
LETTER REQUESTING INFORMATION ON INTERROGATORY OBJECTIONS

[Date]

[Counsel's Name]
[Address]

Dear [Counsel's name]:

I am writing to request some greater definition of the terms of your objections to plaintiff's interrogatories/request for production of documents. You have claimed attorney/client or alternatively work product privilege in refusing to produce any statement of either the defendant or [Name of witness], an eyewitness to the collision.

I would request that you identify by date, general subject matter and name persons giving those statements. Which of those statements do you believe are subject to the work product privilege or fall under the context of attorney/client relationship? Did [Defendant] give a statement? If so, on what date and to whom did she give the statement? Did [Witness] give a statement? If so, on what date and to whom did she give that statement?

If a basis does exist for your objection, I would appreciate receiving the particulars necessary to support such a claim. Otherwise, I look forward to receiving copies of these statements.

In order to assess your claim of work product or attorney/client privilege on any document, we must be provided with the following information as to each document withheld from production:

a. The nature of the document (e.g., report, photograph, chart, diagram, etc.);

b. The parties to the document (author, addressee, recipients) ;

c. The date of the document;

d. The general subject matter of the document; and

e. Specific basis for claim of privilege.

I will calendar ten days in which to receive a response to this letter and consider this process our compliance with [Cite appropriate local rule].

Thank you for your assistance and courtesy in this matter.

Sincerely,

[Signature]

LETTER 6-18
LETTER REQUESTING SUPPLEMENTAL INTERROGATORY RESPONSES 1

[Date]

[Counsel's Name]
[Address]

Dear [Counsel's name]:

With the upcoming depositions to be taken, I would at this time request your supplementation of any and all appropriate interrogatory answers prior to that time. We would particularly ask that you respond to our interrogatories regarding any experts with whom you have consulted or retained in this matter.

It has been many months since these interrogatories were initially answered. Many of your responses to the interrogatories were that you were "investigating" these issues and would supplement your responses in a timely fashion. I would suggest this is an extremely timely occasion for you to supplement your interrogatory answers. Should matters arise in the depositions which were properly subject to the interrogatories, it may be necessary for us to recess rather than conclude those depositions until we have been provided with appropriate responses to your interrogatories.

Thank you for your courtesy in this matter.

Sincerely,

[Signature]

LETTER 6-19
LETTER REQUESTING SUPPLEMENTAL INTERROGATORY RESPONSES 2

[Date]

[Name]
[Address]

Re: [Case name]

Dear [Name]:

With the upcoming depositions to be taken in [State] over the week of [Date] of employees and agents of [Name] Corporation, I would at this time request your supplementation of any and all appropriate interrogatory answers prior to that time. We would particularly ask that you respond to our interrogatories regarding any experts with whom you have consulted or retained in this matter.

It has been many months since these interrogatories were initially answered. Many of your responses to the interrogatories were that you were "investigating" these issues and would supplement your responses in a timely fashion. I would suggest this is an extremely timely occasion on which for you to supplement your interrogatory answers. Should matters arise in the depositions which were properly subject to the interrogatories, it may be necessary for us to recess rather than conclude those depositions until we have been provided with appropriate responses to our Interrogatories and Requests for Production.

Thank you for your courtesy in this matter.

Sincerely,

[Attorney]

LETTER 6-20
LETTER PRECEDING MOTION TO COMPEL ANSWERS TO INTERROGATORIES

[Date]

[Name]
[Address]

Re: [Case name and cause of action number]

Dear [Opposing counsel]:

On [Date], we served your office with Plaintiff's First Set of Interrogatories, the answers to which were due on [Date] according to Rule [Number] of the [State] Rules of Civil Procedure.

We have previously contacted you regarding the insufficiency of your answer to Interrogatory [Number], and are waiting to receive a full and complete answer to that interrogatory according to the [State] Rules of Civil Procedure.

We must ask that we receive the full and complete Answers to Plaintiff's First Set of Interrogatories by [Date] to avoid the necessity of a Motion to Compel and for Sanctions. Please contact us immediately if you anticipate any problems complying with this request. Thank you very much for your cooperation in this matter.

Respectfully yours,

[Attorney]

LETTER 6-21
LETTER REGARDING NON-RESPONSE TO INTERROGATORIES 1

[Date]

[Name]
[Address]

Dear [Opposing counsel]:

I would like to direct your attention to the fact that written interrogatories were served upon your client, [Name], on [Date]. To date we have not received any response to said interrogatories, nor have we been contacted by your office regarding an extension of time within which to respond.

Because more than 35 days since our service of these interrogatories has expired, it is our position that you and your client's time to object to any of the interrogatories has been waived. We are enclosing with this letter a notice of unanswered interrogatories requesting that you serve full and complete answers to the interrogatories propounded to you by plaintiff, [Name], within 10 days of this request. Our office will withhold the filing of any motions to compel answers to interrogatories and request for sanctions out of professional courtesy for the next 10 days.

Thank you for your prompt attention to this matter.

Sincerely,

[Attorney]

Enclosure

LETTER 6-22
LETTER REGARDING NON-RESPONSE TO INTERROGATORIES 2

[Date]

[Opposing Counsel]
[Address]

Dear [Counsel's name]:

We submitted interrogatories to [Responding party's name] and to date have not received these answers. If you have difficulty understanding what information is requested by certain interrogatories, please do not hesitate to call this office for an explanation.

Thank you for your courtesy and cooperation.

[Signature]

LETTER 6-23
LETTER REGARDING NON-RESPONSE TO INTERROGATORIES 3

[Date]

[Name]
Attorney at Law
[Address]

Re: [Case name]
Our Client : [Name]
Our File : [Number]
Date/Loss : [Date]

Dear [Name]:

To date I have received no response from you to the first set of interrogatories propounded by this office to your client, [Name]. Please recall that those interrogatories were dated [Date]. The responses are now long overdue. All objections having been waived by your failure to respond in a timely fashion, I must request that you provide responses, without objections, within ten days.

Should you have any questions or comments concerning this case, please do not hesitate to call. I sincerely appreciate your courtesy and anticipated cooperation.

Very truly yours,

[Signature]

LETTER 6-24
LETTER REGARDING OVERDUE RESPONSE TO INTERROGATORY REQUEST 1

[Date]

[Name]
[Address]

Dear [Name]:

On [Date] Plaintiff served Defendant with a Request for Answers to Interrogatories. The Response was therefore due on [Date].

As our files indicate that your Response has not yet been received, we must request that your answers be provided no later than [Date].

[Signature]

LETTER 6-25
LETTER REGARDING OVERDUE RESPONSE TO INTERROGATORY REQUEST 2

[Date]

[Opposing Counsel]
[Address]

Dear [Name]:

This is to advise you that we have still not received a response to the Request for Answers to Interrogatories served [Date]. The response was due by [Date], and pursuant to your request, we agreed to a 30-day extension. It has now been six months since the interrogatories were first served, and over three months since the extension of time expired.

We would like to avoid having to file a motion to compel answers. However, as we have only three months remaining within which to complete all discovery in this case, we no longer have the luxury of giving you more time on this. We must therefore insist that a response be provided no later than [Date]. Otherwise we will be forced to file a motion to compel answers to interrogatories from your clients.

Thank you for your prompt attention to this matter.

[Attorney]

LETTER 6-26
FOLLOW-UP LETTER REGARDING OVERDUE RESPONSE TO INTERROGATORY REQUEST

[Date]

[Name]
[Address]

Dear [Name]:

This letter is necessitated because you have failed to return my telephone calls and those of the paralegal assisting me with this matter on [Date] and [Date].

As you recall, you requested an extension of time to answer and respond to Defendant's discovery request for an additional thirty (30) days.

When I called you on [Date] about your responses, you stated that appropriate responses would be received no later than the following week. Despite this representation, we have not received any response.

Therefore, this is just a reminder that your client's responses are past due. As you know, we have another settlement conference at [Time] on [Date] before Magistrate [Name]. The purpose of this settlement conference is to narrow the issues at trial. Obviously, your client's answers are important in this regard.

If there is a problem complying with the deadline, please let me know. If not, I expect to receive your client's responses immediately.

[Attorney]

LETTER 6-27
LETTER TO CLIENT RE OVERDUE RESPONSE TO INTERROGATORIES

[Date]

[Name]
[Address]

Dear [Name]:

We are concerned that we have not yet received your response to the following documents which were forwarded to you on [Date].

[List the names and dates of the documents here.]

It is crucial that you understand the importance of the statutory deadlines for responding to these types of documents. The [State] Rules of Civil Procedure state that a party must respond to this type of pleading in [Number] days from receipt of service of this document or the Court may either on its own volition or upon motion by the opposing party, invoke sanctions upon the party who is delinquent in its response. The sanctions which the Court may choose to invoke in cases of this nature are very severe, and range from monetary fines to imprisonment for civil contempt to striking portions or the entirety of your pleadings before this court, which could virtually eliminate your right to [bring claim against . . . /any defenses] in this action

We are sure that you understand that once we have received your response to this document, we must have adequate time to review your responses to protect your rights of privilege and to finalize the document so that it may be filed before the statutory deadline. To that end, we again stress how important it is that we receive the necessary information from you within the next [hours/days]. If there is a problem which will prevent you from being able to produce the material within that period of time, or if there is anything we may do to assist you in this endeavor, please call us immediately so that we may take whatever steps are available to us to try to obtain an extension for you.

We look forward to hearing from you shortly.

Very truly yours,

[Attorney]

LETTER 6-28
LETTER REQUESTING EXTENSION OF TIME TO RESPOND TO INTERROGATORIES 1

[Date]

[Party's Name]
[Address]

Re: [Case name]

Dear [Party]:

This letter is to confirm the extension of time for our client, [Name], to respond to the [Number] set of interrogatories propounded by you on [Date].

Confirmation was received from [Name] of your office on [Date] that responses are now due before or on the [Date].

Thank you for your courtesy and cooperation in this matter.

[Signature]

LETTER 6-29
LETTER REQUESTING EXTENSION OF TIME TO RESPOND TO INTERROGATORIES 2

[Date]

[Name]
[Address]

Re: [Case name and cause of action number]

Dear [Opposing counsel]:

We are in receipt of Plaintiff's First Set of Interrogatories, which were served on [Date]. We have contacted our client regarding the answering of these interrogatories, and have begun to assimilate the information you have requested.

[Unfortunately, our client has suffered a death in his family and has informed us that he must leave immediately to take care of emergency family business in another state. It will be necessary for him to remain out of the state until [Date]. Therefore, we are asking your cooperation in granting our client a three-week extension until [Date] in order to answer the Plaintiff's First Set of Interrogatories.]

[We are having some difficulty in locating some of the information you have requested and would like to request a two-week extension of time in order to answer the interrogatories properly and completely. If you are so gracious as to allow us the two-week extension, our client's Answers to Interrogatories will be due to you on [Date].

We thank you very much for your cooperation in this matter.

Respectfully yours,

[Signature]

LETTER 6-30
LETTER CONFIRMING EXTENSION OF TIME TO RESPOND TO INTERROGATORIES 1

[Date]

[Name]
[Address]

Re: [Case name and cause of action number]

Dear [Opposing counsel]:

This letter is to confirm our telephone conversation today wherein you graciously agreed to grant our client [Name] a two-week extension in which to file the Answers to Plaintiff's First Set of Interrogatories, which were originally served on [Date]. The Answers will now be due on [Date].

We thank you very much for your cooperation in allowing us this additional period of time in which to respond.

Respectfully yours,

[Signature]

LETTER 6-31
LETTER CONFIRMING EXTENSION OF TIME TO RESPOND TO INTERROGATORIES 2

[Date]

[Name]
[Address]

Re: [Case name and cause of action number]
Our Client : [Name]
Our File : [Number]
Date/Loss : [Date]

Dear [Name]:

Please allow this to confirm that your secretary, [Name], has graciously granted my client, [Name], an extension of time within which to respond to your client, [Name]'s Special Interrogatories, Set Number One (1). Therefore, my client's response is now due on or before [Date].

Thank you for your courtesy and cooperation in this matter. Should you have any questions or comments, please feel free to contact me.

Very truly yours,

[Signature]

LETTER 6-32
LETTER CONFIRMING EXTENSION OF TIME TO RESPOND TO INTERROGATORIES 3

[Date]

[Name]
[Address]

Dear [Name]:

This letter is to confirm the extension of time for our client, [Name], to respond to the [Number] set of interrogatories propounded by you on [Date].

Confirmation was received from [Name] of your office on [Date] that responses are now due before or on [Date].

Thank you for your courtesy and cooperation in this matter.

[Signature]

LETTER 6-33
LETTER CONFIRMING EXTENSION OF TIME TO RESPOND TO INTERROGATORIES 4

Interrogatory Extension Letter

[Date]

[Name]
[Address]

RE: [Case name]

Dear [Name]:

This will confirm my conversation today with your secretary, [Name], at which time you granted this office a two-week extension within which to answer or otherwise plead to the first set of interrogatories propounded by defendant, [Name], to plaintiff. The due date for plaintiff's responses is now [Date].

Your courtesy and cooperation in granting this extension is greatly appreciated.

Sincerely,

[Signature]

LETTER 6-34
STATUS LETTER TO CLIENT REGARDING INTERROGATORIES (OR OTHER DISCOVERY)

[Date]

[Name]
[Address]

Dear [Insurance Adjuster]:

The following is a summary of plaintiff's answers to our initial interrogatories.

FACTS

Plaintiff's full name is ______________________________.
He was born ____________________, in ____________________,
and currently resides at ______________________________.
His social security number is ______________________________.
In reference to plaintiff's version of the accident, he states as follows: __________
____
____
____
____
____

With reference to the facts on which plaintiff bases his allegations of negligence, he states: ______________________________
____
____
______________________________.

The plaintiff lists ______________________________
____
____
as witnesses to the accident.

INJURIES AND MEDICAL HISTORY

Plaintiff states that he suffered injury to ______________________________
____
______________________________.

Following the accident, he was hospitalized at ______________________________
____
from ____________________ to ____________________.
His treating physicians were: (list names and addresses) ____________________
____
______________________________.

Plaintiff states that he has had no previous accidents and no accident or illness since the accident here involved.
(Plaintiff states that he has had __________ previous accidents and __________ illnesses and accidents since the accident here involved.)

EMPLOYMENT RECORD

The plaintiff claims to have been employed as a __________________________ for the past ______ years, employed by ______________________________. He claims he was earning $ _____ per hour (or per week, month, etc.) and has lost approximately $ ________ in wages. Lost time since the accident totals ________ days.

SPECIAL DAMAGES CLAIMED

In answer to our interrogatory as to what expenses plaintiff has incurred, he lists the following: ____
____
____
____.

RECOMMENDATIONS

[HAVE ATTORNEY COMPLETE THIS SECTION.]

We will keep you advised as matters further develop herein.

Respectfully yours,

[Attorney]

LETTER 6-35
REPORT TO CLIENT WORKERS' COMPENSATION CARRIER REGARDING PLAINTIFF'S INTERROGATORY RESPONSES

[Date]

[Name]
[Insurance Company]
[Address]

Re: [Case name and cause of action number]
Your Claim No. : [Number]
Insured : [Name]
Date of Loss : [Date]
Our File No. : [Number]

Dear [Name]:

We have received plaintiff's responses to form interrogatories and responses to a document request. The following will summarize those responses.

SUMMARY OF INTERROGATORY RESPONSES

Interrogatories—General Information

[Alan Wade Pease was born on 5/1/57 in Key West, Florida. His California driver's license, number N5379126, was issued on 3/9/90 and had no restrictions. He has lived at 9111 Rosann, Garden Grove, CA 92641 for two years. Prior to that, he lived at 8791 Garden Grove Blvd, Garden Grove, CA 92641 for six months. Prior to that, he lived at 1670 W. Catalpa, Santa Ana, CA 92801 for three years. (Numbers 2.1 to 2.5)

As of approximately May 1993, he had worked in roofing with California Roofing, 12612 Arrow, Garden Grove, CA for three years. He attended Elgin High in Elgin, Illinois, completing 10th grade in 1972. He got his GED in 1980 at AM Tech, Midway City, CA. At the time of the incident, he was working as a laborer for Peterson, 3720 S. Bear, Santa Ana, CA. He was not insured at the time. (Numbers 2.6 to 4.2)

Injuries

As a result of the incident, he was injured in his lower back, legs, neck, shoulder and arms. He suffered physical stress due to physical problems, and not being able to work and provide for his family. He still has pain, which varies in consistency and duration, in his neck, shoulder, right leg, and lower back. The pain is better since surgery (cervical and lumbar laminectomy) but still exists. As a result of the incident, he received treatment at:

1. **Gateway Medical Center** **$791.00**
14251 E. Firestone Blvd., Ste. 102
La Mirada, CA 90638
(213) 802-0208
Orthopedic care on 1/21/92 and 1/24/92

2. **Mark Anderson, M.D.** **$20,422.00**
16300 San Canyon Ave., Ste. 1005
Irvine, CA 92718
(714) 753-0303
Orthopedic care (9 visits) from 2/14/92 to 12/21/92

3. **Irvine Medical Center** **$12,665.00**
16200 San Canyon Ave.
Irvine, CA 92718
(714) 753-2000
Hospitalization and surgery from 3/26/92 to 4/1/92 and from 8/6/92 to 8/8/92.

4. **Hoag Memorial Hosp. Presbyterian** **$208.60**
301 Newport Blvd., Box Y
Newport Beach, CA 92658
(714) 645-8600
Radiology on 4/30/92

5. **West Coast Radiology** **$448.00**
1100 N. Tustin Ave
Santa Ana, CA 92705
(714) 835-6055
Radiology on 2/27/92.

TOTAL MEDICAL EXPENSES **$34,523.60**

Plaintiff received prescriptions for 5mg valium, 30mg delmane, and vicodin from Dr. Anderson. He received a prescription for 600 mg ibuprofen from Dr. Lee at Gateway Medical Center. He took the medications from within the first month following the accident until approximately 9/92. He does not know the cost of the medications to date. He was told by Dr. Anderson that he would need future medical treatment for his neck and back at an unknown time. (Numbers 6.1 to 6.7)

<u>Loss of Income</u>

He is claiming loss of income from his job as a waterproofer, which he began in 9/91. The last day he worked prior to the incident was 1/16/92. At the time, he made $1,608.00 gross salary, based on a 40 hours work week at $12.00 an hour plus overtime. He has not returned to work. His lost income totals **$38,592.00,** calculated at $1,608.00 times 24 months. (Numbers 8.1 to 8.8)

Prior Medical History

In 1988, he had lower back surgery by Dr. Anderson. He had no disabilities immediately before the subject incident. He has sustained no similar injuries since the incident. (Numbers 10.1 to 10.3)

Prior Worker's Compensation Claims

In the last ten years, he filed two worker's compensation claims for the following incidents:

1. On 9/25/87, he had a low back injury while employed with Williams Glass and Mirror, 5421 McFadden Avenue, Huntington Beach, CA 92649. His injury resulted in a lumbar laminectomy. He treated with Dr. Mark Anderson.

   The worker's compensation insurer was Nationwide Mutual Insurance Company, 681 South Parker Street, Orange, CA 92668, Claim number 73-036583-251. He stopped receiving benefits in early 1989.

   The WCAB case number was 88ANA197533.

2. On 9/29/89, he injured his neck, shoulders, lower back, psych (sic) and nervous system while employed with Owen Pacific Company, no address supplied. He does not recall the doctors who treated him.

   The worker's compensation insurer was Workman Comp Indemnity Company of California, no address supplied. The claim number was 77-04-006430. He received benefits from 1/15/90 to 12/10/90.

   The WCAB case number was 89ANA229136. (Number 11.2)

Investigation

On an unknown date, Alan Pease took four (4) photographs of the vehicle he was driving at the time of the incident. His attorney, Steven Schapiro, has possession of those photographs. The California Highway Patrol wrote a report on 1/21/93 for plaintiff and defendant. Plaintiff claims that Maddox violated CVC §22350 by driving at an unsafe speed for the prevailing conditions. (Numbers 12.4, 12.6, and 14.1)

The Subject Incident

The incident occurred on 1/16/92 at 7:30 a.m. on the 55 freeway northbound at 17th Street. Pease was driving a 1986 Mazda pickup truck, number 3R02163. Maddox was driving a black BMW, license number unknown. Neither vehicle had any passengers. Plaintiff's truck was owned by H. S. Peterson Company,

P.O. Box 4199, Huntington Beach, CA 92605, (714) 843-5677. Said truck was leased by Hugo Hernandez. (Numbers 20.1 to 20.2)

Pease was driving from Diamond and Bristol in Santa Ana to a mall in Palm Springs. He took Bristol to the 55 freeway northbound. Immediately before and at the time of impact, plaintiff's vehicle was stopped in the number one lane, and defendant's vehicle was traveling approximately 50 mph in the same lane and direction. After impact, both vehicles were stopped in the number one lane. (Numbers 20.3 to 20.8)

SUMMARY OF DOCUMENTS PRODUCED

Photographs

Plaintiff produced black-and-white photocopies of photographs of a Mazda pickup truck. Two of the photos depict the truck from the rear; two photos depict the rear corners by the tail lights.

Paychecks

The source of the paychecks is not evident. The trade is listed as "laborer." His hourly rate was $13.00; his overtime rate was $19.50.

Pay period ending date	Hours	Gross Salary
9/14/91	8	$104.00
9/21/91	40 + 13	$773.50
9/28/91	40 + 3	$578.50
10/05/91	40 + 11	$734.50
10/12/91	40 + 9	$695.50
10/26/91	40 + 14	$793.00
11/02/91	28	$364.00
11/16/91	40 + 7	$656.50
11/19/91	39	$507.00
12/14/91	30	$390.00
Gross Salary		**$5,596.50**
Average Monthly Gross Salary		**$1,865.50**

Payments from TIC Workers Comp Claim Unit

Temporary Total Disability Payments

Pay period ending	Amount
1/19/92	$336.00

1/30/92	$457.13
2/13/92	$346.67
2/27/92	$346.67
3/12/92	$346.67
3/26/92	$336.00
4/9/92	$672.00
4/23/92	$336.00
5/7/92	$336.00
5/21/92	$336.00
6/6/92	$336.00
6/20/92	$336.00
7/4/92	$336.00
7/18/92	$336.00
8/1/92	$336.00
8/15/92	$336.00
8/29/92	$336.00
8/12/92	$336.00
9/26/92	$336.00
10/10/92	$336.00
10/24/92	$336.00
11/7/92	$336.00
11/21/92	$336.00
12/5/92	$336.00
12/19/92	$336.00
1/2/93	$336.00
1/16/93	$432.96
1/30/93	$432.96
2/13/93	$432.96

Permanent Partial Disability Payments

Pay period ending	Amount
5/4/92	$1.000.00
1/30/93	$478.04
2/5/93	$239.04
2/19/93	$239.04
3/5/93	$239.04
3/13/93	$239.04
3/27/93	$239.04
4/30/93	$239.04
5/14/93	$280.00
5/18/93	$1.000.00
6/5/93	$420.00
6/19/93	$280.00
7/3/93	$280.00
7/17/93	$280.00

Vocational Rehabilitation Payments

Pay period ending	Amount
2/27/93	$432.96
3/13/93	$432.96
3/27/93	$432.96
4/24/93	$432.96
5/1/93	$216.48

Other

Pay period ending	Amount
6/24/92 (Mileage reimbursement)	$136.80
2/13/92 (Penalty for late pymt)	$69.34

Medical Reports for Prior 9/25/87 Injury

1/23/89 10-page report by Brendan Clifford. M.D.: Pease was examined on 1/19/89, at which time he was employed as a bench technician, a job that exacerbated his pain syndrome. Pease felt that cervical movement (which showed normal range of motion and was nonpainful at the extremes) created pain in the low back. The dull and intermittent pain (activity-related and made better by heat) was in his back and at the waist, with some radiation into both buttocks, mostly the right side.

Pease stated that, on 9/25/87, he and 4-5 co-workers were carrying a large and heavy piece of glass upstairs. Pease was about to reach the top of the flight when co-workers pushed the glass up and Pease fell abruptly into a sitting position. He experienced immediate pain in his right hip and buttocks, and he reported it to his supervisor. The company doctor diagnosed low back pain, prescribing Robaxin and Darvocet. **(This is a very different story from that related by Dr. Cummings in his 10/14/87 report.)**

Pease also received chiropractic therapy from Lee Pierce; an exam by neurologist Cummings; and a CAT scan and MRI through neurosurgeon Anderson, who performed a lumbar laminectomy on 11/19/87 at Fountain Valley Regional Hospital.

"Past medical history is negative for hospitalizations." He injured his left hand in 1982, severely lacerating tendons. He also fractured various fingers and his nose while participating in sports.

X-rays of the lumbosacral spine show decreased disc space height between L4 and L5. Exam showed 25% decrease in flexion of the lumbosacral spine. Clinical impression: chronic lumbosacral musculoligamentous strain and status post laminectomy and discectomy with residual, right sciatica. Permanent and stationary. Since Pease gives no history of prior unresolved injuries, all disabilities are due to the 9/25/87 injury. He will need ongoing medical care plus medication, physical therapy, and hospitalization as indicated.

10/14/88 2-page report by Mark Anderson. M.D.: Pease was one-year status-post laminectomy and continued to do well with a minimum of pain and no leg symptomatology. He has a 5% chance of needing future surgery. "Apportionment does not apply due to denial of preexisting history."

8/7/88 1-page report by Anderson: He had returned to rehabilitation and was doing well. His vicodin was renewed.

8/1/88 1-page report by Anderson: **"Approximately 2 days ago, he slipped while walking, sustaining a jolting back injury."** New lumbosacral x-rays did not demonstrate change. Exam showed no change.

5/18/88 1-page report by Anderson: A new set of x-rays demonstrates satisfactory interbody fusion at L4-L5. He had minimal back pain and no leg pain. He had begun vocational rehabilitation and was pleased with his position. His prescription for vicodin was renewed.

5/6/88 1-page report by Anderson: The vocational rehabilitation analyses accommodate the work restrictions set by Anderson.

2/3/88 1-page letter from Southland Neuro. Assoc. of O.C.: regarding claim for surgical monitoring as requested by Anderson and Dr. William Hornstein.

1/4/88 1-page report by Anderson: Had had right posterior calf pain over the holidays that was resolved. Ambulatory with minimal low back pain. Current medication: vicodin and dalmane.

12/4/87 1-page report by Anderson: Wound is well healed. Sutures removed; Pease immobilized in a well-fitting brace. Preoperative leg pain resolved. Disabled for 3 months.

11/19/87 4-page surgical report by Anderson: Assisted by Dr. Theodore Sawyer. Preoperative and postoperative diagnoses: herniated nucleus pulposus, L4. Operation: lumbar laminectomy, L4-5 bilaterally, with posterior lumbar interbody fusion and donor bone graft times five. Condition: satisfactory.

11/19/87 Somatosensory report from Fountain Valley Regional Hospital: normal somatosensory evoked response test with stimulation of the left posterior tibial nerve prior to and after completion of surgery.

11/19/87 3-page admission report by Anderson: With low back pain and right lower extremity radiculopathy since 9/25/87 when he was injured moving a

500-lb pane of glass. Scheduled for lumbar laminectomy and interbody stabilization at F.V. Hosp.

11/6/87 4-page neurosurgical consultation by Anderson: Pease was referred by Dr. Cummings. An MRI scan demonstrated evidence of a very large herniated nucleus pulposus at L4-L5 right with right L5 nerve root displacement. Anderson has recommended posterior lumbar interbody fusion with donor bone graft at L4-L5.

10/28/87 2-page report from Dr. Michael Cummings at Orange Coast Neuromedical Group: EMG and Nerve Conduction Velocities studies (same date - 4 page report) suggest a right L5-S1 radiculopathy. An MRI (dated 10/22/87 - 1 page) revealed a "severe 6-7 mm right posterolateral disc herniation at L4-5, probably of recent origin." Temporarily totally disabled. Ibuprofen recommended.

10/14/87 3-page report by Cummings: In early to mid-September, he was carrying slider doors and noted pain beginning in his right hip and radiating down the posterolateral aspect to the right leg and foot. "He does not recall any discrete injury but the symptoms did arise after this heavy lifting." (See 1/23/89 summary for considerable discrepancy in Pease's version of what happened.)

"On 9-25-87, due to the persistent pain, he went to the Rushmore Clinic" where he was treated with muscle relaxants and Darvocet. He received limited benefit from manipulations from chiropractor Pierce. He has evidence of right sciatica and probably a lumbosacral radiculopathy that may be due to disc herniation. Temporarily totally disabled.

10/6/87 Doctor's first report of injury by Lee Pierce, D.C.: Injured low back while carrying sliding glass doors up some stairs. Diagnosis: lumbar sprain with myofascitis and radiculitis; possible discopathy.

9/26/87 Doctor's first report of work injury by M.A. Afrasiabi. M.D. at Rushmore Medical Center: While lifting glass doors to upstairs, he twisted his lower back and right hip. His employer was notified.

9/25/87 X-ray report from Rushmore Med. Diagnostic Center: Lumbar spine and pelvis films show no evidence of recent bone trauma or destruction.

Date Unknown Work/Comp Questionnaire: "We were carrying sliding doors up some stairs and must have strained myself."

Medical Reports for Prior 10/29/89 Injury

7/9/90 13-page orthopedic report by Martin J. Morris. M.D.: Employed as a glazier for over 7 years when, on 9/29/89 as he lifted rigging over a swing stage, he felt a sharp pain in his neck and dropped the unit, at which time one of the wheels landed on his right foot. He stopped working and went home. In 9/89, he had no residual problems from his 1988 injury, for which he underwent lumbar surgery. He had returned to work in 6/89 and continued to work without problems until the 9/29/89 incident. He returned to work despite low back discomfort and retained an attorney, who referred him to Monarch Medical on 11/2/89, where he was seen by Dr. David Thordarson, an orthopedist. He also received treatment from chiropractor Michael Murphy.

As of 7/9/90, he still had sharp pains in his neck and shoulder, but no problems with his low back. A lumbar MRI on 1/25/90 by Joy Foster (2 pages) revealed findings suggestive of post-operative fibrosis with no evidence of a herniated disc. A cervical MRI the same date (2 pages) was normal. There was no clinical or subjective evidence of a cervical disc problem. No work restrictions resulted from the 9/89 incident. He required no further treatment. He was permanent and stationary. No apportionment indicated. He was employed as a finish carpenter.

6/19/90 15-page report by Robert S. Smith Ph.D. at P.S.Y Health Systems: A comprehensive evaluation of Pease's mental condition was conducted for Workers' Compensation Insurance Company. According to Pease, for 2 months he was employed by Owen Pacific Roofing to travel to construction sites to clean, prime, and caulk joints on the external surfaces of buildings. He was a journeyman bricklayer by trade. He could not recall specific details but, on 10/29/89 while at Crystal Cathedral in Garden Grove, worked for about 5 hours. He had to move his work stage around the building by repeatedly going to the roof to lift the outrigger over a series of channel iron posts that were connected by cables around the rim.

Two days later, he developed left arm, neck and shoulder pain that worsened as he continued working for several more days at a jobsite in Long Beach. When he was unable to operate a Bosin's chair (which required him to briefly support his own weight), he decided something must be wrong medically. He telephoned his employer to report the injury and was told to see his own doctor. Dissatisfied, he decided to contact an attorney and had retained an attorney to represent him in a prior worker's comp claim. His attorney referred him to Dr. Thordarson, a neurologist in Santa Ana. He was told that an MRI revealed damaged cervical discs. He never returned to work and had not resumed physical therapy.

Summary and Conclusions: Psychological factors are playing a contributing role in the continuation of subjective physical distress. He is frustrated by physical limitations imposed by his injury, realistic and understandable reactions to his current predicament, not constituting a mental disorder. He is permanent and stationary, without psychiatric disability.

3/8/90 7-page Final Comprehensive Orthopaedic Evaluation by Dr. David Thordarson M.D. at Monarch Medical: He complains of constant moderate-to-severe neck pain, radiating to the left shoulder and upper extremity; constant, moderate weakness and frequent, slight numbness in his left upper extremity; and moderate, frequent low back pain that radiates to the right lower extremity. His 9/29/89 injury exacerbated a low back condition and resulted in a new onset of left C-6 radiculopathy. Pease was reluctant to undergo cervical anterior interbody fusion as recommended by Thordarson. He was permanent and stationary.

11/16/89 Cervical spine x-ray report from Medical Imaging Center of Huntington Beach: narrow spinal canal (14 mm at C5-C6; otherwise negative). Lumbar spine x-ray report: postoperative changes at L4-L5; mild/moderate narrowing L5-S1 disc space.

11/7/89 6-page initial comprehensive orthopedic evaluation by Dr. Thordarson: Pease stated that, while lifting a 300-lb outrigger, he noted a sudden onset of pain in his neck and low back. Diagnoses: cervical spine strain, with possible herniated disc, with left C-6 radiculopathy; and status post lumbar discectomy and fusion, with reinjury and right L-5 radiculopathy.]

I will notify you when the MSC is reset.

If you have any questions or comments, please do not hesitate to contact me.

Very truly yours,

[Signature]

LETTER 6-36
REPORT TO CLIENT/INSURER REGARDING PLAINTIFF'S RESPONSES TO INTERROGATORIES

[Date]

[Name]
[Insurance Company]
[Address]

Re: [Case name]
Your Claim No. : [Number]
Insured : [Name]
Date of Loss : [Date]
Our File No. : [Number]

STATUS REPORT
Summary of Plaintiff's Responses

Dear [Name]:

We have received plaintiff's responses and further responses to form interrogatories. The following is a summary of plaintiff's responses. We also received documents pursuant to a demand for production. A summary of those documents will be sent to you in another letter.

Interrogatories — General Information

[Alan Wade Pease was born on 5/1/57 in Key West, Florida. His California driver's license, number N5379126, was issued on 3/9/90 and had no restrictions. He has lived at 9111 Rosann, Garden Grove, CA 92641 for two years. Prior to that, he lived at 8791 Garden Grove Blvd, Garden Grove, CA 92641 for six months. Prior to that, he lived at 1670 W. Catalpa, Santa Ana, CA 92801 for three years. (Numbers 2.1 to 2.5)

As of approximately May 1993, he had worked in roofing with California Roofing, 12612 Arrow, Garden Grove, CA for three years. He attended Elgin High in Elgin, Illinois, completing 10th grade in 1972. He got his GED in 1980 at AM Tech, Midway City, CA. At the time of the incident, he was working as a laborer for Peterson, 3720 S. Bear, Santa Ana, CA. He was not insured at the time. (Numbers 2.6 to 4.2)

Injuries

As a result of the incident, he was injured in his lower back, legs, neck, shoulder and arms. He suffered physical stress due to physical problems, and not being able to work and provide for his family. He still has pain, which varies in consistency and duration, in his neck, shoulder, right leg, and lower back. The pain is better since surgery (cervical and lumbar laminectomy) but still exists. As a result of the incident, he received treatment at:

1. **Gateway Medical Center** **$791. 00**
   14251 E. Firestone Blvd., Ste. 102
   La Mirada, CA 90638
   (213) 802-0208
   Orthopedic care on 1/21/92 and 1/24/92

2. **Mark Anderson, M.D.** **$20,422.00**
   16300 San Canyon Ave., Ste. 1005
   Irvine, CA 92718
   (714) 753-0303
   Orthopedic care (9 visits) from 2/14/92 to 12/21/92

3. **Irvine Medical Center** **$12,665.00**
   16200 San Canyon Ave.
   Irvine, CA 92718
   (714) 753-2000
   Hospitalization and surgery from 3/26/92 to 4/1/92 and from 8/6/92 to 8/8/92.

4. **Hoag Memorial Hosp. Presbyterian** **$208.60**
   Newport Blvd., Box Y
   Newport Beach, CA 92658
   (714) 645-8600
   Radiology on 4/30/92

5. **West Coast Radiology** **$448.00**
   1100 N. Tustin Ave
   Santa Ana, CA 92705
   (714) 835-6055
   Radiology on 2/27/92.
   TOTAL MEDICAL EXPENSES **$34,523.60**

Plaintiff received prescriptions for 5mg valium, 30mg delmane, and vicodin from Dr. Anderson.He received a prescription for 600 mg ibuprofen from Dr. Lee at Gateway Medical Center. He took the medications from within the first month following the accident until approximately 9/92. He does not know the cost of the medications to date. He was told by Dr. Anderson that he would need future medical treatment for his neck and back at an unknown time. (Numbers 6.1 to 6.7)

Loss of Income

He is claiming loss of income from his job as a waterproofer, which he began in 9/91. The last day he worked prior to the incident was 1/16/92. At the time, he made $1,608.00 gross salary, based on a 40 hours work week at $12.00 an hour plus overtime. He has not returned to work. His lost income totals $38,592.00, calculated at $1,608.00 times 24 months. (Numbers 8.1 to 8.8)

Prior Medical History

In 1988, he had lower back surgery by Dr. Anderson. He had no disabilities immediately before the subject incident. He has sustained no similar injuries since the incident. (Numbers 10.1 to 10.3)

Prior Worker's Compensation Claims

In the last ten years, he filed two worker's compensation claims for the following incidents:

1. On 9/25/87, he had a low back injury while employed with Williams Glass and Mirror, 5421 McFadden Avenue, Huntington Beach, CA 92649. His injury resulted in a lumbar laminectomy. He treated with Dr. Mark Anderson.

   The worker's compensation insurer was Nationwide Mutual Insurance Company, 681 South Parker Street, Orange, CA 92668, Claim number 73-036583-251. He stopped receiving benefits in early 1989.

   The WCAB case number was 88ANA197533.

2. On 9/29/89, he injured his neck, shoulders, lower back, psych (sic) and nervous system while employed with Owen Pacific Company, no address supplied. He does not recall the doctors who treated him.

   The worker's compensation insurer was Workman Comp Indemnity Company of California, no address supplied. The claim number was 77-04-006430. He received benefits from 1/15/90 to 12/10/90.

   The WCAB case number was 89ANA229136. (Number 11.2)

Investigation

On an unknown date, Alan Pease took four (4) photographs of the vehicle he was driving at the time of the incident. His attorney, Steven Schapiro, has possession of those photographs. The California Highway Patrol wrote a report on 1/21/93 for plaintiff and defendant. Plaintiff claims that Maddox violated CVC

§22350 by driving at an unsafe speed for the prevailing conditions. (Numbers 12.4, 12.6, and 14.1)

The Subject Incident

The incident occurred on 1/16/92 at 7:30 a.m. on the 55 freeway northbound at 17th Street. Pease was driving a 1986 Mazda pickup truck, number 3R02163. Maddox was driving a black BMW, license number unknown. Neither vehicle had any passengers. Plaintiff's truck was owned by H. S. Peterson Company, P.O. Box 4199, Huntington Beach, CA 92605, (714) 843-5677. Said truck was leased by Hugo Hernandez. (Numbers 20.1 to 20.2)

Pease was driving from Diamond and Bristol in Santa Ana to a mall in Palm Springs. He took Bristol to the 55 freeway northbound. Immediately before and at the time of impact, plaintiff's vehicle was stopped in the number one lane, and defendant's vehicle was traveling approximately 50mph in the same lane and direction. After impact, both vehicles were stopped in the number one lane. (Numbers 20.3 to 20.8)]

If you have any questions or comments, please do not hesitate to contact me.

Very truly yours,

[Signature]

CHAPTER 7

DISCOVERY—REQUESTS FOR ADMISSIONS

LETTER 7-1
TRANSMITTAL OF REQUEST FOR ADMISSIONS
COVER LETTER

[Date]

[Name]
[Address]

Dear [Name],

Enclosed is a Request for Admissions regarding certain facts, legal relationships, documents, and other evidence. As you respond to this pleading you are expected to act in good faith, using all information that is readily available to you, including information that is in the possession of your firm or other attorneys or secondary personnel, such as paralegals and secretarial staff. As the Rules of Civil Procedure require, you are to employ and apply your own personal knowledge.

If you cannot fully admit to a specific request, state which part of the request you must deny and which part is acceptable to you. If you deny the request, give your reasons, stating specific facts and conditions which necessitate the denial. If you are simply unable to respond due to a lack of knowledge, so state.

If there is some way we can clarify the question or aid you as you interpret our request, please call. You have thirty days to respond.

Sincerely,

____
[Attorney]

LETTER 7-2
DEMAND FOR RESPONSE TO REQUEST FOR ADMISSIONS

[Date]

[Name]
[Address]

Dear [Name],

This is to notify you that no responses have been received from your client, [Their client 's name], in response to the [Number] set of requests for admission sent by our client, [Your client's name], on or about [Date].

[Local rule number] of the state of [State name] demands responses within [Number] days of your receipt of the same. Therefore your client's answers should have been received on [Date—be sure to include extra days for mailing if provided in your local rules) and are (Number] days overdue as of this writing.

Please contact this office immediately to resolve the situation.

____

[Signature]

LETTER 7-3
SECOND DEMAND FOR RESPONSE TO REQUEST FOR ADMISSIONS

[Date]

[Name]
[Address]

Dear [Name]:

A letter demanding responses to the [Number] set of requests for admission sent by our office to [Their client] on [Date] was [Mailed/hand delivered] to you on [Date]. No response has been received nor has your office attempted to resolve the matter by telephone.

As provided by [State rule number] of the state of [State's name] all requests for admission will be deemed admitted if responses are not received by this office on [Date]. Further, a Notice regarding such admissions will be filed with the court that very day unless you contact our office prior to such filing.

____
[Signature]

LETTER 7-4
LETTER CONFIRMING EXTENSION OF TIME TO RESPOND TO REQUEST FOR ADMISSIONS

[Date]

[Name]
[Law Firm]
[Address]

RE: [Case Name]

Dear [Name]:

This will confirm my conversation today with your secretary, [Name], at which time you granted this office a two-week extension within which to respond to the first set of requests for admissions propounded by defendant, [Name], to plaintiff. The due date for plaintiff's responses is now [Date].

Enclosed with this letter is a form stipulation which I have prepared confirming the extension. Please execute the stipulation and return it to our office, and we will file the same with the court.

Your courtesy and cooperation in stipulating to this extension of time is greatly appreciated.

Sincerely,

____
[Paralegal]
Legal Assistant to
(Name of Attorney)

Enclosure

LETTER 7-5
LETTER CONFIRMING EXTENSION OF TIME TO RESPOND TO REQUESTS FOR ADMISSION 2

[Date]

[Name]
[Address]

Dear [Name]:

This is to confirm the phone call made by [Employee's name] in our office to [Employee's name] in your office on [Date]. As agreed, our client has until [Date] to [Mail/hand-deliver] responses to the [Number] set of requests for admission propounded by [Propounding party] to [Responding party] on [Original date sent].

Thank you for your courtesy and cooperation.

____
[Signature]

LETTER 7-6
LETTER REQUESTING EXTENSION OF TIME TO RESPOND TO REQUESTS FOR ADMISSION

[Date]

[Name]
[Address]

Dear [Name]:

The [Number] set of requests for admission propounded by [Their client] was received by this office on [Date]. At least [Number] attempts have been made to contact you to arrange for an extension for the responses which are due on [Date].

An extension is needed because [e.g., we have been unable to reach our client /or/ responding to the requests will take more time in order to respond fully].

Therefore we request that the response date be extended to [Date]. Unless we hear from you to the contrary we will assume that such an arrangement is satisfactory to both sides.

Thank you in advance for your kindness.

____

[Signature]

LETTER 7-7
LETTER TO CLIENT REQUESTING CERTAIN INFORMATION AND REPORTING ON STATUS OF DISCOVERY

[Date]

[Name]
[Address]

Re: [Case Name]
Our Client: [Client name]
Our File: [Number]
Date/Loss: [Date]

Dear [Name]:

It was a pleasure speaking to you on the telephone yesterday. Enclosed with this letter, please find the contract documents which you had requested.

As we discussed, our firm is representing [Name] in the above referenced lawsuit, and I had previously been dealing with [Name]. Unfortunately, [Name] has been unable to provide me with any information concerning [Name]'s involvement in the lawsuit. I would appreciate any help you may be able to provide.

Among other things, I am interested in the following information:

1. Whether the contract, parts of which are attached hereto, is true and correct.
2. Whether [Name] was the general contractor on the job.
3. Whether [Name] was an electrical subcontractor on the job.
4. Identity of that current employee or officer of [Name] who would have the most knowledge concerning the job involved in this lawsuit.

I am also enclosing with this letter copies of discovery requests which other parties have served on us. As you will note, they include the following:

1. Request for Admissions from [Name];
2. Request for Admissions from [Insurance Company]; and
3. Notice of Deposition of Person Most Knowledgeable with [Name], served by [Name].

Responses to the discovery requests are past due now. However, we are still in a position to deny the Request for Admissions, so long as we do so before the opposing parties bring a motion to have the requests deemed admitted.

Once again, our primary immediate objectives in this case are to locate that [Name] representative who has the most knowledge about this job, and locate [Name]'s job files, if any, for that project. I appreciate your prompt attention to this matter. Should you have any questions or comments, please do not hesitate to call.

Very truly yours,

[Attorney]

LETTER 7-8
SUMMARY OF ADMISSIONS AND DENIALS

[Date]

[Name]
[Address]

Dear [Name]:

The following is a summary of the admissions and denials provided by [Responding party's name] in response to the [Number] set of requests for admission propounded by [Propounding party's name] on [Date].

Admits:

[1) That the New Account Application, Receipt number 12345, and Unconditional guarantee (exhibits "A"–"C") are genuine.
2) That President Smith signed the New Account Application and, in so doing, approved plaintiff for credit.
3) That salesperson Brown initialed Receipt number 12345 and, in so doing, indicated that plaintiff paid for the subject television set in full.]

Denies:

[1) That the standard procedure in April 1986 at ABC Company was to provide the 1985 Unconditional Guarantee.

Comments: ABC Company claims that salespersons provided a 1986 version of the Guarantee. We plan to make every attempt, including interrogatories and a request to produce, to locate a 1986 version. If you have any questions, please do not hesitate to contact us.]

____
[Signature]

LETTER 7-9
SUMMARY OF ADMISSIONS AND DENIALS 2

[Date]

[Name]
[Address]

Dear [Name]:

This letter will summarize everything that each party in this lawsuit has admitted or denied as of this date. Please review it for discrepancies and inform this office if you have any suggestions or questions.

[PLAINTIFF: Admits that she did not have her glasses on at the time of the incident but denies that it contributed to her fall. Admits that she was on medication but denies that it made her dizzy.

RESTAURANT: Admits that the trough was constructed when the kitchen was remodeled ten years ago. Denies that there was a duty to keep it current with today's standards.

ENGINEER: Admits that he constructed the trough. Denies that the design was his own; admits that it was an accepted form of trough 10 years ago. Denies that he had a duty to inform Restaurant.]

Yours truly,
[Attorney]

CHAPTER 8

DISCOVERY—DEPOSITIONS

LETTER 8-1
TRANSMITTAL OF DEPOSITION SUBPOENA

[Date]

[Name]
[Address]

Re: [Case name]
Our Client : [Name]
Our File : [Number]
Date/Loss : [Date]

Dear [Name]:

Please be advised that this office represents [Name] in the above referenced case. Enclosed please find a Deposition Subpoena—Personal Appearance. Defendant [Company] is requesting your attendance at a deposition. Said deposition is scheduled for [Date], at [Time] in our offices. Please make yourself available to attend. I will be contacting you prior to the deposition to discuss any questions you may have. However, in the interim, should you have any questions or concerns, please feel free to contact me.

Very truly yours,

[Attorney]

Encl.

LETTER 8-2
TRANSMITTAL TO WITNESS OF NOTICE OF DEPOSITION

[Date]

[Name]
[Address]

Re: [Case name]
Our Client : [Name]
Our File : [Number]
Date/Loss : [Date]

Dear [Name]:

Enclosed herewith, please find a copy of [Name]'s Notice of Taking Deposition. Please be advised that [Name] is requesting that you bring with you to the deposition certain documents. Please see page 2 of the notice for the documents [Name] is seeking.

Thank you for your courtesy and cooperation. Should you have any questions or comments, please feel free to contact me.

Very truly yours,

[Signature]

LETTER 8-3
NOTIFICATION TO WITNESS OF SCHEDULED DEPOSITION ENCLOSING DEPOSITION TRANSCRIPTS

[Date]

[Name]
[Address]

Re: [Case name]

Insured	:	[Name]
Our File	:	[Number]
Date/Loss	:	[Date]

Dear [Name]:

Please be advised that the [Name]'s attorney has set your deposition for [Date] at [Time]. The deposition will be held at the law firm of [Name] located at [Address]. Please be further advised that the attorney has requested that you produce documents at the time of deposition. Enclosed herewith, please find a copy of the Notice of Taking Deposition (see page 2 for documents to be produced).

If the date and time of your deposition is inconvenient, please contact either myself or my secretary, [Name], and we will try to reschedule the deposition for a more convenient date/time.

In addition, please find enclosed deposition transcripts of [Name], and the report of [Name] (Defendant's expert).

Your courtesy, cooperation, and assistance in this matter is greatly appreciated. Should you have any questions or comments, please feel free to call.

Very truly yours,

[Attorney]

LETTER 8-4
LETTER TO NONPARTY CONCERNING TAKING OF DEPOSITION

[Date]

[Name]
[Address]

Re: [Case name]

As we discussed on the phone today, this office represents [Name] in the above-referenced (case or accident). As I informed you, your testimony concerning the facts of the (case or accident) as witnessed by you will be very helpful to our client. Therefore, I wish to thank you again for agreeing to come to our office, located at [Address], on [Date], at [Time] o'clock to be deposed concerning the (briefly summarize the scope of the deposition).

As we discussed, you will be served with a subpoena requiring your attendance at the deposition. Service of the subpoena, which is required by [federal/state] law, is the method by which you are entitled to witness fees and mileage expenses. It also compels your attendance under penalty of law. Your witness fee will be enclosed with the subpoena.

If you have any problem with attending the deposition at the time and place noted above, please call me at [phone number], or the attorney for whom I work, [name], at [phone number] immediately so that we may reschedule.

Very truly yours,

[Paralegal]
Legal Assistant to
[Attorney]

cc: All parties

LETTER 8-5
NOTIFICATION OF TIME OF DEPOSITION

[Date]

[Name]
[Address]

Re: [Case name]
Our Client : [Name]
Our File : [Number]
Date/Loss : [Date]

Dear [Name]:

Please be advised that your deposition has been set for [Date] at [Time] in our offices. Please meet me here a half hour before the deposition so that we may discuss your testimony.

Thank you for your courtesy and cooperation. Should you have any questions or comments, please feel free to contact me.

Very truly yours,

[Signature]

LETTER 8-6
LETTER STIPULATING TO TAKING OF DEPOSITION

[Date]

[Name]
[Address]

Re: [Case name]: Deposition of [Deponent's name]

Pursuant to our telephone call of [Date], this letter will confirm our agreement on the deposition of your client, [Deponent's name] on [Date], at [Time] o'clock [a.m.][p.m.] at [Address].

As we discussed on the phone, your client will bring certain documents to the deposition, including [List the documents].

If you or your client have a problem with the time and place noted above, please call me at [Phone], or my supervising attorney, [Name], at [Phone], as soon as possible so that we can make alternative arrangements.

Very truly yours,

[Paralegal]
Legal Assistant to
[Attorney]

cc: All parties

LETTER 8-7
LETTER NOTIFYING COUNSEL OF DEFECTIVE NOTICE OF DEPOSITION

[Date]

[Name]
[Address]

Re: [Case name]
Civil No.: [ ]

Dear [Opposing counsel]:

This is to confirm our conversation of [Date]. We have received the Notice of Deposition of [Name of deponent] in the above-captioned case. Pursuant to Rule 32(d)(1) of the Federal Rules of Civil Procedure, we note an error in the notice. Specifically, (the deposition has been noticed subsequent to the discovery cutoff date, which is [Date]) (the name of the deponent has not been included in the notice) (the location of the deposition is greater than 75 miles from the [Name] County courthouse, and therefore outside the statutory jurisdiction) (the notice fails to designate the place where the examination is to be conducted). We request that you correct the error as soon as possible.

By notifying you of the error in the Notice of Deposition, we reserve our right, under Rule 32(d)(1), to object to the deposition, in whole or in part, before trial.

Thank you for your continuing cooperation.

Very truly yours,
[Attorney]
Attorney for (Plaintiff/Defendant)
[Name of party]

LETTER 8-8
LETTER ADVISING CLIENT OF DEPOSITION 1

[Date]

[Plaintiff's name]
[Address]

Re: Case No. __________; in the __________ Judicial District Court in and for __________County, [State), [Plaintiff] vs. [Defendant].

Dear [Name of plaintiff]:

The defendant in the case, [Name], has noticed your deposition for [Day of week], [Month], [Date], 19____. As I have previously explained to you, a deposition is an informal setting in which the defendant's attorney will ask you questions regarding the accident. A court reporter will be in attendance to take down your sworn testimony in written form, and sometime afterwards, we will receive a copy of the transcript which you will be asked to review and sign.

I would like to discuss the deposition in greater detail with you, and request that you contact my paralegal, [Name], to set up a convenient time for you approximately one week in advance of the scheduled deposition.

Please let us know immediately if the scheduled date of the deposition presents a conflict for you.

Very truly yours,

[Attorney]

LETTER 8-9
LETTER ADVISING CLIENT OF DEPOSITION 2

[Date]

[Name]
[Address]

Re: [Case name]

Our Client	:	[Name]
Our File No	:	[Number]
Date/Loss	:	[Date]

Dear [Name]:

The plaintiff in the above matter has requested your deposition, and by law you are required to attend:

DATE:	[Month/Day/Year]
TIME:	[Time]
PLACE:	[Location] [Address]

We will attend the deposition to protect your interest. Please be at the above address about 30 minutes before the deposition so that we can advise you concerning it.

Please sign and return the enclosed copy of this letter to confirm that you will attend and give your telephone number where you can be reached during the day.

In the event any emergency arises which would prevent you from attending the scheduled deposition, contact us without delay. We will advise you promptly if our plans change.

Your cooperation in this matter is essential to a proper defense in this action. If you have any questions concerning this matter, please feel free to contact me at any time.

Very truly yours,

[Signature]

I will attend as requested. Signed: ______________________________

Business Phone: ____________ Home Phone: ____________________

LETTER 8-10
LETTER ADVISING CLIENT OF DEPOSITION 3

[Date]

[Name]
[Address]

Re: Preparation for Deposition
[Case name]

Dear [Name]:

This is to advise you that your oral deposition is scheduled for [Tme] at [Location] and your presence is necessary. This is an important step in the handling of your case. A deposition involves questioning of you under oath before a court reporter by the lawyer for the other side about the facts of your case, your injuries, complaints, elements of your damages, as well as background information about you personally.

Because your deposition is one of the most important parts of your case and because we know that you are not familiar with this procedure, it is absolutely necessary for you to meet with me to discuss the deposition procedure. In fact, the oral deposition may require our talking to you on more than one occasion.

I have scheduled an appointment for you to be in my office on [Date] at [Time], so that we can prepare for your deposition.

Please bring with you to our meeting any medical bills, invoices, or other bills relating to your injuries or damages that you have not previously furnished to our offices. Also, if you have lost wages and have any evidence to prove this, such as check stubs before and after the accident, please bring these along.

Please sign and date the enclosed postcard confirming that you will be present at the time and place specified. Please plan on this meeting taking several hours. It is best that you come without your spouse or children so that we can focus on the deposition preparation without distractions. It is also possible that opposing counsel may wish to depose your spouse at a later date, which is another reason why he should be excluded from this preparation, so that his deposition testimony will be his independent recollection.

I am looking forward to seeing you at our meeting.

Sincerely,

[Signature]
Legal Assistant

LETTER 8-11
LETTER ADVISING CLIENT OF DEPOSITION 4

[Date]

[Name]
[Address]

Re: [Case name]: Notice of Deposition

Dear [Name]:

As we discussed last month, the time has come for you to testify at a deposition about the accident, your injuries, and what your life has been like subsequent to the accident. The deposition is scheduled for [Date], at [Time], at [Address]. Parking is available at [Address]. I have enclosed, for your information, the Notice of Deposition which officially informs all parties of the deposition schedule.

[Name of supervising attorney] and I believe that the deposition will require [Amount of time for the deposition] hours of your time. We know that you will do just fine, and we don't want you to be nervous. Both he and I will be present during the deposition to monitor the questions and to assist you.

We will explain the procedure to you in more detail during our predeposition conference. I have tentatively set aside [Date], at [Time] for this meeting. The only persons present will be [Supervising attorney], you, and me. We will explain what you can expect at the deposition, review the subject matters that we believe will be covered during the deposition, answer all of your questions, show you a videotape of a sample deposition, [conduct a mock examination to give you a feel for a deposition,] and review any documents that will help you remember details of the accident. Plan to spend a couple of hours with us.

I have enclosed a list of suggestions for you to keep in mind in preparing for the deposition. We will go over each of these points during the predeposition conference, and it will be helpful if you take a few minutes to review the list. The more prepared you are for the deposition, the more confident and comfortable you will feel when the day arrives.

Please call me as soon as you get this letter to confirm the date of our predeposition conference.

Very truly yours,

[Legal assistant]
Legal Assistant to
[Attorney]

Enclosures

LETTER 8-12
REQUEST TO REDEPOSE OPPOSING PARTY

[Date]

[Name]
[Address]

Re: [Case name]

Dear [Name]:

As a follow up to our conversation of [Date], wherein I indicated new information has come to light regarding your client's involvement in prior business dealings which has direct impact on the present litigation concerning [Name] Corporation, I am enclosing with this letter pages from deposition transcripts of three witnesses who are members of the [Name] Corporation Board of Directors. You will note from the pages enclosed from the depositions of [Name], [Name] and [Name] that your client is a member of several other boards of directors and has been involved in putting together joint ventures for several other projects similar in nature to [Name] Joint Venture, which is the subject of this litigation.

Prior to taking depositions of these witnesses, we had taken the deposition of your client, [Name]. It is our desire to redepose [Name] so that we may have the opportunity to question him regarding his involvement with other business dealings which we feel are directly relevant to the instant litigation.

You have indicated to me that you feel [Name], having been deposed on [Date] for two full days of testimony, has contributed all of the information within his own personal knowledge that has a direct bearing on the instant litigation. You further indicated to me that you would not make [Name] available for further depositions and intend to oppose a motion to compel attendance of [Name] at a second deposition. I am hopeful that we can come to an agreement prior to the necessity of my making a motion to compel. I propose that you allow your client, [Name], to be redeposed for no more than three hours during which time he will be asked questions limited to the following areas: [List]

Please contact my office within the next ten (10) days, or by [Date], if you are willing to enter into a stipulation for a second deposition of [Name], which will not exceed three hours and which will focus on the limited areas discussed above. If I do not hear from you within the prescribed time, I will be forced to move the court for a motion to compel attendance of [Name] at a second deposition.

Sincerely,

[Signature]
Attorney for Defendant

LETTER 8-13
LETTER TO CLIENT (OR WITNESS) IN PREPARATION FOR DEPOSITION 1

[Date]

[Name]
[Address]

Re:

Dear [Name]:

As you know, your deposition has been scheduled for [Time] on [Date] at [Address].

The following information and instructions are offered in an effort to better acquaint you with what is expected of you and how you can be an effective witness at deposition time:

1. PROCEDURE:

Under our law, the opposing lawyer has the right to take your deposition. This means that you will be put under oath, just as you would be in court, and he will ask you questions relating to the case. His questions and your answers will be taken down by a court reporter. One of your lawyers will be present.

The purpose of the deposition is to pick the mind of the witness of all the facts which he may have in his possession which will assist the lawyers in the preparation and trial of the lawsuit. The lawyers will also use the deposition to: 1) evaluate how you will appear to a jury; and 2) determine the settlement value of the case.

There will be no judge or jury present. After the deposition is over, the reporter will type the questions and answers, and all parties will receive copies. The original will be filed with the Court.

Your deposition when properly given can go a long way in assisting your lawyer in handling your litigation either by way of settlement or at the trial. What *YOU* do at the deposition can help you or hurt you, depending upon your attitude, truthfulness and appearance.

If your case goes to trial this deposition can be used at the trial in cross-examination by the other lawyers if your testimony at trial differs from your testimony at the time of the deposition.

It is extremely important, therefore, that you have everything in mind about the case at the time of the deposition. We will review the case with you before the deposition, but it is helpful if you refresh your recollection before you meet with us.

2. <u>PRE-DEPOSITION RECOMMENDATIONS</u>:

A. REFRESH YOUR RECOLLECTIONS by reading any notes that you made about the case. Visit the scene of the event, if possible, and refresh your recollection concerning visibility, obstructions, distances, speeds and the like.

B. HAVE IN YOUR MIND the *general* figures with respect to your time lost from work, amount of wages lost, doctor and hospital bills. The opposing lawyer will be provided the exact figures, but you should have the general amounts in mind.

C. DO NOT MEMORIZE any statement you have given or anything that you are going to say in answer to questions. You should simply visualize what happened and, in your own words, answer any questions concerning it.

D. DO NOT BRING ANYTHING to the deposition unless instructed to by your lawyer—no records, no notes, no photos, etc.

3. <u>YOUR PHYSICAL APPEARANCE</u>:

You should remember that usually the first opportunity that the opposing counsel has to see you comes at the time of the giving of the discovery deposition. It is important that you make a good impression upon opposing counsel and his client and you should appear at deposition time dressed as you would expect to dress if you were actually going to Court to appear before the jury.

A. You should wear clean, neat clothing.

B. Treat all persons in the deposition room with courtesy.

C. Come prepared to exhibit any and all injuries which you have suffered. If this presents a possibly embarrassing situation, let your lawyer know in advance; he can take care of it.

4. <u>HOW TO HANDLE YOURSELF IN THE DEPOSITION</u>:

We know that you would not deliberately state a falsehood, but it is important that you not be trapped into something that is not true. For this reason, LISTEN TO EACH QUESTION CAREFULLY AND BE SURE THAT YOU UNDERSTAND IT BEFORE ANSWERING. If you do not understand a question, ask the other lawyer to repeat it or rephrase it so you do understand it. When you understand the question, then answer it honestly and in a straightforward manner. If you don't know the answer, say that you don't know or don't recall. No one can remember every minute detail. However, the important things you will remember and you should give an honest and full answer to questions on these points.

In a lawsuit, as in all other matters, honesty is the best policy. Telling the truth requires that a witness testify accurately about what he knows. If you tell the truth and tell it accurately, nobody can cross you up. *Never guess* at an answer!

A. UNDERSTAND THE QUESTION before you attempt to give an answer. You can't possibly give a truthful and accurate answer unless you understand the question. If you don't understand, ask the lawyer to repeat it.

B. TAKE YOUR TIME. Give the question as much thought as it requires to understand it and formulate your answer; then give the answer. Do not give a snap answer without thinking. If you need a break, tell your lawyer. The deposition will probably take several hours and you should be comfortable.

C. GIVE AN AUDIBLE ANSWER so the court reporter can get it. Don't nod your head yes or no, do not answer uh-huh, unh-uh, etc. Speak slowly and clearly.

D. BEWARE OF QUESTIONS INVOLVING DISTANCES AND TIME. If you make an estimate, make sure that everyone understands that you are estimating. Think clearly about speeds, distances and intervals of time. If you do not know an answer, say so! *Do not* give it your best guess.

E. DON'T FENCE OR ARGUE WITH THE LAWYER on the other side. He has a right to question you. Don't answer with a question unless the question you are asked is not clear.

F. DON'T LOSE YOUR TEMPER no matter how hard you are pressed. Lose your temper and you may lose the case. If you lose your temper, you have played right into the hands of the other side.

G. IF ASKED WHETHER you have talked to the lawyer on your side or to an investigator, admit it freely. This is perfectly proper.

H. AVOID JOKING AND WISECRACKS. A lawsuit is a serious matter.

I. NEVER VOLUNTEER ANY INFORMATION—JUST ANSWER THE QUESTION—wait until the question is asked . . . answer it, and stop. If "yes" or "no" will answer the question, give that answer and stop. The other lawyer will probably be friendly and will not "bully" you in any manner. His theory will probably be that the more he can get you to say, the more apt you are to put your "foot in your mouth." An incorrect statement may hurt your case.

J. LISTEN TO YOUR LAWYER—From time to time your lawyer may object to some questions. When he does, stop speaking immediately, listen to his objection and follow his instructions.

In a deposition, many of the Rules of Evidence are different than at trial; DO NOT concern yourself with these matters; your lawyer is protecting your rights.

5. CONCLUSION

REMEMBER: PERHAPS THE MOST IMPORTANT ASPECT OF YOUR LAWSUIT IS YOU AND THE APPEARANCE YOU MAKE. IF YOU GIVE THE APPEARANCE OF EARNESTNESS, FAIRNESS, AND HONESTY, AND IF IN GIVING YOUR DISCOVERY DEPOSITION YOU KEEP IN MIND THESE SUGGESTIONS, YOU WILL BE TAKING A GREAT STRIDE TOWARD SUCCESSFUL AND SATISFACTORY COMPLETION OF THE LITIGATION IN WHICH YOU ARE INVOLVED.

Before the deposition you will have the opportunity to meet with your lawyer, to go over the suggestions contained in this letter, and to ask any questions you may have.

We hope this information has been of help to you in understanding what a deposition is and how important it is to your case.

Sincerely,

[Signature]

LETTER 8-14
LETTER TO CLIENT (OR WITNESS) IN PREPARATION FOR DEPOSITION 2

[Date]

[Name]
[Address]

Re: Your Deposition

Dear [Name]:

As you know, your deposition has been scheduled for [Date], at [Location] at the law offices of [Name].

The following information and instructions are offered in an effort to better acquaint you with what is expected of you and how you can be an effective witness at deposition time. We will, of course, meet with you prior to your deposition to thoroughly discuss what will occur at your deposition and to go through your testimony with you. The purpose of this letter is merely to give you some preliminary background about your deposition.

1. *PROCEDURE*:

Under our law, the opposing lawyer has the right to take your deposition. This means that you will be put under oath, just as you would be in court, and he will ask you questions relating to the case. His questions and your answers will be taken down by a court reporter. Your lawyer will be present.

The purpose of the deposition is to inquire about the facts which he may have in his possession which will assist the lawyers in the preparation and trial of the lawsuit. The lawyers will also use the deposition to: 1) evaluate how you will appear to a jury; and 2) determine the settlement value of the case.

There will be no judge or jury present. After the deposition is over, the reporter will type the questions and answers, and all parties will receive copies.

Your deposition when properly given can go a long way in assisting your lawyer in handling your litigation either by way of settlement or at the trial. What *YOU* do at the deposition can help you or hurt you, depending upon your attitude, truthfulness and appearance.

If your case goes to trial this deposition can be used at the trial in cross-examination by the other lawyers if your testimony at trial differs from your testimony at the time of the deposition.

2. *YOUR PHYSICAL APPEARANCE*:

You should remember that usually the first opportunity that the opposing counsel has to see you comes at the time of the discovery deposition. It is important that you make a good impression upon opposing counsel and his client and you should appear at deposition time dressed as you would expect to dress if you were actually going to Court to appear before the jury.

a. You should wear clean, neat clothing.

b. Treat all persons in the deposition room with courtesy.

c. Come prepared to exhibit any and all injuries which you have suffered. If this presents a possibly embarrassing situation, let your lawyer know in advance; he can take care of it.

3. *HOW TO HANDLE YOURSELF IN THE DEPOSITION:*

We know that you would not deliberately state a falsehood, but it is important that you not be trapped into something that is not true. For this reason, LISTEN TO EACH QUESTION CAREFULLY AND BE SURE THAT YOU UNDERSTAND IT BEFORE ANSWERING. If you do not understand a question, ask the other lawyer to repeat it or rephrase it so you do understand it. When you understand the question, then answer it honestly and in a straightforward manner. If you don't know the answer, say that you don't know or don't recall. No one can remember every minute detail. However, the important things you will remember and you should give an honest and full answer to questions on these points.

In a lawsuit, as in all other matters, honesty is the best policy. Telling the truth requires that a witness testify accurately about what he knows. If you tell the truth and tell it accurately, nobody can cross you up. *Never* guess at an answer!

a . UNDERSTAND THE QUESTION before you attempt to give an answer. You can't possibly give a truthful and accurate answer unless you understand the question. If you don't understand, ask the lawyer to repeat it.

b . TAKE YOUR TIME. Give the question as much thought as it requires to understand it and formulate your answer; then give the answer. Do not give a snap answer without thinking. If you need a break, tell your lawyer. The deposition will probably take several hours and you should be comfortable.

c . GIVE AN AUDIBLE ANSWER so the court reporter can get it. Don't nod your head yes or no, do not answer uh-huh, unhuh, etc. Speak slowly and clearly.

d . BEWARE OF QUESTIONS INVOLVING DISTANCES AND TIME. If you make an estimate, make sure that everyone understands that you are estimating. Think clearly about speeds, distances and intervals of time. If you do not know an answer, say so! *Do not* give it your best guess.

e . DON'T FENCE OR ARGUE WITH THE LAWYER on the other side. He has a right to question you. Don't answer with a question unless the question you are asked is not clear.

f . DON'T LOSE YOUR TEMPER no matter how hard you are pressed. Lose your temper and you may lose the case. If you lose your temper, you have played right into the hands of the other side.

g . IF ASKED WHETHER you have talked to the lawyer on your side or to an investigator, admit it freely. This is perfectly proper.

h . AVOID JOKING AND WISECRACKS. A lawsuit is a serious matter.

i . NEVER VOLUNTEER ANY INFORMATION—JUST ANSWER THE QUESTION—wait until the question is asked, answer it, and stop. If "yes" or "no" will answer the question, give that answer and stop. The other lawyer will probably be friendly and will not "bully" you in any manner. His theory will probably be that the more he can get you to say, the more apt you are to put your "foot in your mouth." An incorrect statement may hurt your case.

j . LISTEN TO YOUR LAWYER—From time to time your lawyer may object to some questions. When he does, stop speaking immediately, listen to his objection and follow his instructions.

k . WAIT UNTIL THE LAWYER HAS FINISHED ASKING HIS OR HER QUESTION. Do not anticipate what the question is before he is finished, and do not start nodding your head or answering until he has finished his question. This is a common mistake by people having their deposition taken because we all do this in casual conversation with others. Even though you know what the question is going to be, wait until the attorney is finished speaking.

l . BE CAREFUL OF QUESTIONS IN WHICH THE ATTORNEY PUTS WORDS IN YOUR MOUTH. An attorney sometimes will phrase the answer himself and ask if that answer isn't correct. For example: "You have had some pain for awhile, but you feel fine now, is that correct?" "You would agree with me, would you not, Mr. Witness, that you have no way of knowing what color the traffic signal was for my client?" These questions are different than merely asking you "Do you have pain now?" or "Are you able to tell us what color the traffic signal light was for my client at the time of the accident?" The difference is the attorney is suggesting an answer to you and asking you to agree with it. Do not be intimidated. Do not let the attorney put words in your mouth unless you *fully* agree with what the attorney has said.

4. *CONCLUSION*

REMEMBER: PERHAPS THE MOST IMPORTANT ASPECT OF YOUR LAWSUIT IS YOU AND THE APPEARANCE YOU MAKE. IF YOU GIVE THE APPEARANCE OF EARNESTNESS, FAIRNESS, AND HONESTY, AND IF IN GIVING YOUR DISCOVERY DEPOSITION YOU KEEP IN MIND THESE SUGGESTIONS, YOU WILL BE TAKING A GREAT STRIDE TOWARD SUCCESSFUL AND SATISFACTORY COMPLETION OF THE LITIGATION IN WHICH YOU ARE INVOLVED.

Before the deposition you will have the opportunity to meet with your lawyer, to go over the suggestions contained in this letter, and to ask any questions you may have.

We hope this information has been of help to you in understanding what a deposition is and how important it is to your case.

____

[Signature]

LETTER 8-15
LETTER TO EXPERT WITNESS IN PREPARATION FOR DEPOSITION 1

ATTORNEY WORK PRODUCT
MAINTAIN SEPARATELY

PERSONAL AND CONFIDENTIAL

[Date]
[Name]

Re: [Case name]

Dear [Name]:

This letter is to remind you that your deposition has been scheduled for [Date] at the hour of [Time]. I will meet with you at [Time] in your office on [Date] to go over the facts and discuss your testimony.

A deposition is the taking of testimony, under oath, in the presence of a court reporter. A transcript will be prepared of your testimony. After you've had a chance to review and correct it, the original transcript will be filed with the defendants' attorney. Your testimony, or parts of it, may be used at trial in an effort to discredit your testimony.

Many times a witness fails to appreciate the importance of deposition testimony. Although there will be no judge or jury present and a deposition is sometimes considered a "dry run," you will be testifying to facts and opinions to which you will be held at the time of trial. Deposition <u>is therefore just as important as the testimony you give at trial and you should prepare for your deposition with the same intensity and concern as if you were preparing for trial</u>.

Although we can't overemphasize the importance of your deposition testimony, there is no reason to be apprehensive with respect to your deposition. If you will carefully consider and follow our suggestions, you will in all probability be an effective witness.

I. SUGGESTIONS

A. Present Your Best Appearance—The demeanor and appearance of a professional is just as important as what he or she has to say. The other attorney will be evaluating your appearance, demeanor and testimony. Please dress professionally, neatly and according to your usual habit. You should wear conservative business clothes to your deposition.

B. Review Records Carefully—Remember that the medical records, if complete and accurate, may well be our first and best source of claims of substandard care. Judges and jurors invariably give great weight to contemporaneous medical records made before parties and medical personnel had any reason or motive to be inaccurate. It is vital that you carefully review medical and hospital records, x-ray reports, x-rays, and any other material you have in connection with this case. A thorough knowledge of the patient's medical course and the records will obviously make you far more effective as a witness and much better prepared to respond to a searching cross-examination. Your testimony should create the impression you are well aware of the patient's course.

C. Be Sure You Understand the Question Before You Answer—Listen carefully to all questions. If you do not understand a question asked by the other lawyer, make no attempt to answer it without first seeking clarification. An inaccurate answer in response to a misunderstood question can materially affect the results of any case.

D. Be Prepared to Admit You Don't Know—Do not feel that just because a question is asked you are expected to know the answer to it. Be able to say "I don't know" without embarrassment.

E. Avoid Exaggeration—Exaggeration is a form of untruthfulness. Do not try to improve upon the facts of this case as this conduct is invariably recognized by the other attorney, who may later be able to exploit any inaccuracies to his advantage. During trial, if the fact finders were to believe you had exaggerated on a material point, they may well surmise that you have exaggerated on other significant matters and could choose to disregard your testimony entirely.

F. Every Question Is Not a Trick Question—Do not look for traps in every question. There are not many trick questions, and, if one comes along, I will help you out by making objections and pointing out the nature of the question. If you try to second-guess each question, you will create the appearance of calculation, hesitation, apprehension, or possibly simple ignorance.

G. Know Your Material—Although you're not expected to know everything there is to know about the medicine in this case, in many instances it is helpful to review the anatomy in question or, in the event medications are involved, to review PDR or a basic pharmacology text concerning drug indications and contraindications.

H. Testify on a Professional Level—It is entirely possible your deposition will be submitted to another doctor for review as a potential expert witness. Although you should avoid overly technical language, you should also avoid any tendency to oversimplify the medicine as you want any expert reviewing your testimony to be impressed by your professionalism.

I. Answer Clearly and Firmly—Speak up so that you can be heard. Answer each question with a verbal response. The reporter cannot record gestures, nods, or shrugs.

J. Take Sufficient Time to Think About Questions—Be thoughtful about your answers. Quick answers suggest either that you are not carefully considering before you answer or that you have rehearsed your answer. We don't want the appearance you have memorized your answers.

K. Do Not Volunteer Information—Answer the question as briefly as possible—answer each question with a "Yes" or "No" where possible, and do not volunteer additional information. Do not supply information not requested by the question even though you may think it is relevant. If the other attorney does not ask you all that you know or does not ask critical questions, do not volunteer information. Under ordinary circumstances, we will not bring out our side of the case during the deposition as all this does is give the other side a better opportunity to prepare for our case before hearing. Many doctors inform us that they are depressed or disappointed following a deposition, feeling they have not been given an opportunity to completely tell, explain or bring out their opinions of the case. This is exactly what we want as we prefer to put our case on at trial, not during your deposition. Please avoid any natural tendency you have to "teach" or "educate" the other attorney, as your purpose is neither to educate the other attorney nor to provide a game plan for our claims

L. Testify Only To What You Know—The law requires only that you testify according to your best memory. If you are uncertain about the answer to a question, indicate this uncertainty in your response. If a question is asked and you need to refer to the records, do so. A deposition is not a memory quiz, and you aren't required to memorize the records before your deposition.

M. Stay Within Your Field of Expertise—Don't offer opinions in areas of medicine that aren't within your area of expertise.

N. Concede Points That Should Be Conceded—Don't regard it as an admission of ignorance to indicate that your opinion is not absolutely conclusive or that you don't know the answer to a particular question. Honesty may require testimony of this nature and prevent your getting out on a limb in an area beyond your expertise.

O. Stick To Your Guns on Firm Opinions and Favorable Facts—Stick to your guns on answers about which you are certain or positive. Generally speaking, there will be conflict in the testimony. Even when your recollection of events or opinion is in conflict with others or the literature, do not water down positive opinions or testimony with qualifying phrases such as "I think" or "I believe." The last thing you want to do is be a limp witness simply because you don't like controversy (that's what lawsuits are all about). Don't be overly conciliatory in the hopes the deposition will end sooner—it won't.

P. Answer All Questions Openly and Honestly—Respond frankly. Any display of embarrassment or reluctance to answer will tend to discredit your testimony.

Q. Your Right to Qualify "Yes" or "No" Answers—Don't allow yourself to be forced into a flat "Yes" or "No" answer if a qualified answer if required. You have a right to explain or qualify your answer if that is necessary for a truthful response. In the same vein, it will occasionally become necessary to explain an answer where you realize an answer without some explanation will be potentially incriminating. Use common sense in answering any question where you feel a limited answer or a simple "Yes" or "No" response will create the wrong impression.

R. The "Did-You-Know" or "Do-You-Recall" Questions—The "Did-you-know" or "Do-you-recall" questions can be trick questions, as answering such questions with a flat "No" may imply that what you were being asked to recall could have happened, but you simply don't remember one way or another. If the proper answer is "It didn't happen," point that out. If you really don't remember, say so. If, however, an event didn't happen or a statement wasn't made, advise the other attorney it isn't a question of recalling or not recalling, but rather "It didn't happen".

S. Hypothetical Questions—The other attorney may ask you to assume certain facts and then proceed to question you concerning compliance with applicable standards accepting those facts as true. This is especially true in diagnosis cases where the patient's version of events differs substantially from what is in the records or was reported to or seen by the physician. You should answer those questions as asked (unless asked to assume facts that are medically impossible or inconsistent with your actual knowledge of events), even if your answers seem unfavorable. Remember, it is up to the attorneys to establish which version of events is more believable and plausible.

T. Familiarity With Standards of Care—You must be familiar with the standards of care in order to testify concerning standards. Factors to consider in this regard are your actual knowledge of standards, acquaintanceships with physicians in the community where the treatment in question occurred, the fact that physicians and/or specialists train in approved medical schools with fairly standardized teaching programs and texts being utilized, the board certification by a national certifying board, your practice at a number of hospitals and an opportunity to verify similar modes of practice, your attendance at local, state and national meetings and opportunity to verify similar modes of practice in other communities, and the fact that with improved communication and literature that is desseminated countrywide, most physicians throughout the country are routinely exposed to prevailing practices.

II. DEPOSITION DEMEANOR

A. Be Professional—Again we can't stress enough the importance of being a pleasant, confident, professional witness. Don't be smug or cavalier, and don't talk down to opposing counsel. Don't use slang or profanity—let the attorney know you are a true professional.

B. Don't Lose Your Temper—If the attorney can provoke you to a display of anger or sarcasm, he may consider this a positive weapon that he can call upon in discrediting your testimony at trial. Unthinking remarks in a deposition may come back to haunt you, as most individuals do not think clearly when angry—i.e., the brain turns off when the emotion turns on.

C. Be Courteous—Be courteous to the other attorney no matter what the provocation. If the attorney is discourteous to you and you don't rise to the bait, you are beating the attorney at his game. If an attorney becomes abusive, we'll intervene. If you're abusive or haughty you may give the attorney a special motive to make a special effort to build a case against you.

D. Don't Get Excited—If it is necessary to admit something you think is "damaging" or "potentially damaging" to our case, do it if a truthful response would require such an admission. However, don't call attention to it by becoming agitated or excited.

E. Be Reasonable—Be able to concede gracefully points which in good faith you should concede.

F. Maintain a Consistent Demeanor—Resist any temptation to show exasperation, boredom or fatigue even though the questioning may be extensive, uninformed or ridiculous. You will beat the attorney at his own game if you maintain your composure.

G. Create Best Possible Impression—Sit upright, hold your head erect and try to avoid nervous mannerisms. We're out to create an impression of the competent, calm, cool, confident physician—the type of doctor the other attorney would want to come to if he or she wasn't defending a case contrary to your opinions.

III. MEDICAL-LEGAL CONSIDERATIONS

Here are some of the more basic medical-legal considerations arising in the typical medical negligence:

A. Standard of Care—As the plaintiff we must generally establish a standard of care for physicians or specialists practicing within the defendant's specialty field (ordinarily by expert testimony), deviation from the standard of care, and some harm resulting from the claimed negligence. Remember, there is a broad range of practice within the so-called "standard of care." A standard of care is not a line above which all good doctors practice and below which a doctor automatically practices bad medicine. Rather, the standard of care may involve a broad range of care encompassing ranges of acceptable practice all the way from excellent care down to the minimally acceptable standard of care. A physician practicing within this wide range of care falls within the so-called "standard." Don't be afraid to concede that there are a number of situations which involve professional judgment. But also remember there are situations when a doctor can be guilty of negligence, even where judgment was involved.

1. Surgical-Medical Judgment—A physician is entitled to be judged prospectively (from the viewpoint of the doctor before the outcome of the case was known), not with the vision of hindsight. Even if a doctor made a mistake in judgment, this does not necessarily mean he practiced below the standard of care unless it can be said that the mistake was a mistake a substantial majority of doctors would not have made under the same circumstances. Judgment calls are protected, and when discussing judgment calls and clinical decisions, be sure to characterize them as such.

2. Conduct to be Judged at the Time of Treatment—Please remember that in terms of informed consent and the treatment in question, a physician is entitled to be judged by then-existing standards of care, not what is being done at this time.

3. Different Schools—Often there are different schools of thought, i.e., different courses of treatment or surgical techniques. A physician is not liable for his selection of a particular course unless his selection is unconsistant with the skill and care of others in his field and speciality. As long as a "respectable minority" of physicians would use the treatment course and/or the surgical technique, the medical care is acceptable even if other doctors would have done things differently. Don't be embarrassed or reluctant to admit you may be of a different school or view with respect to any phase of treatment and would do things differently than others. The fact you do things differently does not mean you set or violate the standard unless there is evidence no other physician would do what you do.

4. Bad-Result Cases—The fact that the patient didn't improve or suffered a complication isn't evidence of bad medicine unless the result was due to inappropriate care. There is no guarantee of cure, of diagnosis or good result in medicine or in the medical-legal arena.

B. Probability Versus Possibility—Anything is possible, and in medical-legal situations it is quite important to understand the distinction between "probability" and "possibility." The law suggests that probability means "more likely than not" or, put another way, a 51 percent or greater probability of a causal link. It is important to distinguish between probabilities and possibilities in testifying. If, for example, something happening after surgery could "possibly" be related to surgery but more than likely was not, there would be inadequate evidence of causation. Keep these distinctions in mind when testifying and be careful to explain when you are talking about "possibilities."

C. Informed Consent—Under [State] law a physician is required to discuss "substantial risks" but not all the risks of a given course of treatment or surgery. The term "substantial" is obviously quite subjective, but generally is held to mean that a doctor is required to disclose major, catastrophic risks which are inherent in the procedure and the more minor risks that occur frequently, e.g., bleeding, infection and the like. The primary requirement is that the patient be informed in some fashion of the magnitude of the proposed surgery or course of treatment in order that he or she may balance the risks against the hoped for benefits and thus give a knowledgeable or informed consent to treatment. This information can be communicated in a multitude of ways while a variety of factors may influence the patient's ability or willingness to either listen to or remember what was said. Even if the patient wasn't informed of a substantial risk, there remains the secondary question whether the patient would have proceeded with the surgery or treatment had the risk been disclosed. Most patients are by nature inherently optimistic when it comes to treatment and believe disclosed risks are complications that happen only to others. A patient who is ill or disabled will accept just about any risk by rationalizing that "it will happen to others, not me."

D. Literature—You may be asked whether you consider certain texts, treatises, journals, articles or publications "reliable authority." This is a condition precedent to cross-examination concerning statements in the literature. Considerations in terms of determining whether literature is "reliable authority" or that you should be bound by the printed word are that medicine is both an art and a science and that there is no "black and white" in medicine nor any Bible. The literature reflects many schools of thought. Much of the literature is woefully out-of-date by the time it is published, especially textbooks. Textbooks are infrequently referred to by the experienced practitioner and are rarely compelling. Remember, too, that there is an unevenness in quality of texts, as a number of doctors may contribute chapters to a text.

Literature is not authoritative simply because it conveys an opinion in writing. Most physicians practice medicine and perform surgery based upon experience and training, not what is written in a book. Don't hesitate to disagree with so-called authorities if, based on your experience and training, you are convinced they are wrong. If you have a sound basis for an opinion, the contrary opinion in an article or treatise will not necessarily discredit your opinion.

You should hesitate to give blanket approval of any text or journal unless you could say you would unequivocally agree with everything said. Rather, you should reserve the right to disagree with opinions expressed in a text or article no matter how authoritative the source, as there probably isn't a book or article in print you would agree with 100 percent. Be prepared for the question "What texts or literature do you consider authoritative or reliable authority?" In answering that question, you may unwittingly be endorsing literature from which the attorney will then attempt to cross-examine you.

If asked what journals you read or subscribe to and whether you consider them reliable authority, remember that many points of view appear in widely read, referred-to journals and the fact an article appears in a respected journal does not necessarily mean a physician must accept it as authoritative. There are virtually millions of articles expressing a multitude of views in a field involving both art and science where the literature could best be described as an adjunctive aid in the real world practice of medicine. You should not feel uncomfortable admitting that you haven't read a particular article or text or stating that you don't agree with the author's opinion. (Remember the Physicians' Desk Reference is a manufacturers' book that does not create any standard of care. The same is true of package inserts and manufacturers' literature.)

We have set aside sufficient time on the day of your deposition to discuss the details of our case. If you will follow my suggestions, we will have more than enough time to cover the substantive issues. Please review this letter carefully before your deposition and review the medical records several times before the day of the deposition, as you should be completely familiar with the records before our meeting.

If you have any questions, think there is anything that should be discussed before our meeting, or don't have complete records, give me a call.

This letter constitutes attorney work product and should not be placed with patient records. Attorney correspondence, correspondence with your insurance carrier, court pleadings, medical literature and the like should be separated from the medical records and placed in a separate medical-legal file. You may, however, bring both files to the deposition, as the other attorney will have no access to your personal file.

Very truly yours,

[Signature]

LETTER 8-16
LETTER TO EXPERT WITNESS IN PREPARATION FOR DEPOSITION 2

[Date]

[Name]
[Address]

Re: [Case name]

Dear [Name]:

As you know, your deposition has been scheduled for [Time] on [Date] at [Address].

The following information and instructions are offered in an effort to better acquaint you with what is expected of you and how you can be an effective expert witness at deposition time:

1. PROCEDURE

You have been declared as an expert witness for trial on behalf of [Client's name]. Therefore, attorneys for the other parties have a right to depose or question you. A court reporter and videographer will be present to record your testimony. An attorney from our office will also be present to represent your interests.

The purpose of the deposition is to give the other attorneys a chance to delve into your expert conclusions and the reasoning behind those conclusions. Your testimony may be used to evaluate how the (jury/judge) will react to you and to determine what effect your testimony may have on settlement possibilities.

No judge or jury will be present during your deposition. However, you will be expected to sign and make corrections to the final typed version of your testimony. The typed transcript might then be used to strengthen or attack your oral testimony during trial.

2. PREPARING FOR YOUR DEPOSITION:

Review your education, work experience, writings, achievements, awards/commendations, and so forth. Contact this office if there is anything in your background that may be unfavorable and might discredit your opinion, or if you have written anything that appears to conflict with the opinion you have reached in this matter.

Visit the scene again, review the photographs, or reexamine the product if it will help your evaluation. Contact this office if you see or hear anything that changes your previous evaluation.

Review all the paperwork that you used to arrive at any conclusions you may have drawn. Double-check any figures you used in mathematical equations.

3. PHYSICAL APPEARANCE:

Please dress as you would if you were going to appear in court before a judge and jury. Your testimony will have more of an impact on the attorneys present if you appear knowledgeable and powerful.

4. DURING THE DEPOSITION:

Be prepared to discuss the following: your qualifications, educational background, work experience, writings.

Be prepared to divulge other testimony you have given in depositions and trials, whether you have testified for plaintiffs or defendants, what your conclusions have been, and so on.

Be prepared to list everything (materials, writings, information, statistics) that you used to arrive at your expert opinions.

Be prepared to discuss your fees and expenses and the payment schedule that you expect to receive for your evaluation, deposition and court testimony.

Be prepared to explain why you were hired, specifically which issues you were asked to evaluate, or what you were asked to do or accomplish.

Remember that your opinions must be based on reasonable probability; you do not necessarily have to have relied on proven scientific experiments and conclusions.

If you are asked a question that contains technical errors, ask the attorney (with the corrections inserted) if that is the question he or she had in mind. Do not answer a technically incorrect answer as it stands, no matter how persistent the questioning attorney remains.

If you are asked a question with an obscure technical term with which you are unfamiliar or that may have two meanings, do not hesitate to admit that you are not familiar with the term or to ask for clarification.

Answer with an unqualified "Yes" or "No" only if you are absolutely sure that the question contains no errors. It is permissible to ask for a question to be repeated or rephrased if you did not understand or could not hear. It is also permissible to say that you do not remember or do not know, if that is truly the case.

Refrain from nodding your head, or saying "Uh-huh" or 'Uh-uh," or speaking simultaneously with the attorney, as the court reporter must record everything that is said.

Be prepared to answer difficult, leading, or argumentative questions.

Avoid exaggerating, arguing, or being condescending, as that will only serve to irritate the attorney and possibly hurt your position as an unbiased expert.

The examining attorney is not allowed to abuse the deponent. If you interpret the attorney's question or mannerism as abusive, hesitate before answering the question. If that question is not allowed in a deposition, I will interject an objection. If I do not object, be prepared to answer the question calmly and rationally.

Do not converse with any of the attorneys other than during the deposition in the question-and-answer session. Do not speak with them before or after the deposition or during breaks. Remember that they may be trying to find ways to impeach you. If they want to hire you for another matter, they can approach you after the trial is over.

5. CONCLUSION:

You may be asked to speculate, for example, divulge whether you might do what the plaintiff or defendant did in the same circumstances, without regard to all the expert information you retain. Remember that such a question cannot banish hindsight from the reasoning of the person answering such a question, nor can it delete your vantage point with your superior knowledge and background.

If there are any written materials or items that you think you might need to explain your theories or conclusions, check with the attorney before taking them to the deposition.

An attorney from this office will meet with you before the deposition. If you have any questions regarding the facts of the case, please do not hesitate to contact this office before the date of your deposition.

Sincerely,

[Signature]

LETTER 8-17
TRANSMITTAL OF TRIAL EXHIBITS TO EXPERT WITNESS

[Date]

[Name]
[Address]

Re: [Case name]
OCSC Case No. : [Number]
Date of Loss : [Date]
Our File No. : [Number]

Dear [Name]:

My apologies for the delay in sending the trial exhibits to your office. The exhibits should arrive at your office on or before [Date]. They have been sent UPS—ground service.

If you have any questions or comments, please do not hesitate to contact this office.

Very truly yours,

[Signature]
Legal Assistant to [Attorney]

LETTER 8-18
LETTER TO EXPERT WITNESS TRANSMITTING VARIOUS DOCUMENTS AND SUMMARIZING CASE

[Date]

[Name]
[Address]

Re: [Case name]
OCSC Case No. : [Number]
Date of Loss : [Date]
Our File No. : [Number]

Dear [Name]:

Enclosed is a copy of the deposition transcript of [Name], a copy of the Eveready one-page report regarding leakage, and a summary of the facts of this case. The trial in this matter is scheduled to take place in the [County] Superior Court, commencing on [Date].

Summary of the Facts

This case involves battery alkaline burns to plaintiff's buttocks which allegedly occurred during a drive from [Place], to plaintiff's home in [Place], on March 25, 1990. On that date, plaintiff installed eight (8) Eveready Energizer "D" size batteries, which he had allegedly purchased that morning, into his JVC stereo cassette player, which he had received from his sister as a Christmas gift in 1989. Plaintiff installed two of the subject batteries backwards.

After installing the batteries, plaintiff drove up to [Place] to go skiing. When plaintiff arrived at the resort, he allegedly placed the cassette player on the driver's seat of his truck.

When he arrived back at the truck to return home late that evening, plaintiff moved the cassette player and sat on the seat where the radio had been resting. About halfway down the mountain, plaintiff noticed an excruciating pain in his buttocks.

If you have any questions or comments regarding this action, please do not hesitate to contact this office.

Very truly yours,

[Signature]
Legal Assistant to [Attorney]

LETTER 8-19
LETTER TO OPPOSING COUNSEL REGARDING EXCHANGE OF EXPERT INFORMATION

[Date]

[Name]
[Address]

Re: [Case name]
OCSC Case No. : [Number]
Date of Loss : [Date]
Our File No. : [Number]

Dear [Name]:

As you know, we have already scheduled the deposition of your expert to take place on [Date]. I have just discovered that the formal Demand for Exchange of Experts was inadvertently sent to plaintiff's prior counsel. Technically, this means that there is no formal Demand filed by any party in this action, and therefore, there can be no proper designation of experts pursuant to Section 2034.

Because you have the burden of proof, it would seem that it would be in your best interest to have an exchange of expert information which would be effective in the eyes of the Court. Accordingly, I am serving an additional copy of the Demand for Exchange of Expert Witness Information. This additional copy which is being served at this time will not change the previously scheduled deposition of Dr. [Name].

At this time, I plan to list my expert witnesses on the previously scheduled exchange date of [Date].

If you have any objection to the service of this Demand, please notify me immediately. Thank you for your assistance.

Very truly yours,

[Signature]

LETTER 8-20
NOTIFICATION OF CHANGE IN DATE FOR EXCHANGE OF EXPERT WITNESS INFORMATION

[Date]

[Name]
Attorney at Law
[Address]

[Name]
[Law firm]
[Address]

[Name]
Attorney at Law
[Address]

Re: [Case name]
Our Client : [Name]
Our File : [Number]

Dear [Counsel]:

Please recall that the demand for exchange of expert witness information recently served by this office specified [Date], as the date for the exchange. However, I have since been advised that [Date] falls on a Sunday this year. Therefore, under [State] Civil Code Section 10, the appropriate exchange date would be the following Monday, [Date].

In order to avoid confusion, I ask that each of you sign a copy of this letter on the line provided and return the signed copy to my office, acknowledging the agreed-upon exchange date. I sincerely appreciate your anticipated courtesy and cooperation. Should you have any questions or comments, please do not hesitate to call.

Very truly yours,

[Attorney]

LETTER 8-21
REPORT TO CLIENT/WORKERS' COMPENSATION CARRIER OF INTENT TO ATTEND PLAINTIFF'S DEPOSITION

[Date]

[Name]
[Insurance Company]
[Address]

Re: [Case name]
Your Claim No. : [Number]
Insured : [Name]
Date of Loss : [Date]
Our File No. : [Number]

Dear [Name]:

Defendant has sent out a notice to take plaintiff's deposition on [Date]. Unless you instruct me otherwise, I will attend plaintiff's deposition so that we may obtain more information concerning the facts of this case and determine plaintiff's ability as a witness.

I will prepare a deposition summary for your review.

Very truly yours,

[Attorney]

LETTER 8-22
FAX MESSAGE WITH NOTICE OF ABSENCE FROM DEPOSITION AND REQUESTING COPY OF TRANSCRIPT

TO: ____
NAME LOCATION

FROM: ____
SENDER'S NAME

RE: ____
CASE NAME

****

MESSAGE : Please be advised that [Name] will not be attending the [Date] deposition of [Name]. However, we would like to request a copy of the transcript. Thank you.

****

NUMBER OF PAGES (INCLUDING THIS SHEET): 1

DATE: ______________________ TIME: ____________

IF YOU HAVE ANY QUESTIONS OR PROBLEMS WITH THIS TRANSMISSION, PLEASE CALL [TELEPHONE]

LETTER 8-23
TRANSMITTAL OF DEPOSITION TRANSCRIPT WITH CORRECTION REQUEST 1

[Date]

[Attorney]
[Firm Name]
[Address]

Re: [Case name]; Cause No. [Number]

Dear [Name]:

Enclosed please find your copy of the depositions of [Names] as taken on [Date] in the above-referenced matter. Also enclosed are the original correction sheets to their depositions.

Please make arrangements for them to read your copy of their depositions and execute the original correction sheet to our office so that we may file them with the original depositions.

Since federal law requires that original depositions be filed within 30 days of their availability to the witnesses, we would appreciate your executing the original correction sheets within 30 days from the receipt of this letter and returning the same to our office on or before [Date].

Sincerely,

[Signature]
Court Reporter Service

Enclosures

LETTER 8-24
TRANSMITTAL OF DEPOSITION TRANSCRIPT WITH CORRECTION REQUEST 2

[Date]

[Name]
[Address]

Re: [Case name]

Dear [Name]:

Your deposition in the above-entitled action which was taken on [Date] has now arrived in our office for your review and corrections, which must be accomplished within thirty (30) days or by [Date]. We are sending you a copy of the transcript which you can mark up with pencil and return to us. We will then have corrections typed on a separate piece of paper and send it to the court reporter to be attached to your deposition. It would be helpful to us if in addition to correcting the deposition transcript itself, you prepared a list on a separate piece of paper listing your corrections by page and line and incorrect word along with correct word or phrase.

Please remember that you may not rewrite or change any portion of your deposition transcript. You are merely to check it for accuracy as you recall your testimony. You may wish to correct spelling of certain names or places. You may also wish to correct matters of fact. If you have a serious problem with the way the transcript has recorded your answers, please contact our office immediately so that we can call it to the attention of the court reporter. She will then compare the transcript with her tape and make the necessary corrections. Occasionally there are mistakes made in the transcript which can be corrected by the court reporter by referring back to the original tape.

It is important that we have your corrections within the statutory time period or we will lose the opportunity to make corrections in the transcript, and inconsistencies or inaccuracies will remain part of the record.

If you have any questions regarding this procedure or need assistance, please do not hesitate to contact our office. Thank you for your cooperation and prompt attention to this request.

Sincerely,

[Signature]

LETTER 8-25
TRANSMITTAL OF DEPOSITION TRANSCRIPT WITH CORRECTION REQUEST 3

[Date]

[Deponent's Name]
[Address]

Re: [Case name]

Dear [Deponent]:

Enclosed please find the transcript of your deposition in the [Name] case taken on [Date]. Please review the transcript and make any changes or corrections on the amendment sheets enclosed. Please sign both the signature page and the amendment sheets, have your signature notarized, and return them to us in the enclosed envelope. You do not need to return the transcript to us.

Thank you for your courtesy and cooperation.

[Signature]

LETTER 8-26
TRANSMITTAL OF DEPOSITION TRANSCRIPT WITH CORRECTION REQUEST 4

[Date]

[Name]
[Address]

Re: [Case name]
Our Clients : [Names]
Our File No : [Number]
Date/Loss : [Date]

Dear [Name]:

Enclosed is your original deposition taken on [Date], in the above-captioned case. We are sending it to you at this time for your review, correction, and signature on the witness line on page [Number]. Please date and sign where indicated.

If you do make changes, please draw a single line through words to be changed, write the change above it in ink, and place your initials in the right-hand margin. Please do not obliterate the answer as originally transcribed.

Please return the signed original deposition within five days to this office in the self-addressed, stamped envelope provided.

If you have any questions regarding the above, please do not hesitate to call this office. Your cooperation in this matter is appreciated.

Very truly yours,

[Signature]

LETTER 8-27
TRANSMITTAL OF DEPOSITION TRANSCRIPT WITH CORRECTION REQUEST 5

[Date]

[Name]
[Address]

Re: [Case name]

Dear [Name]:

I have enclosed a copy of your deposition in the above-captioned case. Please review it and make any necessary corrections on the amendment sheet which is enclosed separately. Please sign both the amendment sheet and the enclosed signature page and have your signature notarized.

You are welcome to keep this copy of your deposition. Please return the amendment page and notarized signature page to me within TEN (10) days so that I may file them with the court. If they are not filed with the court within this time period, the court reporter will file your deposition with the court without benefit of any amendments you may wish to make.

Please call me at [Telephone] if I may answer any questions for you.

Very truly yours,

[Signature]

Enclosures

LETTER 8-28
TRANSMITTAL OF DEPOSITION CORRECTION SHEET FOR SIGNATURE

[Date]

[Name]
[Address]

Re: [Case name]

Dear [Name]:

Enclosed is a correction sheet for your deposition transcript on which the changes noted in your letter of [Date] have been typed.

Please review the correction sheet, sign it before a notary, and return the completed packet to my attention. Should you note any misinterpretations of your handwritten copy, please line through the error, write in the word(s), and initial the handwritten change(s) on the correction sheet. Feel free to call me if you have any questions.

Thank you for your cooperation.

Sincerely,

[Signature]

Enclosure

LETTER 8-29
NOTIFICATION THAT DEPONENT HAS SIGNED DEPOSITION TRANSCRIPT

[Date]

[Attorney]
[Firm]
[Address]

[Attorney]
[Firm]
[Address]

Re: [Case name]
Our Client : [Name]
Our File : [Number]
Date/Loss : [Date]

Dear [Counsel]:

Please be advised that [Name] signed his deposition transcript on [Date]. Please be further advised that [Name] made no changes to the transcript. This office will retain the original transcript.

Should you have any questions or comments, please feel free to contact me.

Very truly yours,

[Signature]

LETTER 8-30
LETTER TO CLIENT REQUESTING DOCUMENTS MENTIONED IN CLIENT'S DEPOSITION

[Date]

[Name], Insurance Manager
[Company]
[Address]

[Name]
[Company]
[Address]

Re: [Case name]
Our File : [Number]
Date/Loss : [Date]

Dear Messrs [Names]:

Please recall that I am representing the interests of your company in the above-referenced lawsuit. I request your further assistance in preparing our defense.

We recently deposed [Name], who was the project manager for your company on this job. [Name] testified that, throughout the course of the job, he kept daily logs and records of weekly safety meetings held among company employees. I would appreciate it if you could search your records and provide me with all copies of any such daily logs or reports of safety meetings.

Should either of you have any questions or comments about this request, please do not hesitate to call. I sincerely appreciate your courtesy and coöperation and look forward to hearing from you soon.

Very truly yours,

[Signature]

LETTER 8-31
TRANSMITTAL OF DEPOSITION TRANSCRIPTS

[Date]

[Name]
[Address]

Re: [Case name]
Insured : [Name]
Our File : [Number]
Date/Loss : [Date]

Dear [Name]:

Enclosed herewith, please find the following deposition transcripts for your review:

1. Volume 1 and 2 of [Name];

2. [Name]; and

3. [Name].

Should you have any questions or comments, please feel free to contact me.

Very truly yours,

[Signature]

LETTER 8-32
DEPOSITION DISTRIBUTION REQUEST

[Date]

[Court Reporters]
[Address]

Re: [Case name]; Cause No. [Number]

Dear Court Reporter:

Enclosed is the original correction sheet for the deposition transcript of [Name] taken in the above-entitled action.

Please process accordingly and distribute to all parties of record as required.

Sincerely,

[Signature]

Enclosure

LETTER 8-33
RESCHEDULING OF DEPOSITION 1

[Date]

[Name]
[Address]

Re: [Case name]

Deposition of [Name]

Dear Opposing Counsel:

This will confirm my conversation with your secretary, [Name], today, [Date], at which time arrangements were made to continue the deposition of our client, plaintiff [Name], from [Date] to [Date]. We appreciate your cooperation in agreeing to this continuance which has been necessitated by serious Illness in the family forcing our client to travel out of town to care for her mother. We will notify you when she returns and confirm at that time that this deposition date is firm.

Thank you for your courtesy in agreeing to this continuance. This office will make arrangements for a court reporter and the deposition will go forward at [Time] on [Date] at the law offices of [Name], [Address].

Thank you again for your courtesy and cooperation.

Sincerely,

[Signature]

LETTER 8-34
RESCHEDULING OF DEPOSITION 2

[Date]

<u>Via Facsimile</u>

[Attorney]
[Firm]
[Address]

[Attorney]
[Firm]
[Address]

Re: [Case name]
Our Client : [Name]
Our File : [Number]
Date/Loss : [Date]

Dear Counsel:

Please allow this to confirm the conversation between our offices of last week. Mr. and Mrs. [Name]'s depositions will be continued from Tuesday, [Date], to Friday, [Date]. Mrs. [Name]'s deposition is to start at 9:00 a.m. and Mr. [Name]'s deposition at 10:00 a.m. Please allow this to further confirm that Mr. [Name]'s deposition previously set for Friday, [Date] at 10:00 a.m. will now be held Friday, [Date] at [Time]. The depositions will be held at [Location], located at [Address].

Thank you for your courtesy and cooperation in this matter. Should you have any questions or comments, please feel free to contact me.

Very truly yours,

[Signature]

LETTER 8-35
RESCHEDULING OF DEPOSITION 3

[Date]

[Name]
[Address]

[Name]
[Address]

[Name]
[Address]

Re: [Case name]
Our Client : [Name]
Our File : [Number]
Date/Loss : [Date]

Dear Gentlepersons:

Please allow this to confirm that the deposition of [Name] previously set for [Date], at [Time] has been continued to [Date], at [Time]. The deposition will still be held at [Location].

Should you have any questions or comments, please feel free to contact this office.

Very truly yours,

[Signature]

LETTER 8-36
RESCHEDULING OF DEPOSITION 4

[Date]

[Name]
[Address]

Re: [Case name]
Our Client : [Name]
Our File : [Number]
Date/Loss : [Date]

Dear [Name]:

Please be advised that the time of the your deposition on [Date] in our office has been changed from [Time] to [Time]. Please meet me here a half hour before the deposition so that we may discuss your testimony.

Thank you for your courtesy and cooperation. Should you have any questions or comments, please feel free to contact me.

Very truly yours,

[Signature]

LETTER 8-37
RESCHEDULING OF DEPOSITION 5

[Date]

[Name]
[Address]

Re: [Case name]
Our Client : [Name]
Our File : [Number]
Date/Loss : [Date]

Dear [Name]:

Enclosed herewith, please find a copy of Price Roofings Amended Notice of Taking Deposition. Please notice that your deposition has been changed from [Time] to [Time]. Said deposition will be in our offices. Kindly meet me here a half hour early.

Thank you for your courtesy and cooperation. Should you have any questions or comments, please feel free to contact me.

Very truly yours,

[Signature]

LETTER 8-38
RESCHEDULING OF DEPOSITION 6

[Date]

[Firm]
[Address]

ATTN: [Name]

Re: [Case name]
O/client : [Name]
Our File : [Number]

Dear [Name]:

Pursuant to my conversation with [Name] of your office, this will confirm that the deposition of the most knowledgeable person of [Party] as to issues referred to in your Notice of Deposition has been continued from [Date] to [Date], at [Time] in your office.

Thank you for your courtesy and cooperation in this matter.

Very truly yours,

[Signature]

cc: [Names]

LETTER 8-39
RESCHEDULING OF DEPOSITION 7 (WITH ATTACHED AGREEMENT BY ADDRESSEE TO ATTEND)

[Date]

[Name]
[Address]

Re: [Case name]
Our Clients : [Names]
Our File No : [Number]
Date/Loss : [Date]

Dear [Name]:

Your deposition previously set for [Date], has been continued to [Date] at [Time]. The deposition will still be held at the law firm of [Name], located at [Address].

Please meet me at [Firm] at [Time] so we may discuss your testimony. Please sign the second page indicating that you have noted the change of the deposition date and that you will be attending the deposition.

In the interim, should you have any questions concerning this matter, please feel free to contact me.

Very truly yours,

[Signature]

I have noted the continuance of my deposition and will attend as requested.

Signed: ______________________

Business Phone: ________________ Home Phone: ____________________

LETTER 8-40
LETTER MEMORIALIZING ORAL AGREEMENT REGARDING RESCHEDULING DEPOSITIONS

[Name]
Attorney at Law
[Address]

Re: [Case name]
Our Client : [Name]
Our File : [Number]
Date/Loss : [Date]

Dear [Name]:

Please allow this letter to memorialize the telephone conversation which I had with Greg of your office on this date. Greg advised me that neither Dr. Shiffman or Dr. Nishigaya will be available to give deposition testimony on Monday, [Date], the date currently set for their depositions. Greg advised me that Dr. Nishigaya is out of town and could not be reached until Tuesday. His deposition has therefore not been rescheduled. However, it was agreed that pretrial discovery cut-off rules will be waived if necessary to complete Dr. Nishigaya's deposition prior to trial, and that I will have an opportunity to depose Dr. Nishigaya prior to any deposition of Dr. Einbund.

We also agreed that Dr. Shiffman's deposition will be continued to [Date], at 5:00 p.m. That deposition will take place in Dr. Shiffman's office at [Address].

I sincerely appreciate your courtesy and cooperation in this matter. Should you have any questions or comments, please do not hesitate to call.

Very truly yours,

[Signature]

LETTER 8-41
LETTER TO CLIENT'S INSURER SUMMARIZING EXPERT'S DEPOSITION TESTIMONY

[Date]

[Name]
[Insurance Company]
[Address]

Re: [Case name]

Insured	:	[Name]
Claim No.	:	[Number]
Date of Loss	:	[Date]
Our File No.	:	[Number]

Dear [Name]:

On [Date] I took the deposition of plaintiff's expert, Charles H. Braithwaite. The following will summarize the important portions of his deposition testimony.

IMPRESSION OF WITNESS

Deponent is a Caucasian male who appears to be in his sixties. He has gray hair and is balding. He came to the deposition dressed in a suit. He appears to be honest, although he is not a particularly effective communicator. As will be explained below, he had very little information to impart regarding many of the areas at issue in our case. If called upon as a witness to testify, he will probably make a fair impression.

PERSONAL BACKGROUND

Deponent is a chemical engineer who is currently employed as a legal consultant. Among his varied past is a three-year period, forty years ago, when he worked at Westinghouse doing electrical insulation design work. Enclosed for your review is a copy of his curriculum vitae.

GENERAL TESTIMONY

He has no experience designing or manufacturing batteries. Even basic questioning disclosed that he has very little knowledge regarding battery technology. He believes that virtually all batteries sold over the counter are alkaline batteries. As an exemplar to use in our case involving Energizer alkaline batteries, he chose Eveready's Super Heavy Duty Battery. He has no knowledge regarding safety devices that are incorporated into modern batteries which are used to release pressure and avoid explosions.

At one point in the deposition he stated that he has no experience in the design of batteries and, therefore, is not competent to testify regarding a design defect. At another point in the deposition, he testified that a potential design defect exists regarding improper or inadequate insulation materials. He admits that he has not opened an Energizer battery to determine which insulation materials are used or the amount of such materials. With respect to a manufacturing defect, he speculates that the insulation may have been inserted improperly causing leakage. He admits that he does not know for certain if there were any manufacturing defects in any of the subject eight batteries. He believes that the warning was inadequate because it was too small and did not adequately differentiate the consequences from throwing a battery into a fire and the result of putting a battery in backwards.

He does not know why batteries should not be re-charged. He speculates that this is a sales gimmick to encourage further sales of batteries. He also admits that he does not know why batteries should not be mixed with used or other types of batteries. He believes this latter warning is designed to encourage consumers to buy more batteries. As an example of the packaging of the batteries, he produced a packaging for the Super Heavy Duty Eveready Batteries. He has not seen the packaging for the Energizer batteries. He does not know whether or not plaintiff actually read any of the warnings.

It is his understanding that two of the batteries were put in backwards. He believes that this caused these two batteries to be drained of power. He also believes that the two backwards batteries would cause two other batteries to be rendered ineffective, resulting in the operating power of the radio coming from the four remaining batteries. He did not seem to realize that the line of batteries in this particular radio consisted of three batteries in a row.

He admits that he has not examined the subject radio. He does not know whether or not it had a cassette player attached as part of the radio. His testing of the batteries indicated that battery no. 2 and no. 3 contained no charge. Battery no. 5 was weak. Batteries no. 1, 4, 6, and 8 were active.

Absent actual physical puncture, he believes that there are only two mechanisms which would cause leakage. The first has to do with a deterioration of the insulation material. The second possible cause has to do with the corrosion of the metal portion of the batteries. He does not know which of these two mechanisms was the cause of the leakage in our case.

Although he tried to give an explanation, it is clear that he does not understand how putting a battery in backwards can cause it to leak.

He believes that the design of the Eveready Super Heavy Duty Battery is superior to the design of the Eveready Energizer Battery because the manner in which the ends are sealed is such that it is more likely that leakage will occur from the Energizer battery, than from the Super Heavy Duty battery.

He believes that the subject batteries were probably defective because he would not expect them to leak on the same day they were purchased. He thinks that they were defective because there would not have been sufficient time for corrosion or deterioration to occur, causing leakage.

COMMENTS REGARDING TESTIMONY

I have never deposed an expert who knew less about the subject of the litigation than Dr. Braithwaite knows about batteries. I was absolutely amazed at his ignorance. The list of factual errors seemed unending. Plaintiff's counsel has utterly wasted his money by retaining this expert.

This deposition merely serves to strengthen my opinion expressed earlier to you that this is a defensible case. If plaintiff's counsel tries to prosecute this case with this expert he will look like a laughing stock.

As a cost-saving vehicle, I continue to believe that a binding arbitration should be considered as one of our options. If we agree to a binding arbitration, it must be before a judge who will not be coerced into "splitting the baby" to achieve "fairness." Additionally, I continue to believe that we should agree to a binding arbitration only if the floor is at or near zero. The trial date remains set for [Date]. Please let me know the results of your conversations with Eveready concerning a possible binding arbitration.

Very truly yours,

[Signature]

Enclosure: Curriculum Vitae

cc: [Names]

LETTER 8-42
REPORT TO CLIENT/WORKERS' COMPENSATION CARRIER REGARDING DEPOSITION OF PLAINTIFF

[Date]

[Name]
[Insurance Company]
[Address]

Re: [Case name]
Your Claim No. : [Number]
Insured : [Name]
Date of Loss : [Date]
Our File No. : [Number]

STATUS REPORT
Deposition of Plaintiff

Dear [Name]:

On [Date] I attended the deposition of plaintiff ALAN PEASE. The following will summarize the important portions of his deposition testimony.

IMPRESSION OF WITNESS

Deponent is a Caucasian male who appears to be in his mid-thirties. He has dark hair and wears a mustache. He is soft-spoken, and although his memory is lacking in some areas, he does appear credible. If called upon as a witness to testify, he will probably make a fair to good impression.

PERSONAL BACKGROUND

He was born on May 1, 1957, in Key West, Florida. He ended his common-law marriage to Angela Kay Harp in 1977. He married his current wife, Deborah Reber, on April 1, 1991. His son, Nathan, is fifteen years old.

At the time of the incident, he was living at 9111 Roseanna, Garden Grove, California. He currently resides at 880 Yorba, Orange, California.

He obtained a GED Certificate in 1977. He has had subsequent computer courses as part of his rehabilitation from the 1987 work-related accident. Following these computer courses, he worked for a short period of time at Detector Systems in Stanton, California, assembling circuit boards. He did not like this job, so he started working for a roofing subcontractor in Garden Grove. He did this job for four or five months before he started in July 1989 for Owens Pacific on Compton Blvd., Los Angeles, California. He did caulking work for this roofing company.

Because of his 1989 industrial accident, he did not work again until 1991. At that time, he started working again for the roofing subcontractor. In about October 1991 he started working for Master Builders. He worked there until his automobile accident on January 16, 1992.

He did not work again until July 1993, when he started working as a salesman in a pawnshop.

He was paid $100.00 per day as a roofer. At Master Builders, he was paid $12.00 per hour, plus time and a half for overtime. He currently makes $200.00 per week working at the pawnshop.

His orthopedic surgeon, Dr. Anderson, has informed him that he will no longer be able to work in the construction field because of his neck and lower back injuries.

PRIOR WORK INJURIES

In September 1987 he was working at Williams Glass & Mirror and was injured while carrying a heavy piece of glass. Six or seven men were carrying a piece of glass weighing 200 lbs. up three flights of stairs. Plaintiff tripped and was pinned under the glass. He immediately began experiencing pain in his right buttocks and down his right leg. He was treated for this injury by a chiropractor and various orthopedic doctors. His orthopedic surgeon was Dr. Anderson. Dr. Anderson performed the laminectomy in November 1987.

He had a good result from the surgery and did not undergo any further treatment other than follow-up treatment, until the industrial accident in 1989. After the surgery, Dr. Anderson did tell him that he must limit the time he works and the amount of weight he can carry. Between 1987 and 1989, plaintiff was still active, including playing volleyball, basketball and golf. In September 1989 he was injured working at Owens Pacific, while lifting a beam weighing 200 lbs. to 300 lbs. He immediately experienced pain in his shoulders, arms and neck. An MRI was taken of his neck following this incident. He was examined by Drs. Thordarson, Morris and Smith. Although he denies his low back was injured in the 1989 accident, the chiropractic records indicate that he complained of low back pain following that accident.

JANUARY 16, 1992 AUTOMOBILE ACCIDENT

The accident occurred at approximately 7:30 a.m. He was proceeding northbound on the 55 freeway, and was on his way to pick up a co-worker. At approximately 17th Street, the traffic came to a stop. He brought his 1986 Mazda pickup to a complete stop. He then looked down at a clipboard in his seat and then looked up. He then immediately felt a "very hard" impact from the rear. This impact took place three to four seconds after he initially came to a stop. This impact caused his vehicle to move forward (causing skid marks) seven to ten feet long.

The accident occurred in the number one (fast) lane. At no time prior to the impact did he see the defendant's vehicle. The impact "knocked me silly." At the time of the impact, his pickup was in neutral. His foot was on the brake. He was wearing his seat belt when the collision occurred.

Both drivers exited their vehicles while still in the fast lane. Defendant asked plaintiff why he had stopped. Plaintiff indicated that he had stopped because the traffic had stopped. The drivers then parked their vehicles on the side of the road and exchanged information.

INJURIES

Immediately following the impact, he started to experience a "horrendous" headache. Later on that day, he started feeling a dull, throbbing, burning soreness in his shoulders, arms, and right buttocks. The soreness became worse and he stayed in bed the next day. The pain in his buttocks continued to get worse and began to travel down his right leg, down to his calf.

He does not believe he sought medical treatment until February 1992. At that time, he saw a doctor at Gateway Medical Clinic.

He treated with this clinic for a short period, but found that the therapy was not helpful. He eventually went back to see his orthopedic surgeon, Dr. Anderson.

Defense counsel asked no questions regarding the second back surgery in 1992.

At this time, he feels "pretty good." His neck, shoulders, right leg and buttocks still hurt when he overextends himself, or when the weather becomes rainy. When this happens, it feels to him as if he has a severe charley horse. He is unable to move when he has the pain. At this time, he is also numb in his right foot.

As a result of his injuries, he is no longer able to aggressively participate in sports. Prior to the accident, he went biking five to twenty-five miles every weekend. He has only been biking four or five times since the incident. He also no longer is able to play basketball in the summer with his son. In addition, he is limited in his ability to play golf or go hiking. Prior to the accident, he went jogging about three-quarters of the days of every week. He is no longer able to do this.

LITIGATION PLAN

You and I have discussed the Mandatory Settlement Conference which has been scheduled to take place on **AUGUST 19, 1993,** you indicated to me you would not be opposed to a short continuance of the MSC.

You have indicated to me that you would determine whether or not the worker's compensation claim is completely closed.

Regarding my evaluation of this case, it appears that liability is reasonably clear. The focus of the discovery in this case is the apportionment of plaintiff's injuries among the three work-related accidents. Defense counsel will strongly argue that many of the expenses incurred following the automobile accident were incurred as a result of prior injuries. During the deposition of plaintiff, several of the records were produced regarding the prior industrial accidents. I will have these summarized and sent to you.

If you have any questions, please do not hesitate to contact me.

Very truly yours,

[Signature]

LETTER 8-43
DEPOSITION SUMMARY LETTER 1

[Date]

[Name]
[Address]

Dear [Client]:

The following is a summary of the deposition of Joseph Doe taken June 21, 199_, before we entered this case.

GENERAL INFORMATION

Doe's home is in Fountain Valley, California. He has been the president of XYZ for about 18 months. His business, located in Huntington Beach, sets up filing systems in physicians' offices.

ERC CORPORATION

ERC owns and operates XYZ and other medical facilities, including ABC, the clinic that is the subject of this action. Doe worked for ERC between January 198_ and January 198_. At ERC he was responsible for certain administrative activities that included personnel, food services and engineering. Part of his time every day was spent at various facilities. During the summer of 198_ he was physically present at ERC for about 4 hours every morning.

MODIFICATION OF FACILITIES AT ABC

Doe oversaw the construction and engineering at ABC. They renovated a number of areas, including the laundry room in the basement. However, the room never functioned as a laundry because the drain pipes connected to it always seemed to back up. Therefore, it was used strictly for storage.

SCENE OF ACCIDENT

Doe was not present when plaintiff stumbled over a carpet in the middle of the defunct laundry room. However, Doe was at the scene within three hours of the incident and found that the light switch turned on the overhead fluorescent lights after about a five-second delay. He was not informed that there had been an accident. He went into the room to get supplies.

SAFETY MEETINGS

ERC suggests that its facilities hold safety meetings regularly. However, Doe does not personally attend them or verify that they took place. According to minutes of previous meetings, the storage room was supposed to be kept locked with only a few persons having keys. Doe does not know of anyone who might have given a key to plaintiff, who was not authorized to have one.

COMMENTS

Pleadings received in this case before we entered it will be summarized next. If you would like a copy of the deposition transcript of Joseph Doe, please contact our office.

Very Truly Yours,

[Attorney]

LETTER 8-44
DEPOSITION SUMMARY LETTER 2

[Date]

[Name]
[Address]

Dear [Name]:

The following is a summary of the deposition of John Doe, witness to the accident, which was taken on June 30, 1986 on behalf of plaintiff.

GENERAL INFORMATION

John Doe has lived at 123 Main Street one block south of the accident site, for twelve years. He was born on 10/30/50 and is married with two children. He is general manager and owner of his automotive repair shop, XYZ Company, located three blocks north of the accident site. He does not drink. He does not wear glasses. His hearing is excellent.

BEFORE THE ACCIDENT

Doe arose at 7:00 a.m. and ate breakfast, leaving his home at 8:30 a.m. Since it was raining, he took an umbrella. He began walking north on Main Street to go to work. He arrived at the intersection of Main and First Streets at about 8:35 a.m.

As he waited for the green light to cross from the southwest corner to the northwest corner, Doe noticed a red sedan stopped in the left turn lane on Main heading south. He also saw a blue sedan in the left turn lane on Main Street heading north. When the arrow for the lane Doe could see turned green, the red and blue cars began to enter the intersection. The crosswalk light was still red.

THE ACCIDENT

When the blue sedan reached the part of the intersection fronting Main Street's southbound traffic, Doe heard brakes screech. He observed a green sedan hit the blue sedan on the right rear door and send the blue sedan spinning over to within three feet of the corner where Doe stood. The driver of the green sedan rushed over, apologizing, and opened the driver's door of the blue sedan. The driver, his seat belt still fastened, was bleeding from his forehead and seemed dazed.

AFTER THE ACCIDENT

The city police arrived within five minutes. A female officer tended to the blue sedan's driver while a male officer questioned witnesses, including Doe.

An ambulance arrived within another few minutes and two attendants placed the driver on a stretcher before taking him away.

Doe gave a statement two weeks later to an insurance representative for the driver of the blue sedan.

COMMENTS

The driver of the red sedan will be deposed at a later date and you will be notified. We plan to subpoena the police records and the witness statement which Doe made to the insurance representative.

If you have any questions to ask or information to offer, please do not hesitate to contact this office.

[Signature]

LETTER 8-45
LETTER TO COURT REPORTING FIRM WHEN ORDERING TRANSCRIPT ON DISK

[Date]

[Name]
[Address]

Re: [Date] Deposition of [Name of Deponent]: Deposition Transcripts on Disk

Dear [Name]:

This is to confirm the time, place, and date of the deposition of [Name of deponent]. The notice of deposition is attached for your reference. As we discussed over the phone, we expect [Name of deponent]'s deposition to last for five days.

In addition to any paper copy requested, we need disks containing the deposition transcripts. The disks should conform to the following criteria:

1. [ASCII text file on 5-1/4-inch floppy disks, either 360 Kb DSDD or 1.2 Mb] [DiscoveryZX™/CAT-Links™ indexed file on 3-1/2-inch disks, 720 Kb]. An ASCII file should be in the "Amicus" format

2. Page and line numbers imbedded in the file must match the hard-copy transcripts

3. Page-number lines should not contain any text other than the page number itself. For example, do not reference page numbers with text such as "Page 100" or "J. Doe 100," or "Doe Vol. I at 100"

4. Omit headers, trailers, underlining, and printing codes in the ASCII file

5. Use the following convention when naming files: [DOE.VI (for Doe's deposition, Vol. 1)] [DOE1029.DEP (for Doe's October 29 deposition)] [DOE-VI.ARK (for Doe's deposition, Vol. 1, in the lawsuit called *Arkadia v. State*)].

If you have any questions about the criteria set forth above, please give me a call.

Very truly yours,

[Paralegal]
Legal Assistant to [Attorney]

Attachment

LETTER 8-46
LETTER OBJECTING TO FORM OF WRITTEN DEPOSITION QUESTIONS

[Date]

[Name]
[Address]

Re: [Case name]; [File number]
Deposition of [Name of deponent] on Written Questions
Objection to Form of Direct Questions

Dear [Name]:

We are in receipt of the Notice of Deposition on Written Questions and Direct Questions served on [Date]. We have reviewed the questions and, pursuant to Rule 32(d)(3)(C) of the Federal Rules of Procedure, object to certain of the questions as to form:

Question 22: Isn't it true that the Bank of Columbia required written confirmation of the collateral required, as described in answer to question 21?

Objection: Leading question, prohibited by Rule 611(c) of the Federal Rules of Evidence.

Question 29: When did you stop beating your wife?

Objection: Argumentative.

I request that these questions either be eliminated or rephrased prior to the deposition. If they are not eliminated or rephrased, I reserve my client's right to raise these objections at trial.

Very truly yours,

[Signature]
Attorney for [Plaintiff/Defendant]

CHAPTER 9

DISCOVERY—EXAMINATIONS AND INSPECTIONS

LETTER 9-1
LETTER ADVISING CLIENT OF INDEPENDENT MEDICAL EXAMINATION

[Date]

[Name]
[Address]

Re: Your Insurance Medical Exam on [Date of Exam]

Dear [Name]:

Your insurance company has scheduled an insurance medical exam which you must attend. This exam has been scheduled for [Date] by [Doctor] at [Address].

You may submit the hours you have to miss from work as lost wages through your insurance carrier. Your employer should provide a statement calculating your hourly wage and the time absent from your job, and submit it to the insurance company directly, requesting payment under your no-fault policy.

Enclosed is an instruction and evaluation form that provides you with instructions regarding this examination. Please complete this form *confidentially* after your examination and outside of the doctor's examining room.

Please contact our office before your exam with any questions you may have and for further instructions.

[Signature]

LETTER 9-2
LETTER TO CLIENT WHEN OPPOSING PARTY HAS REQUESTED INDEPENDENT MEDICAL EXAMINATION 1

[Date]

[Name]
[Address]

Dear [Name]:

The defendant's insurance company has scheduled an independent medical exam which you must attend. Pursuant to [State] law, the defendant's insurance company is entitled to a medical exam by a doctor of its choosing. The medical exam has been set for [Date] with [Doctor] at [Address].

It is important that you contact our office before this exam so that we may give you further instructions and answer any questions you may have. I have enclosed a form for you to complete *confidentially* after you have been examined by the doctor.

I look forward to hearing from you before this exam.

[Signature]

LETTER 9-3
LETTER TO CLIENT WHEN OPPOSING PARTY HAS REQUESTED INDEPENDENT MEDICAL EXAMINATION 2

[Date]

[Name]
[Address]

Re: Accident Date: [Date]

Dear [Name]:

As you know, [Name]'s attorney has requested an independent medical examination to verify the extent of your injuries and the 15 percent overall permanent disability rating by Dr. [Name]. This is a legitimate request during the discovery process, and we have agreed to it on your behalf. The examination is currently set for Monday, [Date] at [Time], and will be conducted in the offices of Dr. [Name], [Address]. I will attend the independent examination with you on [Attorney]'s behalf.

We would like to meet with you prior to this examination to discuss it with you. Please call me to schedule a convenient time to come in.

I look forward to meeting with you before [Date].

Very truly yours,

[Name]
Legal Assistant

LETTER 9-4
LETTER TO CLIENT WHEN OPPOSING PARTY HAS REQUESTED INDEPENDENT MEDICAL EXAMINATION 3

[Date]

[Name]
[Address]

Re: [Case Name]

Dear [Name]:

By law, the defendant is permitted to have you examined by a doctor on his behalf. A request has been forwarded for you to be examined by Dr. [Name], [Address] [Telephone Number].

Only advise the doctor of the **general** nature of how your injuries occurred. Do **not** go into any details concerning admissions of fault. However, as to your injuries, be as detailed as possible. **Give the doctor a complete description of all injuries you sustained and all your complaints and problems relating to those injuries that still exist.** Inform him of all prior conditions and claims also.

If an appointment is not specified, or if you wish another time, please call the doctor's office and make the arrangements. Be sure to advise our office of the new date of examination. After the evaluation is completed, please call so that I may mark my records accordingly.

Thank you for your anticipated cooperation.

Very truly yours,

[Attorney]

LETTER 9-5
NOTIFICATION OF RESCHEDULING OF INDEPENDENT MEDICAL EXAMINATION

[Date]

[Name]
[Address]

Re: [Case Name]
Our Clients: [Names]
Our File No: [Number]
Date/Loss: [Date]

Dear [Name]:

Please allow this to confirm that the Independent Medical Examination of your client, [Name], set for [Date], has been continued. [Name]'s IME will now be taken on Tuesday, [Date], at [Time] by Dr. [Name] at [Address].

Should you have any questions or comments, please feel free to contact me.

Very truly yours,

[Attorney]

LETTER 9-6
LETTER INFORMING DEFENSE ADJUSTER OR ATTORNEY OF DOCTOR'S KNOWN REPUTATION AS INSURANCE DEFENSE DOCTOR

[Date]

[Adjustor or Attorney]
[Address]

Dear [Defendant's Adjuster or Attorney]:

Your office has advised that you wish to schedule an insurance medical examination by [Name of Doctor]. While I certainly do not dispute that you have the right to have [Name of Client] examined by a physician of your choice, I object to the use of [Name of Doctor].

I object to [Name of Doctor] to examine [Name of Client] for his [neurological, orthopedic, etc.] condition on the basis that he has a known reputation in the legal, medical and insurance communities as an insurance company doctor who will not render an unbiased opinion, but rather will render an opinion that will either minimize the seriousness of [Name of Client]'s condition, attribute his condition to causes other than this accident, or insinuate that [Name of Client]'s condition is exaggerated for purposes of receiving compensation. [Name of Doctor] has been involved in several of our cases and in each instance he has always rendered a biased opinion in favor of the insurance company, which is why he is used so frequently by insurance companies in this state. Therefore, in fairness to the evaluation of this case, I think we should select an individual who does not have a reputation as being a biased examiner for insurance company interests.

Please contact me at your earliest convenience so that we may resolve this situation. In the interest of fairness and justice, I request that [Name of Client] be examined by a qualified, competent and unbiased professional who will conduct a fair and competent exam.

Thank you for your cooperation and assistance.

[Signature]

LETTER 9-7
LETTER TO CARRIER CONCERNING DOCTOR'S REPUTATION TO RESTRICT BENEFITS

[Date]

Claims Division
[Name of Company] Insurance
[Address]

Re: Your Insured: [Name]
Our Client: [Name]
Date of Accident: [Date]
Your Claim No.: [Number]

Dear [Insurance adjuster]:

I am writing this letter with regard to the insurance company medical examination that you have scheduled for my client [Name] for [Date] with [Name of Doctor], a neurosurgeon.

[Name of Doctor]'s opinions, as you are aware, apply only the most conservative criteria for diagnosis and treatment of medical and more specifically [Name of Specialty] problems. [Name of Doctor]'s approach and opinions in this regard are well known throughout the medical, legal and insurance communities. We believe that you expect and that [Name of Doctor] will submit reports now or in the future which you will seek to use to limit or preclude treatment and therapies for [Name of Client] pursuant to prescriptions, recommendations, or referrals of her treating physicians or other health care professionals.

The law in this state as enunciated by our trial courts has been that, when treatment has been undertaken by an insured that is prescribed by a competent medical practitioner, it must be covered even if other practitioners suggest that other or no treatment at all is appropriate. An insured who opts for legitimately prescribed treatment has a right to rely on his insurance coverage to pay for what he contracted.

I hope that payment of medical care will not be an area of contention and that you will allow [Name of Client] to pursue, without interference, any treatment or care based upon bona fide recommendations made by various, competent medical practitioners with whom [Name of Client] has treated.

Additionally, notification of this examination was sent directly to my client without a copy to me. In the future, please provide me with copies of all correspondence directed to my client by you.

Sincerely,

[Signature]

cc: [Client's Name]

LETTER 9-8
REQUEST FOR CONFERENCE REGARDING COMPELLING OPPOSING PARTY TO SUBMIT TO INDEPENDENT MEDICAL EXAMINATION

[Date]

[Name]
[Firm]
[Address]

Re: [Case Name]
Our Client: [Name]
Our File: [Number]
Date/Loss: [Date]

Dear [Name]:

Although I did not personally appear at the Status Conference on [Date], and I understand that you did not either, I was advised by [Name] of our office that Judge [Name] requested that our offices attempt to resolve informally the issues surrounding our Motion to Compel your client's IME. [Name] said the judge indicated that he would most likely grant our motion but did not want to waste court time if we could resolve it informally.

Please give me a call at your earliest convenience so that we may discuss the matter in more detail. I sincerely appreciate your courtesy and cooperation and look forward to hearing from you soon.

Very truly yours,

[Attorney]

LETTER 9-9
LETTER REGARDING AGREEMENT TO SHARE COSTS OF INDEPENDENT MEDICAL EXAMINATION

[Date]

[Name]
[Firm]
[Address]

Re: [Case Name]
Our Client: [Name]
Our File: [Number]
Date/Loss: [Date]

Dear [Name]:

Thank you for your letter of [Date]. I understand your reluctance to pay Dr. [Name]'s bill in this situation. Please be advised that we will be bringing a motion to compel plaintiff's attendance at an IME, and seeking sanctions for her failure to do so in the past.

However, it is my understanding that you had agreed to share in IME costs. Please advise me if it is still your intention to share in the costs of the IME which we have rescheduled for [Date], at [Time].

I sincerely appreciate your cooperation and look forward to hearing from you.

Very truly yours,

[Attorney]

LETTER 9-10
LETTER ADVISING INSURER OF VARIOUS INVESTIGATION AND DISCOVERY MATTERS

[Date]

[Name]
[Insurance Company]
[Address]

Re: [Case Name]
Insured: [Name]
Our File: [Number]
Claim No.: [Number]
Date/Loss: [Date]

Dear [Name]:

I enclose a copy of Dr. [Name]'s report of his examination of Mr. [Name]. While his report is somewhat vague, I will tell you that he told me that Dr. Newquist is tops and that it is reasonably certain that the incident caused the low back pain due to the proximity of the first onset of pain and the incident. We should not hold the hope of successfully getting Dr. Newquist to testify that the two are not related. Dr. Einbund did tell me that the low back pain reaction is unusual, which is why he added the one sentence on page 5 of his report under recommendations, but, as I said, he verbally told me Dr. Newquist's opinion that the incident that caused the pain will hold up.

I have been advised that Price Roofing has filed bankruptcy. As they have a [Amount] policy, I do not believe this will impact on us but we should be prepared to file a Motion for Relief of Stay for the insurance proceeds. To date, counsel for Price has not asserted the bankruptcy stay.

Should you have any questions or comments, please do not hesitate to call. Plaintiffs' deposition got continued to [Date], the deposition of Jerry Bleinks of Price and Jim Barisic have been continued to [Date] and the deposition of Dr. Newquist is tentatively set for [Date]. We still have a Mandatory Settlement Conference set for [Date] at [Time] in Department [Number].

Very truly yours,

[Attorney]

LETTER 9-11
NOTIFICATION OF PREMISES INSPECTION 1

[Date]

[Name]
[Address]

Re: [Case Name]
Our File No.: [Number]

Dear [Name]:

This letter shall confirm the telephone conversation of today's date, wherein you agreed to attend the property inspection in the above-referenced matter presently set for [Date] at [Time]. The property is located at [Address].

Enclosed please find a photocopy of plaintiffs' complaint to help familiarize yourself with this matter.

Thank you for your courtesy and cooperation in this matter.

Very truly yours,

[Attorney]

LETTER 9-12
NOTIFICATION OF PREMISES INSPECTION 2

[Date]

[Name]
[Company]
[Address]

Re: [Case Name]
Insured: [Name]
Our File: [Number]
Date/Loss: [Date]

Dear [Name]:

Please be advised that [Name] has agreed to allow an inspection of his property at [Address] on Saturday morning, [Date]. I have advised [Name] that we anticipate arriving sometime between 10:00 and 11:00 a.m.

I live very near the subject premises and would suggest that we meet at my residence between 10:00 and 10:30 on Saturday morning. I reside at [Address]. I understand that you will be traveling south and suggest you take the following route: [Directions]

My home is the rear unit of two located on a single lot. Should you have trouble finding my home, please feel free to call at [Telephone Number].

Should you have a problem with the date or time scheduled, please call me or my secretary, [Name], at the phone number listed on this letterhead. I sincerely appreciate your courtesy, cooperation and assistance and look forward to meeting you.

Very truly yours,

[Attorney]

LETTER 9-13
CONFIRMATION OF AGREEMENT FOR PREMISES INSPECTION

[Date]

[Name]
[Address]

Re: [Case Name]
Our Clients: [Name]
Our File: [Number]
Date/Loss: [Date]

Dear [Name]:

It was a pleasure speaking with you on the telephone recently. Please allow this letter to confirm that you have graciously agreed to allow an inspection of your property at [Address] by myself and my safety engineer, [Name]. [Inspector] plans his inspection for Saturday, [Date] at approximately 10:30 a.m. and will be traveling down from Los Angeles. I will call you on Saturday morning to confirm.

I would sincerely appreciate some notice from you should the date and time contemplated present problems for you. Please call me should you have any questions or comments.

Very truly yours,

[Attorney]

CHAPTER 10

TRIAL AND POST-TRIAL

LETTER 10-1
LETTER ADVISING CLIENT OR WITNESS OF TRIAL DATE 1

[Date]

[Name]
[Address]

Re: Trial Notice

Dear [Name]:

We have been advised that your case has been tentatively scheduled for trial at [Time] on [Date] and thereafter until reached and concluded at the [County name] County Courts Building, [Address].

We cannot be absolutely certain that your case will be tried on that date due to its position on the list of cases scheduled for trial at the same time, as well as the possibility of an adjournment or postponement for various reasons accepted by the court.

Upon receipt of this letter, immediately call Joe Jones, a paralegal with our firm, to advise us:

1. Where you can be reached on short notice; and

2. To schedule an appointment, if necessary, to review your file.

We will need to receive by return mail, if not recently supplied, an accurate accounting of your medical expenses and lost wages, along with a list of all persons who may testify on your behalf about the incident or the effect of the injuries on you. If this information is not promptly supplied, we may be prevented from providing testimony on these issues at the time of trial.

Thank you for your anticipated cooperation.

Very truly yours,

[Attorney]

LETTER 10-2
LETTER ADVISING CLIENT OR WITNESS OF TRIAL DATE 2

[Date]

[Name]
[Address]

Re: [Style or caption of case]

Dear [Name]:

This is to advise you that the trial of the above-entitled matter has been scheduled, on a stacked basis, starting on [Date]. In cases of this nature, the Court, as a matter of judicial economy, stacks several cases back to back so there will not be any periods of time wasted between trials. As a result, it is very difficult to know the exact date and hour the trial will commence. We do wish to advise you at this time that you should be available during that entire week.

We ask that you keep us advised of your whereabouts at all times since we will need to be in contact with you to give you a more accurate trial date and to discuss this case with you in detail.

If for any reason you find you will not be available during this time please call our office immediately because your testimony is necessary at trial.

Very truly yours,

[Attorney]

LETTER 10-3
LETTER ADVISING CLIENT OR WITNESS OF TRIAL DATE 3

[Date]

[Name]
[Address]

Re: [Style or caption of case]

Dear [Name]:

We have received notice from the Court that the trial date on the above-referenced case has been set for Monday, [Date]. We anticipate that the trial will last at least the entire week of [Date], and it may possibly carry over into the following week. We would like to offer your testimony early in the trial presentation, so it is likely that we would need you to testify either in the afternoon session on [Date], or during the morning session on Wednesday, [Date]. We also need to schedule some time before your court testimony to review the case with you and prepare you to testify.

Please check your calendar for the week of [Date], and advise us immediately if you foresee any conflicts in scheduling which would prevent you from being available to testify during the time frame outlined above.

To assist you in preparing for this trial, I am enclosing a copy of the transcript of the deposition you gave in this case on [Date], so that you can review it at your convenience.

In reviewing my file I find that I have not yet received the reference articles you agreed to send me on this matter when we last discussed the case in [Date]. Please see if you can locate those materials and forward them to me at your earliest convenience.

Again, thank you for your assistance to our trial team in preparing this case for trial. I shall look forward to hearing from you soon to confirm your availability for the trial.

Very truly yours,

[Paralegal]

Enclosures: [List Documents]

LETTER 10-4
LETTER ADVISING CLIENT OR WITNESS OF TRIAL DATE 4

[Date]

[Name]
[Address]

Re: [Case Name]

Incident: [Day, Date, Time, Place]

Dear [Name]:

Trial in the above-referenced case has been scheduled to begin as indicated below:

Date: [Day and date]

Location: [Court Title, Street Address, Major Cross Streets, and Courtroom Identification]

Parking Information: [Site and Method of Payment, e.g., meters accept only quarters or parking paid to attendant when exiting lot]

Judge's Name: Courtoom Telephone:

It is anticipated that your testimony will be required on [Day and Date] at approximately [Time]. Remember to bring your glasses if you need them for reading, as well as [diary, calendar, documents, etc. that you want the client to bring]. Please meet [Attorney] in front of the courtoom at [Time], which is one-half hour before the [Morning/Afternoon] session begins. This will give you an opportunity to discuss your testimony.

We cannot guarantee that your testimony will begin exactly as scheduled. Therefore, we suggest that you provide information as requested below so that we may inform you of any last-minute changes.

Home phone: ________________ Business phone: ________________

Pager number: ________________ Vehicle phone: ________________

Alternate contact person/phone: ________________________________

When you attend trial, we request that you dress appropriately for the courtroom. If you have any questions, please do not hesitate to call myself, my legal assistant [Name], or my secretary [Name].

Sincerely,

[Attorney]

LETTER 10-5
LETTER ADVISING CLIENT OR WITNESS OF TRIAL DATE 5

[Date]

[Name]
[Address]

Dear [Name]:

This letter is to advise the trial of [Caption] is still scheduled to commence during the week of [Date]. It presently appears that we will need your testimony some time on [Day and Date]. I will attempt to give you a better estimate of when on that date as time of trial draws near. However, for the time being, please advise if there is any problem in your appearing in court on that date.

I anticipate that we will shortly have a subpoena served upon you to preserve our right to call you as a witness. Please do not hesitate to give me a call if you have any problems concerning either your testimony or this anticipated trial time.

Very truly yours,

[Signature]

LETTER 10-6
LETTER ADVISING CLIENT OR WITNESS OF TRIAL DATE 6
(ENCLOSING TESTIMONY MATERIALS)

[Date]

[Name]
[Address]

Re: Trial Preparation Conference

Dear [Name]:

This will confirm our telephone discussion of this date concerning scheduling an appointment for your trial preparation conference with [Attorney] for Tuesday, [Date] at [Time].

I am enclosing a photocopy of the Answers to Interrogatories which were filed on [Date] together with the transcript of your deposition which was taken on [Date], in this case. Please take time to read these materials to refresh your recollection before your meeting with [Attorney]. As you review these documents, please jot down any questions you may have about them or about the case and bring your questions with you to the trial preparation conference.

If you should have a conflict which would prevent you from attending the meeting on [Date], please let us know as soon as possible so that we can reschedule. Otherwise, we will plan on seeing you in our offices on that date.

Very truly yours,

[Paralegal]

Enclosures

LETTER 10-7
LETTER ADVISING WITNESS OF TRIAL DATE 1
(TRAVEL CONFIRMATION)

[Date]

VIA CERTIFIED MAIL

[Name]
[Address]

Re: Scheduling of Trial Testimony
_______________ v. _______________

Dear [Name]:

I'm writing to notify you of the date we anticipate needing your trial testimony in the above-referenced matter.

We plan to have you testify on [Date]. Therefore, we will need you to arrive in [City] on [Date] in order to prepare you for your testimony the following day. The length of your testimony is estimated to be one-half day.

Courtesy hotel reservations have been made for you at [Location]. This establishment is located close to the [Courthouse] where the trial will take place. If you plan to stay elsewhere, please call me so I can cancel the reservations.

If there are any changes in the schedule, we will contact you immediately. Please call me if you have any questions.

Sincerely yours,

[Paralegal]

LETTER 10-8
LETTER ADVISING WITNESS OF TRIAL DATE 2

[Date]

[Name]
[Address]

Re: [Case name]
Our Client: [Name]
Our File : [Number]
Date/Loss : [Date]

Dear [Name]:

This law firm represents [Name] in the above referenced law suit. You may recall providing a declaration on their behalf concerning this matter about two years ago.

The case has never been resolved and is now set for trial on [Date] at 8:45 a.m. in [Court] Department [Number], [Address]. In order to defend [Clients] from what we believe to be a groundless lawsuit, we may desire your cooperation and assistance as a witness concerning the [Subject]. I assure you it is my desire to cause you as little inconvenience as possible, and if I need your testimony, it would entail only a brief appearance for you. I would cooperate fully to arrange as convenient a date and time as possible for you, and you would be entitled to statutory witness fees.

I understand you have spoken to my legal assistant, [Name], and have arranged to meet me at [Time] on [Date] in our office. I sincerely appreciate your anticipated courtesy and cooperation and look forward to meeting you. A map is enclosed for your convenience.

Very truly yours,

[Attorney]

LETTER 10-9
LETTER ADVISING WITNESS OF TRIAL DATE 3

[Date]

[Name]
[Address]

Re: [Case name]
Insured : [Clients]
Our File : [Number]
Date/Loss : [Date]

Dear [Name]:

The above referenced case has been set for a prospective trial date of [Date]. The Court has set no specific time for commencement of the trial. However, should the trial commence as scheduled on that date, it will take place in Department [Number] [Court], located at [Address].

If the trial commences as scheduled, I would anticipate needing your testimony sometime during the second week of trial. Please advise me if you anticipate any irresolvable calendar conflicts. Should you have any questions or comments, please do not hesitate to call. I sincerely appreciate your professional courtesy and cooperation in defense of this lawsuit.

Very truly yours,

[Attorney]

LETTER 10-10
INITIAL LETTER TO EXPERT WITNESS INCLUDING NOTICE OF TRIAL DATE

[Date]

[Name]
[Address]

Re: [Case name]
OCSC Case No.: [Number]
Date/Loss : [Date]
Our File No. : [Number]

Dear [Name]:

Thank you for agreeing to act as an expert witness in this case.

This action involves burns to plaintiff's buttocks which allegedly occurred as a result of leaking "D" size batteries. I represent Eveready Battery Company in this action. Discovery has thus far disclosed that plaintiff installed the batteries backwards in his radio. The batteries contained a warning that the batteries may leak, causing personal injuries, if installed backwards.

The trial is currently scheduled to begin on [Date]. Because of various factors, this trial could move.

I will forward to you additional records under separate cover. If you have any questions regarding this case at this time, please do not hesitate to contact me.

Very truly yours,

[Attorney]

LETTER 10-11
OFFER OF ON-CALL OPTION TO TRIAL WITNESS 1

To: [Name]
[Address]

Re: [Case name]

Dear [Name]:

You have been given a Civil Subpoena and asked to appear as a witness in this case to help the Court and jury reach a true and proper verdict.

We have the greatest system of justice in the world. This system is based on the fact that witnesses, like jurors, perform an important civic function when they take time out from their personal lives to participate in a trial.

The Court requires every attorney to have the witnesses available to testify when needed and without keeping the Court and the jury waiting.

We could ask all witnesses to be in Court and wait their turn to testify. However, this would result in many witnesses having to wait around the Courtroom when they could use their time to better personal advantage. The only other practical way to reduce the waiting time of a witness is to put the witness on what lawyers call "telephone call". This requires that a witness who has been subpoenaed promise to be available to appear in Court on approximately two (2) hours' phone notice and requires the witness give the lawyer phone numbers where the witness can always be reached. NATURALLY WE WILL TRY TO GIVE YOU AS MUCH ADVANCE NOTICE AS POSSIBLE.

We want to be fair with every witness. We leave the choice up to you. If you would prefer to be in Court every day and wait for your turn to testify, it will be necessary for you to appear at the time and place shown on the subpoena. If you prefer to be put on phone call, please sign one copy of this letter and return it to the undersigned so we can present it to the Court if requested.

Very truly yours,

By: [Attorney]

I, [Name] can be reached by phone at the following numbers:

between 9:00 A.M. to 5:00 P.M.: ______________________________

before 9:00 A.M. and after 5:00 P.M.: ___________________________

Please put me "on phone call". I promise to appear in Court within two (2) hours after being phoned at the number which I have given you above. Of course, I would appreciate as much advance notice as possible.

[Date]

[Signature]

LETTER 10-12
OFFER OF ON-CALL OPTION TO TRIAL WITNESS 2

[Date]

[Name]
[Address]

Re: [Case name]
Insured : [Name]
Our File : [Number]
Date/Loss : [Date]
Trial Date: : [Date]

Dear [Name]:

You have been subpoenaed to appear to testify at the trial of the above-referenced matter. So that you will not be greatly inconvenienced by having to sit in court for an unknown period of time until you are called to testify, you may agree to be put on a three hour "On Call" basis (or sufficient notice to allow for travel time). We request that you be available or, in the alternative, call and let this office know where you can be reached.

Please fill in the last section of this letter and return it immediately in the self-addressed stamped envelope if you wish to be placed on a three-hour "On Call" basis.

Thank you for your anticipated courtesy and cooperation in this matter. Again, please complete and immediately return the agreement to be placed on call.

Very truly yours,

[Attorney]

[Case name]

I, [Name], agree to be placed on a three-hour "on-call" basis for the trial in the [Case name] case that is scheduled to begin on [Date] at [Time] in the [Court] located at [Address].

My residence phone number is: ______________________________

My business phone number is: ______________________________

A third contact number is: ______________________________

[Date] [Name]

LETTER 10-13
OFFER OF ON-CALL OPTION TO TRIAL WITNESS 3

[Date]

[Name]
[Address]

Dear [Name]:

Enclosed please find a subpoena ordering your presence at the trial of this matter on [Date] at [Time] in [Room] at [Address]. Because we expect that your testimony will not be needed immediately, I want to extend an offer for you to agree to be available on a [Number]-hour notice to come to court.

Once we give you notice, you would have to agree to arrive at the courthouse prepared to testify within [Number] hours. We will give you more than [Number] hours if it is at all possible.

If you agree to be placed on [Number] hours' notice to come to the courthouse and to spare yourself a lot of wasted time sitting in the halls, please fill in the spaces provided below. Then sign and date the letter and return it in the enclosed postage-prepaid, self-addressed envelope.

If you cannot agree to place yourself on call for the trial, we will not have an agreement concerning your testimony, and you must arrive pursuant to the subpoena at the time and place shown on the subpoena.

Please do not hesitate to call if you have any questions or comments.

Very truly yours,

[Attorney]

I agree to be placed on a [Number]-hour notice to attend the trial as indicated in the letter above.

[Date]	[Name]
____________________	____________________
Daytime telephone	Work or alternate telephone number

LETTER 10-14
NOTIFICATION TO COURT OF SCHEDULING CONFLICT WITH TRIAL SETTING

[Date]

[Presiding Judge]
[Court]
[Address]

Re: [Case name]
Our Client : [Name]
Case No. : [Number]

Dear Judge:

Please be advised that I am representing plaintiff/cross-defendant [Name] in the above referenced case. The case is currently set for trial on [Date], in [Court], Department [Number], at [Time].

Pursuant to [Court] Local Rule No. [Number], I hereby notify the court that another case in which I am involved as trial attorney has been set for trial in [Court], Department [Number], [Location], on [Date]. That case is captioned [Case Name], Case No. [Number]. The five year deadline for bringing that action to trial would have expired in June of 1991 had the parties not stipulated to extend the deadline until December 15, 1991. I therefore anticipate that case will likely proceed to trial on [Date]. I believe these facts tend to indicate that [Case Name] may not proceed to trial on the date to which it has been assigned. All other parties to this lawsuit have been notified through counsel of these circumstances.

Should you have any questions or comments regarding this matter, please feel free to contact me.

Very truly yours,

[Attorney]

LETTER 10-15
NOTIFICATION OF TRIAL SETTING

[Date]

[Name]
[Address]

Re: [Case name]
Our Client : [Name]
Case No. : [Number]

Dear [Name]:

Please be advised that the trial in the above referenced case has been set for [Date], at [Time] in Department [Number] of the [Court] located at [Address].

Should you have any questions or comments, please do not hesitate to call.

Very truly yours,

[Attorney]

LETTER 10-16
LETTER TO CLIENT'S INSURER REGARDING VARIOUS PRETRIAL MATTERS

[Date]

[Name]
[Company]
[Address]

Re: [Case name]
Insured : [Name]
Claim No. : [Number]
Our File : [Number]
Date/Loss : [Date]

Dear [Name]:

On [Date] plaintiff's counsel's motion to withdraw as counsel of record was granted. Plaintiff is currently proceeding In Pro Per, unless he can find a new attorney.

The Court declined our request to send the case back down to Municipal Court. Instead, we obtained a trial date in the Superior Court for [Date] at [Time] in Department [Number] of the [Court]. I will prepare a pretrial report under separate cover.

Please let me know if you have any questions at this time.

Very truly yours,

[Attorney]

LETTER 10-17
TRANSMITTAL TO OPPOSING COUNSEL OF STIPULATED DOCUMENTS TO BE EXECUTED

[Date]

[Name]
[Address]

Re: [Case name]
OCSC Case No.: [Number]
Date of Loss : [Date]
Our File No. : [Number]

Dear [Name]:

Pursuant to the local fast track rules, I enclose the following:

1. Stipulation to Facts and to Admissibility of Tangible Evidence.
2. Joint List of Controverted Issues.
3. Joint Statement of the Case.
4. Joint List of Witnesses.
5. Joint Requested Voir Dire Questions.
6. Defendant's Motion in Limine on Insurance Coverage.
7. Exhibits not previously produced.
8. Statement of Compliance.

Please review the proposed documents and let me have any comments or suggestions you may have. With respect to ANSI Standards, I am currently not aware of any which deal with specific installation requirements. I have, however, included the one paragraph dealing with the insertion of batteries backwards. You are, of course, welcome to perform any research you wish on applicable standards or rules.

When I receive any additions from you telephonically, I will make the changes in my office and will send the revised documents back to you for your execution. Please then sign all the documents where indicated, and return them to me for filing with the Court.

I look forward to discussing these issues with you.

Very truly yours,

[Attorney]

Enclosures: As Listed Above

LETTER 10-18
TRANSMITTAL OF REVISED STIPULATED DOCUMENTS TO BE EXECUTED

[Date]

VIA FEDERAL EXPRESS
[Name]
[Address]

Re: [Case name]
OCSC Case No.: [Number]
Date of Loss : [Date]
Our File No. : [Number]

Dear [Name]:

Enclosed are the revised documents we discussed telephonically. Please execute them and return them to me via overnight mail, so that I may file them with the Court on Friday.

Thank you for your assistance.

Very truly yours,

[Attorney]

Enclosures: –Stipulation to Facts and to Admissibility of Tangible Evidence
–Joint Statement of the Case
–Joint List of Witnesses to be Introduced at Trial
–Joint Requested Voir Dire Questions

LETTER 10-19
TRANSMITTAL OF JOINT CASE MANAGEMENT STATEMENT

[Date]

[Name]
[Firm]
[Address]

Re: [Case name]
O/client : [Name]
Our File : [Number]
Date/Loss : [Date]

Dear [Name]:

Enclosed please find a copy of the executed Joint Case Management Statement. Due to the time constraints we have filed the statement directly with the court. Upon receipt of the conformed statement, we will forward a copy to your office.

Should you have any questions, please do not hesitate to contact this office.

Very truly yours,

[Attorney]

LETTER 10-20
LETTER NOTIFYING WITNESS OF RETRIAL

[Date]

[Name]
[Company]
[Address]

Re: [Case name]

Dear [Name]:

The United States Court of Appeals for the Seventh Circuit has now reinstated our Company's breach of contract claims arising out of the breakdown of our opponent's quality review program. These issues are now in the process of being remanded to the United States District court for retrial.

It has not yet been finally determined which witnesses will be necessary for this next phase of litigation. However, your participation remains a possibility.

Enclosed is a copy of the Court of Appeals' decision for your review. If you have any questions, feel free to call the senior litigation attorney, [Name], or our Company's legal assistant assigned to this matter, [Name].

Thank you for your continuing interest.

Sincerely,

[Attorney]
Senior Counsel

Enclosure

LETTER 10-21
LETTER TO CLIENT/INSURER REPORTING TRIAL OUTCOME IN DETAIL

[Date]

[Name]
[Company]
[Address]

Re: [Case name]
Insured : [Name]
Our File : [Number]
Claim No. : [Number]
Date/Loss : [Date]

Post-Trial Report

Dear [Name]:

As you know, in the above case we represented the developer, seller and general contractor of residential tract homes. Plaintiffs were homeowners. [Name] claims to have been struck in the head by a cement roof tile, knocked out and injured. A herniated disk at L4 L5 was diagnosed approximately 2 1/2 months later and a laminectomy was performed.

[Name], the roofing subcontractor, was a Co-Defendant. However, they had filed bankruptcy. While there was still coverage for the personal injury there was no coverage for the property damage.

There was no defense for the roof itself. Our own expert found more wrong with the roof than did Plaintiff's. We had a Cross-Complaint against [Name] for equitable indemnity only as there was no contractual indemnity provision.

You had previously authorized settlement in the amount of $75,000.00. At the Settlement Conference in March, 1992, we and Co-Defendants offered a package settlement of $75,000.00 (with our contribution being $25,000.00). Plaintiff's demand was $250,000.00. At the conference Defendants had agreed to go up to a $100,000.00 joint settlement (our contribution being $34,000.00) but it was never offered because Plaintiff was "offended" by our $75,000.00 offer.

Thereafter, I attempted to settle our clients out separately and to that end offered Plaintiffs $40,000.00. Plaintiff refused to settle us out alone because he did not want to give up the strict liability cause.

Midway through trial we entered into a reverse Mary Carter agreement with Co-Defendant Price that our maximum exposure would be the property damage ($16,356.00 plus $25,000.00) in exchange for our not calling our expert or our employee. We had already discussed that our expert and our employee would testify the roof was defective which could come back to us since we had a duty to inspect Price's work.

The jury came back finding against our client on the strict liability for the property damage only ($16,356.00) and against both our clients and Price for negligence. The negligence was divided 50%/50%. They awarded $24,726.90 for economic damages (the medical and loss of earnings for the 10-week post-surgery period) and $25,666.00 for non-economic pain and suffering. The jury gave nothing on Mrs. Robinson's loss of consortium claim.

In speaking with the jury afterward, there were 2 people who do not believe it ever happened; unfortunately that is not enough for a defense award. However, I believe their input helped to keep the damage award low. As you know, the jury really disliked Mrs. Robinson. Your decision not to waive costs in exchange for the dismissal of her claim thereby leaving Mrs. Robinson in as a Plaintiff seems to have been the pivotal event. We will have to remember this on future loss of consortium claims.

Price's counsel is convinced that we both are entitled to all our costs from Mrs. Robinson since she did not prevail on her loss of consortium claim (and she was not included in the property damage claim where Mr. Robinson did prevail). I am not yet convinced this is correct, but will prepare a cost bill anyway.

It has been a pleasure handling this file with you, I hope you are as pleased with the outcome as I am. Should you have any questions or comments, please do not hesitate to call.

Very truly yours,

[Attorney]

LETTER 10-22
TRANSMITTAL OF CLIENT'S DOCUMENTS POST-TRIAL

[Date]

[Name]
[Company]
[Address]

Re: [Case name]
Our Clients : [Names]
Our File No. : [Number]
Date/Loss : [Date]

Dear [Name]:

We have completed the post-trial items and will be satisfying the judgment in the near future. I am closing out my file and am returning the original plans and construction progress file to you before they end up in storage limbo.

Very truly yours,

[Attorney]

LETTER 10-23
POST-TRIAL REPORT TO CLIENT'S INSURANCE CARRIER

[Date]

[Name]
[Company]
[Address]

Re: [Case name]

Insured	:	[Name]
Claim No.	:	[Number]
Date of Loss	:	[Date]
Our File No.	:	[Number]

Post-Trial Report

Dear [Name]:

Even though you were present throughout much of the trial, including the reading of the defense verdict, I write you this report so that you will have a summary of the trial for your file and so that the personnel at Ralston Purina, Eveready and American Drug Stores will be made aware of the significant developments which occurred during the trial.

We appeared ready for trial on August 9, 1993. Because this case was the oldest one on the docket, we were able to begin the trial and pick a jury that day. The original panel included, to the dismay of plaintiff's counsel, five or six engineers. Plaintiff's counsel used every one of his peremptory challenges and stated to me that he wished he had a dozen more. The jury that was ultimately selected included a mechanical engineer, an insurance broker, a registered nurse, a sales manager responsible for coordinating repairs to JVC stereos (it was a JVC unit at issue in our case), and a plant manager for a lighting company.

On the first day of trial, plaintiff testified, trying his best to convince the jury that his actions were reasonable in not obtaining medical care for the first two days. I believe that I was successful during my cross-examination of pointing out to the jury that no "reasonably prudent person" would have failed to seek medical care for two days.

The next witness was plaintiff's expert chemical engineer, Charles Braithwaite, Ph.D. He testified that the two batteries leaked because of a manufacturing defect or a defect in the design of the "insulation" material. He also criticized Eveready's warning as being much too small and confusing. As you know from my prior reports, there was no scarcity of subjects upon which I could cross-examine him.

I pointed out to the jury that Dr. Braithwaite had purchased Eveready's Super Heavy Duty battery to use as an exemplar. The doctor thought this was an alkaline battery. I am pleased to confirm for you that I was able to set him straight on the difference.

Dr. Braithwaite's testimony regarding his lack of knowledge of the system, which allows the battery to vent, was also easy to critique. In addition, I was able to cause the jury to question his comments regarding the warning, by pointing out to them that Dr. Braithwaite didn't even know why the warning contains some information. For example, he believed that one reason why Eveready warns not to recharge the battery is so that Eveready's sales will increase.

In contrast, the testimony of Eveready's Manager of Standards and Product Safety, Terrence N. Telzrow, went quite well. I believe that Mr. Telzrow's testimony dazzled the jury, both with his qualifications (Chairman of the ANSI, IEC and NEMA Committees), but also with his personable approach to testifying. He came across as a real teacher, informing the jury about battery technology and the risks of not heeding Eveready's warning about putting the battery in backwards. Mr. Telzrow was able to use a "multi-media" approach to his testimony by providing oral testimony, diagraming battery technology on the board, referring to blow-ups of the batteries involved and using the actual parts of an Energizer battery to demonstrate for the jury exactly how the battery vents when it is charged.

Plaintiff's counsel called plaintiff's mother, a registered nurse, to testify regarding the steps plaintiff took to seek medical advice during the two days before he actually saw a doctor. I do not believe this testimony went particularly well for plaintiff because I was able to get the mother to testify that after she told him to see a doctor, he waited approximately another thirty hours.

In my opinion, the most effective testimony for plaintiff came from plaintiff's expert plastic surgeon, Daniel Mills, M.D. Dr. Mills testified that, based on his experience with chemical burns, the skin develops a protective layer after twelve to fifteen hours and no further burning takes place. I addressed this testimony in closing argument by pointing out to the jury that once plaintiff felt the excruciating pain in his buttocks, he drove another two hours home, without going to an emergency room or calling a doctor. When he arrived home, he looked in the mirror and noticed that his buttocks were black. At that point, he simply went to bed. In the morning, he awoke and again saw that his buttocks were black. He was still in pain at that time. Nevertheless, he did not go to the doctor. I pointed out to the jury that all of these actions took place within the first fifteen hours. I argued to the jury that no reasonable person would wait that long before seeking medical treatment.

In closing argument, plaintiff's counsel asked the jury for payment of past medical bills of $1,579.00 and future medical bills of $22,800.00. He also asked for pain and suffering damages. At the conclusion of his argument, he asked the jury to return a verdict in the amount of $79,229.00.

The jury deliberated for approximately one hour and fifteen minutes. Because of the various theories of liability, a special verdict form was used. I was able to convince the judge that the issue of breach of warranty should not go before the jury because the defendants had proved that the product had been misused. The case ultimately went to the jury on the theories of strict liability design defect, manufacturing defect and failure to warn, as well as a general negligence theory. The special verdict form was written so that if the jury first found that there was no defect and that there was no negligence on the part of the defendants, the jury would not even have to consider plaintiff's comparative negligence or the damages issues. When the jury came back, we learned that the jury did not even address the damages or comparative negligence issues because they found that there was no product defect and that defendants were not negligent.

When the judge polled the jury, it was determined that all twelve jurors found that there was no negligence. On the issue of strict liability design defect, two of the jurors answered "yes" to the question asking whether or not there was a product defect. When the judge questioned these jurors, both of them admitted that while they thought there may be a defect, plaintiff did not meet his burden of proving a defect. If this is true, then they obviously should have voted no. Because we already had our requisite nine "no" votes, I decided not to pursue the matter because the judge may have ordered the jury back into deliberations.

As you know from talking to the jurors after the trial, the two that voted yes on the strict liability theory said that there was a defect because the batteries leaked. Obviously, these two jurors did not understand the more technical aspects of our defense. I am sure that had the vote been closer, the more astute jurors would have made an effort to explain to these jurors that the batteries were designed to vent so as to avoid a serious explosion when the pressure built up.

At this time, we must decide whether or not it would be useful to pursue costs from plaintiff. Because we did receive a defense verdict, we are, of course, entitled to a judgment against the plaintiff in the amount of the costs we expended in this case. As a practical matter, it may be difficult to actually obtain the money from [Name]. I understand from his testimony that he is still going to school. Once you have had an opportunity to consider this issue, please contact me so that we may discuss how best to proceed.

It has been a pleasure working with you on this file and in obtaining this just result.

Very truly yours,

[Attorney]

LETTER 10-24
LETTER PRAISING EXPERT WITNESS'S PRESENTATION OF TESTIMONY AT TRIAL

[Date]

[Name]
[Company]
[Address]

Re: [Case name]
OCSC Case No. : [Number]
Date of Loss : [Date]
Our File No. : [Number]

Dear [Name]:

Even though I took an opportunity in my post-trial report to discuss Mr. Telzrow's testimony during the recent jury trial in this case, I would like to take this opportunity to let you know how important his testimony really was to our defense.

We went into the trial confronted with the testimony of plaintiff's expert regarding alleged design and manufacturing defects. Although plaintiff's expert's theories were incorrect, they were presented in a plausible manner by an individual with a Ph.D. in chemical engineering and the author of seven patents.

Mr. Telzrow rose to this challenge magnificently. In my prior report, I explained the methods he used during the trial to "teach" the jury. By the time he was done, he had developed a true rapport with the members of the jury. His unique combination of independent qualifications (Chairman of ANSI, IEC and NEMA Committees) and his personable approach to testifying, certainly makes him a formidable adversary to anyone who wishes to bring a battery action against Eveready.

As I told him during the trial, he really is a dream witness. If I had a wish list to create the perfect battery expert, I could do no better than Mr. Telzrow.

I have already given him my heartfelt thanks for his assistance in obtaining the defense verdict. I trust that you realize what a genuine asset he is to Eveready.

Thank you for your assistance in coordinating my pretrial work in this case.

Very truly yours,

[Attorney]

LETTER 10-25
LETTER MEMORIALIZING ORAL AGREEMENT REGARDING WAIVER OF COSTS AND POST-TRIAL MOTIONS

[Date]

[Name]
[Address]

Re: [Case name]
OCSC Case No.: [Number]
Date of Loss : [Date]
Our File No. : [Number]

Dear [Name]:

This serves to confirm our telephone conversation on [Date].

In exchange for an agreement not to pursue costs in this matter, you and your client agree not to file any post-trial motions in this matter and agree not to appeal the judgment.

Please have this letter executed where indicated below and return the original to my office.

Thank you for your assistance.

Very truly yours,

Accepted:

[Attorney]

By: ______________________________
[Attorney]

By: ______________________________
[Attorney]

LETTER 10-26
TRANSMITTAL OF COPY OF JUDGMENT AND NOTICE OF JUDGMENT

[Date]

[Name]
[Company]
[Address]

Re: [Case name]
Insured. : [Name]
Claim No. : [Number]
Date of Loss : [Date]
Our File No. : [Number]

Dear [Name]:

Enclosed for your file is a copy of the Judgment and the Notice of Entry of Judgment.

Pursuant to the instructions of [Name], in exchange for an agreement that plaintiff will not appeal or make any post-trial motions, we have agreed not to pursue costs against [Name].

I will close my file at this time. It has been a pleasure working with you toward a successful resolution of this case.

Very truly yours,

[Attorney]

Enclosures: –Judgment
–Notice of Entry of Judgment

LETTER 10-27
WITNESS THANK-YOU LETTER

[Date]

[Name]
[Address]

Re: [Case name]

Dear [Name]:

Enclosed you will find the decision of the Court in the [Case Name] matter. This decision supports the position of our client, [Name], that his employer's corporate employee manual represented a binding promise of health benefits.

Needless to say, we are very happy with the Court's decision. The clear and objective testimony you presented as an expert in employee benefits management helped greatly to support our client's position.

Sincerely,

[Attorney]
Senior Legal Assistant

Enclosure

LETTER 10-28
COVER LETTER ENCLOSING JUROR QUESTIONNAIRE

[Date]

[Name]
[Address]

Re: [Case Name]

Dear [Juror Name]:

You recently served on a jury in the [Court Name and Location]. I represented [Client Name] at that trial. I would appreciate it if you would answer the questionnaire enclosed with this letter and return it to me in the envelope provided. Your answers will assist me in improving my skills as a trial lawyer and improve my ability to see the case from a juror's point of view.

(OPTIONAL PARAGRAPH)

After you have had a chance to read through this questionnaire and think about your answers, I would appreciate it if you would contact me to discuss the case. If you prefer, [state other options for action, depending on what the attorney wants to do].

You are not required to respond at all, but I would very much like to hear from you as I feel your comments about this case would be valuable to me as an attorney. If you would be willing to discuss this case with me, please contact me at your earliest convenience.

Very truly yours,

[Trial Attorney]

CHAPTER 11

MISCELLANEOUS LEGAL LETTERS

LETTER 11-1
TRANSMITTAL LETTER TO CLERK OF COURT

(DATE)

RE: Cause No. ______________________________, In the ____________________ Judicial District Court in and for ______________ County, __________, _______ ____________ vs. ______________________________

- -

(CLERK OF COURT)

____

____

Dear Sir:

We enclose ______________________________ in the above styled and numbered cause which we request that you file among the papers in this cause. Please acknowledge receipt and filing of this instrument by placing your file mark on the enclosed copy of this letter and returning it to us. A self-addressed, stamped envelope is enclosed for your convenience in returning the copy to us.

A copy of this pleading has been furnished to the attorneys for the plaintiff(s)/ defendant(s).

Very truly yours,

(Attorney's Name)
For the Firm of ____________
State Bar No. ______________

___/___

Enclosures

cc: ______________________________
____
____

LETTER 11-2
NOTICE OF INTENT TO MAKE CLAIM UNDER CLIENT'S MEDICAL PAYMENTS COVERAGE

[Date]

[Insurance Company]
[Address]

Re: Your Insured: [Name]
Your Policy Number: [Number]
Accident Date: [Date]

Gentlemen:

This law firm represents [Name] who was injured in an automobile accident on [Date], in Washington, D.C., when his automobile, which he was then operating, was struck by a vehicle operated by [Name] of [Place]. Under [Name]'s policy, he is entitled to medical payments benefits not to exceed $20,000 per person for expenses incurred within one year of the accident date. [Name] is currently under the care of a physician and it is unknown at this time when he will be released.

The purpose of this letter is to put [Insurer] on notice of our intent to make a claim under [Name]'s medical payments coverage at a future date. This letter should not be interpreted as a demand for payment at this time.

If you need any further information or have any questions, please do not hesitate to contact me.

Very truly yours,

____

[Attorney]

LETTER 11-3
DEMAND TO CLIENT'S INSURER FOR MEDICAL PAYMENTS

[Date]

[Insurance Company]
[Address]

Re: Your Insured: [Name]
Your Policy Number: [Number]
Accident Date: [Date]

Gentlemen:

As we advised you in our letter of [Date], this law firm represents your insured, [Name], for injuries sustained in an automobile accident on [Date], in [Place], when his vehicle, which he was driving at the time, was struck from the side by a motor vehicle operated by [Name] of [Address].

As a result of this accident, [Name] incurred the following medical expenses:

Washington Hospital Center (1/1/87 to 2/17/87)	$28,787.60
Dr. Samuel L. Jones	775.00
Dr. Robert T. Smith	2,250.00
Capitol Area Ambulance Service	50.00
Radiology	300.00
Drug Fair	272.19
People's Drug	+ 37.95
TOTAL MEDICAL EXPENSES:	$32,472.74

For your information, we are enclosing copies of the above-referenced bills, along with the Washington Hospital Center record in its entirety, and reports from Drs. Jones and Smith. Also enclosed is a photostatic copy of [Name]'s policy declaration sheet for your reference.

(insert appropriate demand paragraph here)

If you have any questions or need additional information, please do not hesitate to contact me.

Very truly yours,

____

[Attorney]

Enclosures

LETTER 11-4
LETTER TO CARRIER RE: SUSPENSION OF CLIENT'S MEDICAL PAYMENT BENEFITS

Re: Your Insured/My Client: [Name]
Claim No.: [Number]
Date of Accident: [Date]

Dear [Claims Adjuster]:

I am writing this letter in response to yours of [Date of letter] in which you state with regard to [Name of client] that you will be unable to extend further personal injury benefits for medical treatment resulting from the accident of [Date of accident]. This notice of refusal to pay for further medical care is based upon the examination that was conducted by [Name of IME doctor] at the direction of your insurance company and his opinion that [Name of client] had achieved maximum medical improvement.

As you are no doubt aware, [Name of IME doctor]'s opinions apply only the most conservative criteria for diagnosis and treatment of medical and [Orthopedic or other specialty] problems. [Name of IME doctor]'s approach and opinions in this regard are well known throughout the medical, legal, and insurance communities.

The law in this state is that when treatment has been undertaken by an insured which has been prescribed by a competent medical practitioner, it must be covered under [State statute cite], even if other practitioners suggest that other treatment or no treatment at all was appropriate.

I hope that you will allow [Name of client] to obtain treatment in accordance with recommendations of those physicians who have been treating him. He hopes, and through me requests, that you will honor your side of the contract and allow him to receive reasonable and necessary medical care arising out of the accident of [Date of accident].

[Signature]

LETTER 11-5
REQUEST THAT CLIENT PAY COURT REPORTERS

[Date]

[Name]
[Address]

Re: [Case name]
Your Claim No. : [Number]
Insured : [Name]
Date of Loss : [Date]
Our File No. : [Number]

Dear [Name]:

Enclosed is invoice number [Number] in the amount of $[Amount] from [Court Reporters].

Please issue a check made payable to:

[COURT REPORTERS]
[Address]
Tax I.D. #: [Number]

Please direct payment to their offices. If you have any questions, please contact our office.

Very truly yours,

[Signature]

Enclosure: Invoice

LETTER 11-6
FOLLOW-UP ON REQUEST THAT CLIENT PAY COURT REPORTERS

[Date]

[Name]
[Address]

Re: [Case name]
Claim No. : [Number]
Insured : [Name]
Date of Loss : [Date]
Our File No. : [Number]

Dear [Name]:

Enclosed is invoice number [Number] in the amount of $[Amount] from [Name] Court Reporters. Said invoice was initially forwarded to you for payment on [Date]. Please check to see if payment was made.

If you have any questions, please contact our office.

Very truly yours,

[Signature]

Enclosure: Invoice

LETTER 11-7
TRANSMITTAL OF CHECK FOR DESIGNATION FEES

[Date]

[Name]
[Address]

Re: [Case name]
Our Client : [Name]
Our File : [Number]
Date/Loss : [Date]

Dear [Name]:

Enclosed herewith, please find my principal's check in the amount of $[Amount] representing designation fees. Please be advised trial has been set for [Date] in [Location]. Should you have any questions or comments, please feel free to contact this office.

Very truly yours,

[Attorney]

LETTER 11-8
REQUEST THAT CLIENT'S INSURER PAY TRIAL FEES

[Date]

[Name]
[INSURANCE COMPANY]
[Address]

Re: [Case name]
[Court] Case No.: [Number]
Date of Loss : [Date]
Our File No. : [Number]

Dear [Name]:

Please have two checks prepared and sent to my office. The first check will be for the first three days of trial. This check should be made payable to the [Name] County Clerk in the amount of $[Amount]. This check will cover the voir dire reporter fee of $[Amount], together with the daily jury fee of $[Amount] and the daily defendant's half of the reporter's fee in the amount of $[Amount].

Please make the second check out to the [Name] County Clerk in the amount of $[Amount]. This check will cover the daily jury fee and the daily reporter's fee for Friday, if necessary. I understand from our prior conversation that you will have the checks delivered to my office on Thursday.

Thank you for your assistance.

Very truly yours,

[Attorney]

CHAPTER 12

PARALEGAL OFFICE MANAGEMENT

LETTER 12-1
REPLY TO RESUME (INTERVIEWED—UNABLE TO OFFER JOB)

[Date]

[Name]
[Address]

Dear [Name]:

I am sorry to tell you that I am unable to offer you the paralegal position in the [Name of department] department at [Law firm] that we discussed recently.

I do want you to know, however, that it was not an easy decision and that I and the members of the [Name of department] group with whom you spoke enjoyed meeting you and wish you the best of luck in your job search.

Very truly yours,

[Paralegal]

LETTER 12-2
JOB OFFER LETTER

[Date]

[Name]
[Address]

Dear [Name]:

This will confirm the offer of employment which I extended to you for the position of [Name of group] paralegal at a salary of $[Amount] per month.

In addition to your salary, we have a comprehensive benefits program that significantly adds to the overall financial package. The firm provides medical and dental coverage for you as an individual or for your family. We offer personal time off and we recognize 10 holidays. Also, we have a liberal vacation policy.

The [Name of group] group and I enjoyed meeting with you and were very impressed with your interviews. We all feel that you will make a positive contribution to [Law firm] and we look forward to your acceptance of this offer.

Please indicate your acceptance by signing, dating, and returning the enclosed copy of this letter in the envelope that has been provided. Meanwhile, if you have any questions, please feel free to call me at [Telephone number].

We look forward to having you join us at [Law firm].

Sincerely,

[Paralegal]

LETTER 12-3
JOB ACCEPTANCE ACKNOWLEDGMENT AND FIRST DAY PROCEDURES

[Date]

[Name]
[Address]

Dear [Name]:

I am pleased to acknowledge your acceptance of our offer of employment as a paralegal with a starting salary of $[Amount] per month. We are looking forward to having you join us on Monday, [Date].

When you arrive for work please come to the 12th floor at 9:00 a.m. and ask for [Name]. She will explain the [Law firm] benefits to you, will help you fill out the appropriate insurance forms, and will be able to answer any questions you may have.

Please bring with you either a passport, a driver's license and social security card, or a driver's license and birth certificate on your first day. We need to view this documentation in order to verify your eligibility to work as required by the Immigration Reform and Control Act of 1986.

We believe you will find your association with [Law firm] to be a rewarding, challenging, and enjoyable experience.

Very truly yours,

[Paralegal]

LETTER 12-4
REPLY TO RESUME
(INFORMATIONAL INTERVIEW FOR INTERESTING CANDIDATE WITHOUT EXACT EXPERIENCE)

[Date]

[Name]
[Address]

Dear [Name]:

This letter is in response to your recent inquiry into the possibility of employment as a paralegal at [Law firm].

At present, the only positions available are for paralegals with specialized paralegal experience. However, if you would like to come into the office and discuss the situation in general terms, I would be happy to meet with you. Please telephone my assistant, [Name], at ext. [Number], if you would like to arrange an appointment. Thank you for your interest in [Law firm].

Very truly yours,

[Paralegal]

LETTER 12-5
REPLY TO RESUME (INFORMATIONAL INTERVIEW FOR FUTURE COLLEGE GRADUATE)

[Date]

[Name]
[Address]

Dear [Name]:

This is in response to your recent letter with respect to the possibility of employment as a paralegal at [Law firm] upon your graduation from [College].

At present, I cannot predict what specific paralegal positions might become available this summer. However, if you would like to come into the office and discuss the situation in general terms, I would be happy to meet with you. Please telephone my assistant, [Name], at ext. [Number], if you would like to arrange an appointment.

Thank you for your interest in [Law firm].

Very truly yours,

[Paralegal]

LETTER 12-6
REPLY TO RESUME (INTERVIEW FOR INTERESTING CANDIDATE FOR FUTURE OPENINGS)

[Date]

[Name]
[Address]

Dear [Name]:

Thank you for your recent inquiry concerning employment as a paralegal at [Law firm].

Although your qualifications and experience do not exactly correspond to our present needs, I would be happy to meet with you if you would be interested in coming into the office to discuss possibilities that might arise in the future. Please telephone my assistant, [Name], at ext. [Number], if you would like to arrange an appointment.

Very truly yours,

[Paralegal]

LETTER 12-7
REPLY TO RESUME (NO JOB OPENINGS—INFORMATIONAL INTERVIEW)

[Date]

[Name]
[Address]

Dear [Name]:

Thank you for your recent inquiry with respect to the possibility of employment as a paralegal at [Law firm].

At present, we do not have any openings for paralegals. However, if you would like to come into the office for an informational interview, I would be happy to meet with you. Please telephone my assistant, [Name], at ext. [Number], if you would like to arrange an appointment.

Very truly yours,

[Paralegal]

LETTER 12-8
LETTER FOLLOWING UP ON INFORMATIONAL INTERVIEW—NO JOB OPENINGS

[Date]

[Name]
[Address]

Dear [Name]:

Thank you for coming into the office on [Date] for an exploratory interview. I enjoyed meeting with you.

As you already know, we do not have any openings at the present time; however, I will keep your resume on file and notify you if any appropriate positions become available in the near future.

Thank you for your interest in [Law firm].

Very truly yours,

[Paralegal]

LETTER 12-9
REPLY TO RESUME (ANNOUNCED JOB ALREADY FILLED)

[Date]

[Name]
[Address]

Dear [Name]:

Thank you for responding to our recent job announcement.

I am sorry to inform you that the position for which you have applied has been filled. I will, however, keep your resume on file to refer to in the event that an opening arises to which your capabilities seem suited.

Very truly yours,

[Paralegal]

LETTER 12-10
REPLY TO RESUME
(NO INTEREST IN THIS PARTICULAR RESUME)

[Date]

[Name]
[Address]

Dear [Name]:

Thank you for your recent inquiry with respect to the possibility of employment as a paralegal at [Law firm].

Having carefully reviewed your resume, I regret to tell you that your qualifications and experience do not exactly correspond to our current needs. I shall, however, keep your resume on file to refer to in the event that an opening arises to which your capabilities seem suited.

Thank you for your interest in [Law firm].

Very truly yours,

[Paralegal]

LETTER 12-11
REPLY TO RESUME (INEXPERIENCED PARALEGAL—JOB OPENING FOR EXPERIENCED PARALEGAL)

[Date]

[Name]
[Address]

Dear [Name]:

This is in response to your recent inquiry with respect to the possibility of employment as a paralegal at [Law firm].

Unfortunately, the only positions available at this time are for paralegals with specialized paralegal experience. I will, however, keep your resume on file to refer to in the event that an opening arises to which your capabilities seem suited.

Thank you for your interest in [Law firm].

Very truly yours,

[Paralegal]

LETTER 12-12
REPLY TO RESUME (NO JOB OPENING IN SPECIALTY AREA)

[Date]

[Name]
[Address]

Dear [Name]:

This is in response to your recent inquiry with respect to the possibility of employment as a paralegal at [Law firm].

Unfortunately, there are no positions available at this time for paralegals in your area of expertise. I will, however, keep your resume on file to refer to in the event that an opening arises to which your capabilities seem suited.

Very truly yours,

[Paralegal]

LETTER 12-13
REPLY TO RESUME (NO JOB OPENING)

[Date]

[Name]
[Address]

Dear [Name]:

Thank you for your recent inquiry with respect to the possibility of employment as a paralegal at [Law firm].

I am sorry to tell you that at present our paralegal staff is at full capacity. I shall, however, keep your resume on file to refer to in the event that an opening arises to which your capabilities seem suited.

Thank you for your interest in [Law firm].

Very truly yours,

[Paralegal]

LETTER 12-14
REPLY TO REFERRED RESUME (NO JOB OPENING)

[Date]

[Name]
[Address]

Dear [Name]:

[Name] forwarded your resume to me. Thank you for your inquiry with respect to the possibility of employment as a paralegal at [Law firm].

Unfortunately, at present our paralegal staff is at full capacity and I do not anticipate any openings soon. I shall, however, keep your resume on file in case an unanticipated opening does occur. In the event of such an opening, I shall contact you to ascertain your availability.

Thank you for your interest in [Law firm].

Very truly yours,

[Paralegal]

LETTER 12-15
REPLY TO RESUME
(EMPLOYMENT PRIOR TO LAW SCHOOL)

[Date]

[Name]
[Address]

Dear [Name]:

This is in response to your recent inquiry with respect to the possibility of employment as a paralegal at [Law firm] prior to attending law school.

I regret to tell you that the firm requires a minimum two-year commitment of employment from all paralegal applicants.

Best of luck with your law school career, and thank you for your interest in [Law firm].

Very truly yours,

[Paralegal]

LETTER 12-16
REPLY TO RESUME
(EMPLOYMENT UPON GRADUATION FROM COLLEGE)

[Date]

[Name]
[Address]

Dear [Name]:

This is in response to your recent letter with respect to the possibility of employment as a paralegal at [Law firm] upon your graduation from [College].

At present, I cannot predict what specific paralegal positions might become available this summer. I shall, however, keep your resume on file to refer to in the event that an opening arises to which your capabilities seem suited.

You should be aware that the firm requires a minimum two-year commitment from all paralegal applicants.

Thank you for your interest in [Law firm].

Very truly yours,

[Paralegal]

LETTER 12-17
TERMINATION OF LEASE LETTER 1

[Date]

[Name]
[Address]

Re: CONTRACT NO. [Number] LEASE AGREEMENT—Suite [Number]

Dear Building Manager:

The purpose of this letter is to formally document the understanding reached during our meeting last Tuesday. We agreed to make the February payment and allow [Name] to retain the security deposit, plus [Firm] will provide $2,000 as the buy-out amount for the balance of the agreement.

[Firm] has turned over the keys to Suite [Number] and it is understood that [Name] may lease the suite to others.

At some future date, [Firm] may be meeting with opposing counsel and the judge in connection with the out-of-court settlement reached in this case. It is my understanding that should [Firm] need an office or place to meet, [Name] will try to accommodate this need at no additional cost to [Firm].

I appreciate your willingness to negotiate on the expenses involved in closing this contract.

Sincerely,

[Paralegal]

LETTER 12-18
TERMINATION OF LEASE LETTER 2

[Date]

[Lease Co.]
[Address]

Re: CONTRACT NO. [Number] LEASE FOR OFFICE SPACE

Dear Leasing Agent:

The purpose of this letter is to provide formal notification that [Firm] has vacated the office premises located at the corner of [Location] in the City of [Name]. As you are aware, we expected to lease the premises for at least four months, however, the litigation has been settled out of court.

The keys were returned to your corporate offices this Monday. My understanding is that the final cleaning of the office space will be done by your cleaning staff at no additional cost to [Firm].

I appreciate your willingness to negotiate on the expenses involved in closing this contract. Thanks for your cooperation in working with us.

Sincerely,

[Paralegal]

LETTER 12-19
LETTER TO TEMPORARY AGENCIES
REGARDING TEMPORARY CODING PROJECT

[Date]

[Vendor]
[Address]

Re: Temporary Coding Project

Dear [Name]:

Thank you for the opportunity to work with you on the XYZ coding project. In order for the project to run smoothly and effectively for all parties, we would like to outline some project considerations:

1. All coding will take place on [Location of coding, including floor and contact person]. We ask that none of the temporary coders go beyond the coding area and not to any of the offices located above the floor unless otherwise instructed.

2. The coders are to work from 8:30 a.m. to 5:30 p.m. with an hour off for lunch. All persons need to take a lunch break away from coding. A 40-hour work week is expected.

3. The coding will be completed on paper; therefore, all coders need legible handwriting and be able to code between 20 and 25 pages per hour. All documents will be checked for accuracy.

4. The project length will be anywhere from 6 weeks to 3 months. However, we reserve the right to terminate the project at any time.

5. We are employing temporary coders from several agencies and request that all agencies pay their coders $[Amount] per hour. Any persons making more or less than this amount may cause motivation or morale problems. Also, please educate your employees as to any agency benefits, such as insurance, holidays or bonus pay.

We will identify three persons to assist with quality control and one person to act as a document archive librarian (must be familiar with Lotus). Because their duties will differ from the coders, we will pay an additional $1.00 per hour per person so that each person may get $.50 per hour more, equalling $[Amount] dollars per hour.

6. A lunch room is located on the coding floor and includes such amenities as: refrigerator, microwave, free coffee and soft drinks.

7. Key personnel: The ALS manager is [Name] and the coding advisor is [Name]. [Name] is the attorney liaison. All invoices should be submitted to: [Name], Director of Personnel.

8. Each coder is expected to sign a Confidentiality Agreement from the agency for this project. Any discussion of the project or document contents outside the office, within the elevator or with personnel outside of the project is grounds for termination.

9. The project will commence on [Date], with coder training beginning at 8:30 a.m. The training will last approximately one day.

10. If any coder is not able to perform the coding duties, we expect credit for his or her training and coding time. If a coder terminates his or her employment with the agency prior to the end of the project, then we do not expect to be charged for the time it takes to train a new person.

11. We ask that a person from your agency be designated to collect time sheets, paychecks, or handle personnel issues such as: illness, tardiness, and monitor lunch or break times on behalf of your agency.

We look forward to working with you on this project. If you have any questions, please let me know.

Sincerely,

[Paralegal]

INDEX

All references are to letter number.